KENNETH WILLIAMS

JUST WILLIAMS
an autobiography

J M Dent & Sons Ltd
London Melbourne

By the same Author

Acid Drops
Back Drops

First published 1985
Reprinted 1985 (4 times)
© Kenneth Williams 1985

This book is set in 11/12pt VIP Sabon by
D. P. Media Limited, Hitchin, Herts
Printed and bound in Great Britain by
Mackays of Chatham Ltd, for
J M Dent & Sons Ltd
Aldine House, 33 Welbeck Street, London W1M 8LX

British Library Cataloguing in Publication Data

Williams, Kenneth
  Just Williams.
  1. Williams, Kenneth   2. Actors——Great Britain
  ——Biography
  I. Title
  791'.092'4   PN2598.W5/

ISBN 0-460-04688-5

List of Illustrations

Chapter One

'You must understand what I'm trying to tell you,' the schoolmaster said to me. 'As a prefect you have certain responsibilities; if you mock teachers you might succeed in amusing people, but you'll also succeed in undermining your own authority. Don't you see that?'

I nodded dumbly.

'I'm telling you this for your own good,' he continued. 'A facetious front may win you popularity but you won't be taken seriously when you want to be sincere. People won't believe you and that will hurt you, won't it?'

'I suppose so,' I replied, pretending agreement, but in fact I understood nothing of what he was trying to tell me.

The rebuke was born of an incident in the playground of Manchester Street Junior School, King's Cross, London. I had been impersonating the master, surrounded by a cluster of admirers, when he had suddenly appeared behind me. I had continued, unaware of his presence, until my tiny audience stopped giggling and eyed me warningly. He sent them back to the classroom; I was detained for the reprimand. But I'm afraid it was water off a duck's back.

As a young actor I was to do the same thing during a production of *Peter Pan* at the Scala Theatre. I was backstage, entertaining some of the actors with an impression of the director, Cecil King, when someone coughed embarrassedly. I turned, saw Cecil, and realised he'd witnessed the whole thing.

'Well, one of us is terrible,' he muttered and stumped away.

Similar happenings with disparate endings, they illustrate the risks involved in humour. Middle age may be chivalrous but youth is invariably unkind. It's not had time to weigh the consequences.

My youth was spent in a working-class area of London where I learned a lot about derision but precious little about diplomacy. The cockney penchant for pricking the bubble of pretension was ever-present. Lines like, 'All kid gloves and no drawers' were reserved for the meretricious; 'Spit in her eye and it wouldn't choke her' denoted aplomb; while 'I should cocoa' implied deep scepticism.

I came into the world on the 22nd of February 1926 at Bingfield Street, off the Caledonian Road, where my parents and my elder sister, Pat, shared two rooms. 'You arrived on the Monday at about 2.30,' my mother, Louisa, told me later. 'I remember because it was early closing day and Charlie had the afternoon off.'

Charlie was my father. He managed a hairdresser's shop in Marchmont Street where his rude responses to feminine requests never seemed to lose him customers. 'Henna dye on your head?' he'd say incredulously. 'D'you want to look like a tart?' And brushing aside any protests, he did their hair *his* way. 'Stick to your own colour,' he'd tell them. 'You can't improve on nature. You ought to know that. You're old enough and ugly enough.' He always used this last line to finalise any argument.

Some years later we moved to rooms over the shop, and Louisa frequently reproved him for the way he talked to his customers. But he would brook no argument. 'You look after your business, my lady, and I'll look after mine,' he told her, conveniently forgetting that the two jobs frequently intermingled. For Louisa was always being called away from housework to do shampooing in the ladies' saloon, and manage the till in the gents'.

On these latter occasions she delighted in gossiping with the men who were waiting for a chair. Confiding her ambition to see Loch Lomond to a train driver he told her, 'I'll take you for nothing – you can go in the guard's van.' 'Oh, yes,' cried Louisa, 'as first class baggage!', and everyone fell about in the ensuing laughter.

Charlie didn't approve of this hilarity. 'This is a hairdresser's shop, not a music hall,' he would say, 'and you've marked up this till all wrong!' Louisa's maths were not her strong point and he would have to reckon the sums all over again.

My own maths were pretty bad, too, and when he learned of my lack of numeracy from bad school reports, he admonished me roundly. 'How do you expect to get on in the world if you can't add up?'

'I shall seek other kinds of employment,' I returned airily, using the accent of the governing classes. That always infuriated him.

'Don't talk to me as if you've got a plum in your mouth!' he snapped. 'If you can't handle figures you'll never get a trade.

Sooner or later you'll realise that you'll get nowhere if you haven't got a trade.'

I pointed out that I earned better marks in Art, but he was unimpressed. 'Drawing is no good unless you can do cartoons. There's money in cartoons. You can't do cartoons.'

I admitted that I couldn't.

'Well, what *are* you good at?'

I seized upon acting. 'I'm in the school play. I've got a very important part.'

He snorted. 'Acting is no good. The women are all trollops and the men are nancies.' Loose morals and effeminacy were two things he abhorred and he thought the theatre epitomized both.

'You'd better work at the drawing,' he eventually conceded, 'you might work up to cartoons. I'll have to have a word with one of your masters and find out what you get up to at that school.'

What indeed did I get up to? I sat through most of the lessons blissfully ignorant of their import. My head was full of fanciful conspiracies; I would whisper 'O.G.' to my friend, Wreyford Palmer, and wait impatiently for the school break when we would disappear to a remote corner of the recreation ground and play 'Our Game'. This consisted of a rambling Ruritanian plot in which I was the King, forced to abdicate by the sinister power and guile of Wreyford's Prime Minister. We made up the dialogue and the roles as we went along, pretending we were wearing cloaks and swords in castle fortresses far from the grimy world of King's Cross.

There weren't only day-dreams at school; at home I went to bed and had nightmares. Voices urged me towards a vacant throne: 'Claim your kingdom, defy your foes.' In somnambulance I hurled missiles at my adversaries. In actual fact I was sleepwalking and throwing flower pots from the window sill on to the street below. One of them hit my mother's crony, Florrie Plume, who rushed to a neighbour's house where my parents were visiting.

'I might have been concussed,' she expostulated. 'It's a good thing my head was covered – I'm only standing here now because of this felt hat!'

Louisa was aghast. 'But I left him in bed – he was asleep!'

'Well, he's on the windowsill now, and your marigolds are all over the pavement.'

They returned to find me wandering about the house in my pyjamas and guided me back to bed.

'Always bloody acting and calling attention to himself,' complained my father darkly; but a doctor's advice was sought, potions were prescribed, and Florrie Plume took to walking home on the other side of the street.

For all my neglect of study at school, the one thing I did acquire there was an appreciation of poetry. During English lessons, the teacher would ask a pupil to stand and recite an appropriate passage; most of us nine-year-olds mumbled it senselessly or spoke with self-conscious embarrassment. But one day the light dawned for me. I was delivering Antony's speech, 'Friends, Romans, Countrymen,' and I suddenly realised the power and persuasion of the rhetoric; I knew that I was presenting an argument and I gave it meaning and immediacy. It succeeded. I felt the surprised attention of the class, and afterwards the master took me aside and suggested I should be in the school play.

Poetry and performing fused for me. The episode is vivid in my mind to this day. It had nothing to do with careful perusal or imitation: it was instinctive, involuntary and authentic. I was inwardly exultant. I felt like someone at the door of a treasure house. Words would supply the keys to open it. I thought I'd be through in a trice. I didn't know then that the proper performance lay in an endless search for the harmony between content and form. I was only at the beginning of comprehending form: content was a long way off.

One of my school reports ended with the words: 'Quick to grasp the bones of a subject, slow to develop them.' I affected indifference when my father read it to me. It sounded like a reluctant vulture on someone else's prey. Secretly, though, I was incensed by this cryptic summary of my potential.

There was consolation in our local Methodist chapel. When Dr Beacham thundered from the lectern: 'Of making many books there is no end; and much study is a weariness of the flesh,' I practically rose in the pew to agree. I enjoyed the drama and the simplicity of his homilies. They echoed Keble's dictum on Faith: 'All the lore its scholars need: Pure eyes and Christian hearts.' God clearly didn't care whether one passed exams or not, as long as one could see properly. And as for the Christian heart bit, I naturally assumed I'd got one.

4

I decided to join an organisation dedicated to the service of others. Too young for the Boy Scouts, I was accepted into the Wolf Cubs who met in the chapel gymnasium. There my enthusiasm quickly palled. All the animal jargon seemed foolish, calling a lady 'Arkela' was ridiculous, and the physical exertion was distasteful. Eventually I fled in horror from choruses of 'Dib dib' and the smell of BO, and decided it was not for me.

Thereafter most of the evenings found me closeted in my bedroom reading Rupert Brooke or listening to 78 rpm records on my wind-up gramophone. I was solitary, apart from the odd encounter with my sister's boyfriends.

Pat was a champion swimmer, three years my senior, good at her lessons and popular with her classmates; she was attractive and greatly sought-after. An endless succession of athletic youths rang our front door bell. She would sometimes ask me to put them off. 'Say I've got to stay in tonight 'cos I'm helping Mum.' I would comply most of the time but once I marched up to the door and told the hapless caller, 'She doesn't want to see you tonight, she's meeting another bloke.' I was jealous of the ease with which she collected good-looking admirers and often tried to put a spoke in her wheel. Invariably my mischief backfired.

Once one of her beaux called Dennis protested: 'But we're going swimming together'. 'That's all right', I quickly replied, 'I'll come with you instead.' His embarrassed disappointment didn't deter me. I ran for towel and costume and walked with him to Finsbury Public Baths, talking nineteen to the dozen. 'It's no good you expecting loyalty from Pat,' I confided. 'She's off with someone different every night, but don't worry, I'll keep you company. I can recite poetry.'

I was halfway through *The Lady of Shalott* before he interrupted, 'I think that stuff's boring.'

I gulped back my discountenance. 'I'll sing you a song instead,' I suggested brightly, and began a spirited rendering of 'Deep Purple'. After a few notes Dennis said, 'Oh do shut up. You can't sing either.' I stopped dead in my tracks, mortified. He continued walking.

'No wonder my sister doesn't want to meet you,' I cried. 'You're ignorant! All brawn and no brain. You're a buffoon.' By now I was shouting at his retreating back.

I ran home furiously. I didn't want to go to any rotten

swimming pool anyway, I thought, and that's the last time I bother trying to entertain any of her boyfriends.

I settled for the books, the gramophone and an awful lot of talking to myself. My exhibitionism concealed a sense of inadequacy. The real self was a vulnerable, quivering thing which I did not want to reveal; showing-off, affectation and play-acting I used like a hedgehog uses his spines. The façade was not to be penetrated. My parents respected this privacy. 'He's up in his room,' they'd tell visitors. 'He likes to be on his own,' and I was undisturbed in my private world where artists were heroes and the imagination was king.

Charlie told me later that a master at my next school, the Stanley Central in Mornington Cresent, had said to him that I suffered from an inferiority complex. This sort of diagnosis was very fashionable at the time. I thought it was rubbish. I didn't think I was inferior at all. I had a very high opinion of my capabilities. If I hadn't yet found a way to articulate my aspirations I didn't doubt that they existed. Though energy was not being channelled creatively I felt that time would eventually reveal the process. I thought I was special all right. Already I could see myself as a budding actor.

But in truth a theatrical career had only remote possibilities for me. Apart from its immorality in my father's eyes he also pronounced it financially parlous: 'I've had them in the shop with their la-di-da voices and their blow-waves: they haven't got two ha'pennies to rub together. You want to steer clear of that lot!'

After consulting with my teachers, Charlie decided that drawing was my only talent worth pursuing and after persuading me that what I needed was 'a career with prospects', at the age of fourteen I was sent to Bolt Court, the School of Lithography in Fleet Street. I passed the oral examination and was accepted for training as a litho draughtsman.

It was 1940 and the war caused the evacuation of the younger pupils of the school to Bicester. I was first billeted with a family, but after a few weeks working an allotment alongside an elderly ex-veterinary surgeon called Mr Chisholm, I asked him to let me share his rambling old house at 19 Sheep Street. For me, it was a magical abode and no home has ever usurped its place in my affections. It was lit by oil lamps and candles, there was a book-lined drawing-room, a kitchen and a surgery on the ground floor, and upstairs there were four-poster beds and ornate dressing tables in huge bed-rooms, overlooking a weed-tangled garden, with a coach-house in the rear. It was Aladdin's cave as far as I was concerned.

Mr Chisholm lumbered through its halls and passages bawling ballads and reciting poetry, while Mrs Woods, his house-keeper, countered with Evangelical hymns sung in a quavering contralto. They were often in noisy conflict, and when she straightened her bonnet in the evenings and announced, 'I'm off to the Salvation Army now,' he'd cry, 'Go bang your tambourine, woman, we'll have a bit of poetry,' and then he would roar through 'The Charge of the Light Brigade' or the 'Loch Achray', while I sat goggle-eyed at the power of his voice and his extraordinary memory. He knew long passages by heart and had a natural feel for measure and stress.

I was encouraged to hold forth as well, and he would warn me against the dangers of elision and extol the value of the pause. 'The silence only works if you've created the sound,' he would say. The sound with him was invariably dramatic, whether in poetic diction or veterinary anecdotes. He once described how he'd been called out in the middle of the night to deal with a sick cow which was calving. 'I had no anaesthetic and no time. One of them held the lamp and the other one had this pole-axe. I could only save the one, you see. I had to slit her belly and grab her calf, while he came down in one stroke and cut her head off.' He smacked his open palm with the edge of his other hand, making the scene as vivid as the death of Nelson.

When my mother arrived with her friend, Edie Smith, to visit my new home, she didn't share my enthusiasm. 'Terrible beds! Those flock mattresses have never been turned. The one we slept in was all humped. I was in the dip and Edie was up on the high bit. She kept rolling down on me. We couldn't stop laughing. And when old Mr Chisholm walked in wearing that long nightshirt and holding his candle, I nearly died. 'Course he'd heard us giggling; wanted to know if we were all right. We hardly slept all night. And that breakfast. Oh dear. I took one look at that kitchen range and my stomach went over. I tried to warn Edie but she had the eggs and bacon. When we got outside afterwards she asked why I'd been making faces at her and I told her I'd seen the mice droppings in the frying pan. She was nearly sick on the spot. She said she'd rather face the bombs in London than spend another night in Bicester. Honestly, I don't know how you can stay there!'

In the event I didn't stay long; at fifteen I was regarded as adult enough to face the London air-raids and I resumed my studies with the older boys at Bolt Court in Fleet Street. After struggling with perspective drawing and lettering, I was apprenticed to Edward Stanford, the cartographer in Long Acre. Since much of the work was flat-bed printing on lithographic stones, it necessitated writing in reverse. At last my lefthandedness was no longer a disadvantage and my lettering began to improve.

By now it was 1942 and evacuation had made me more adventurous. I joined the Sea Cadets. After work at the drawing office, I cycled home, changed into sailor's attire and went to Nautical classes in Paddington Street. I'd been apprehensive about joining for my arrogant exterior was often provocative to other youths and I had a horror of fisticuffs. But my fears were dispelled by my cousin Ronnie Hayden who agreed to enrol me. He had a profile like George IV, great confidence and strength enough to deter any aggressor.

We were taught knots, boxing the compass, and how to take lead soundings: there were trips on the river, church parades and desperate attempts to dance the hornpipe. Alas I didn't absorb very much. I was only really interested in dressing up.

When my sister arrived home on leave from the WRAF we had our photographs taken together in uniform and I was at pains to see that my hat was angled so that the band was hardly distinguishable. If you couldn't read 'Sea Cadets' on it, I thought, people would take me for the real thing. I imagined that this sort of primary training would ensure that when I was called up for the forces, I would automatically go into the Navy.

Draughtsmen at work had told me about the survey ships and that there was a good chance I'd get into hydrography. Deck-work and engine rooms held no attraction for me, but the idea of swanking around in bell-bottoms and working on the odd navigation chart seemed a delightful way of serving conscription.

Things were looking promising. Apart from chums in the Sea Cadets, I found another friend at Stanfords: he was Val Orford who worked in the Ordnance Survey section. He lent me books, guided my reading, and arranged my first memorable visit to the theatre. We saw Shaw's *The Doctor's Dilemma*. I was entranced and fascinated. Never before had I heard such lively argument and such irreverent wit. I was shocked and attracted by the figure of Dubedat – his contemptuous dismissal of materialism and his impassioned plea for art found an immediate response in me. This was the sort of part I wanted to play – these were the aesthetics I wanted to proclaim.

I began reading all Shaw's plays and Val provided me with a volume of the *Prefaces*. It seemed propitious that there was an amateur drama group just round the corner from my parents' home in Marchmont Street and I went along to the Mary Ward Settlement in Tavistock Place, determined to put all my theories about acting into practice.

Because of the war there was a shortage of men and I was welcomed by a bevy of theatrical ladies who said they'd teach me deportment, vocal technique, how to apply make-up and how to succeed on the stage. Outwardly complaisant I secretly scorned their advice. I thought that all I had to do was to learn the lines and then deliver them with enormous conviction direct to the spectators. My style must have combined something of the preaching fervour of our Methodist minister with the hauteur of Charles Laughton, my favourite actor. My first role for the group was Gaston in Guitry's *Villa for Sale*. It was also my last. I looked far too young for the part and wore a moustache to affect maturity. Half of it fell off when I started speaking and I held what remained with my fingers. There were giggles from the audience at the gomphotic delivery which ensued, and the group never asked me back again. After the performance people murmured sympathetically backstage, and although I ranted about the ineffective spirit gum, my ego was definitely round my ankles.

Between the theory and the practice, there is a gulf; between the idea and the act there is an abyss which can only be crossed by a tightrope. This involves a balancing act and if the rope is slack, or the steps are tentative, you wobble. Enough wobbling leads to teetering confusion. 'Pride goeth before destruction' all right, and it was to be many years before I understood the professional tightrope, let alone the dynamism that keeps it taut.

In February 1944, shortly after my eighteenth birthday, I received a summons to appear before a Medical Board apropos of my fitness to serve in the forces. At a drill hall in Duke Street, I stood in embarrassed nakedness before various gentlemen seated at trestle tables. They shook their heads in disbelief over my feeble physique and pale complexion. I overheard whispered asides from which I vaguely discerned the word 'anaemia', but I hadn't a clue as to its significance.

I was eventually despatched, with a sealed letter, to an address in Harley Street, where a pathologist stuck needles into my finger-tips and withdrew samples of blood. It was all very Bela Lugosi and vampirish. I was left shaken and disturbed. A solicitous lady in a white coat showed me to the door commiserating: 'Don't worry, dear, I shouldn't think you'll be called up.' I didn't know whether to feel grateful or insulted. I thought that if that lot at Duke Street couldn't decide whether I was fit or not, there must be something wrong with me. I became convinced I was another Keats: talented but sickly, doomed to a short life, ending in an alien clime.

That night, at the Sea Cadet Class, I was mournfully preoccupied; naval training seemed utterly pointless. When my glumness was questioned, I averred that I was not long for this world – 'I'll probably have to be nursed in Italy,' I moaned balefully. Cousin Ronnie looked sceptical. 'We're at war with Mussolini. More likely you'll end up in the Royal Free.'

In the event I ended up in Carlisle Castle and I was far from supine. There were endless days of square-bashing, rifle drill, bayonet practice, kit-cleaning, barrack-room bawdiness and exhaustion. My preference for the Navy was ignored; I was conscripted into the Army, given the medical grading B2 and sent to train with the Border Regiment in Cumberland.

I was appalled by the subsequent invasion of privacy. I'd been away from home before – evacuation had seen to that – but I'd always had my own room. I'd never had to undress daily in front of other people. I found it greatly demeaning and I clung to propriety by removing trousers and underpants separately, and then quickly girding the pyjama bottoms under the shirt. This was rumbled the third night – there was a chorus of derision.

'Frightened of showing us your willy, Casey?' they cried (for my initials were K.C. and that became my nickname in the squad).

'Nonsense,' I protested lamely. 'I was just trying to keep warm in this freezing dump.'

But I was stung into bravado and did the obligatory flash to catcalls and whistles down the room.

After that I made no attempt to conceal my nudity. It was just as well that I overcame my inhibition for there followed a succession of medical examinations. My B2 grading occasioned concern and after a lot of prodding from various doctors I was removed from Carlisle. I was sent with a pathetic group of pale and skinny conscripts to Hereford PDC where a burly PT Sergeant informed us at the top of his voice: 'This is a Physical Development Centre which specially caters for weaklings like you. You scrawny horrible creatures come in here looking like something out of the workhouse, but after we've finished with you, you go out looking like athletes! Do you hear me?' We all made nervous noises of assent and scurried away to our Nissen huts, whispering our conjectures about the transformations in store.

In the morning we each began a series of remedial exercises carefully chosen to put right whatever physical weaknesses we possessed. These were done in the open countryside, in the gymnasium and in the swimming pool. At meal times we were shown into mess-halls where rationing might never have existed: meat and fish were supplied in plenty, along with wheat-bread and fresh butter. Everyone seemed to put on weight, and at the end of six weeks, a special assault course had to be completed to prove the success of the PDC. Wearing a full pack, ammunition pouches and rifle we had to traverse various hazards and surmount rigorous obstacles. There was a river-crossing where the preceding soldier threw you a rope on which you swung over the water. I slung my rifle over my shoulder, grabbed the rope, sailed through the air with all the grace of a trapeze artist, and landed neatly on the other side.

Full of triumph, I turned for applause to the PT Sergeant who was following our progress on a bicycle. 'And what have you done with the bloody rope?' he demanded, getting off the bike and pointing to the river where it was hanging dejectedly midstream. 'You're supposed to hold on to it and throw it back over the water to the next man waiting to cross.'

The soldiers on the opposite bank were castigating me loudly and gesturing their disgust. 'Oh dear, I never thought,' I muttered helplessly.

11

'Well, you'd better start thinking now,' he barked. 'Hold your rifle high in one hand, go into the middle of the river, get hold of the rope and throw it to your mates.'

'But I'll get wet,' I said fatuously.

'You're wet already, you stupid little soldier,' he exploded, 'you're the wettest rotten rookie in the whole rotten squad! Now get in that river sharpish!'

He gave me a hefty shove and I was up to my neck in water, wading towards the rope.

'Do the breast stroke, Casey!' shouted the laughing conscripts on the other side as I paddled single-handedly and threw them the rope. I emerged with squelching boots and soaking uniform to start the wall-scaling and the route march. The water-laden equipment seemed to weigh a ton, my feet began to blister painfully and at the halfway mark I was struggling far behind the rest.

I suddenly thought, 'To hell with it', sank in a tired heap on the ground, and gave up. The sergeant returned on the bicycle. 'It's no good,' I panted. 'I'm all in.'

He eyed me ruefully. 'You'll be all in for the duration if you sit there doing the dying swan. If you don't pass the officer at the finishing post, you spend another six weeks here and do it all over again.'

I shuddered at the thought and made a face. He continued relentlessly: 'You'll have to do course after course. They'll keep you at it till you *do* pass.' I said I was built for comfort not for speed, and he walked back to his bike. I thought I was going to be disqualified.

He turned in the saddle and said shortly,'Get on my cross bar.'

I was too astonished to argue. He took my pack and hitched it to his own shoulders. I straddled the rail and he pedalled furiously along a circuitous route, hidden from the assault course. Within a few yards of the checkpoint he made me dismount.

'Hop over that hedge and stagger in with the rest.'

I began to burble profuse thanks but he brushed them aside and returned my pack.

'You haven't seen me since the river, remember.'

'No – I mean, yes, of course.'

'Get going them and for gawd's sake look tired.'

I trotted off and in five minutes I was feigning breathlessness at the finishing post where a waiting officer clicked his stop-watch and ticked my name on a clipboard.

'Nicely done, soldier,' he said approvingly.

I thought secretly, yes it was done nicely, very nicely indeed. Aloud I replied, 'Thank you, sir', and walked away feeling like an espionage agent concluding his first rendezvous.

In the sixth week I was shoved before another Medical Board who beamed their approval of my physical improvement. 'You've made excellent progress,' I was told. 'You are re-graded to A1' and I returned to Carlisle Castle for primary training, convinced that I was destined for the infantry. Why else this ceaseless combat work? All these exertions wouldn't improve my draughtsmanship. Obviously the army wasn't going to put me to the drawing-board, they intended me to fight. At the Castle I quickly slipped back into the old routines and the discipline of the PDC gave me a distinct advantage over the others. The corners had been rubbed off; the rhythms had been established.

At the passing-out parade, my squad was declared the best and we rushed back to the barrack room loud and boastful in our pride. There were celebrations, and in the evening we gave an impromptu concert in the gymnasium where my impressions of Winston Churchill and Nellie Wallace won vigorous applause.

The next day we were lined up before an officer who announced the regiments to which we were posted. My surname meant that I was practically the last to know. He read out posting after posting to combat units and my heart sank as I listened. What use was I going to be with a rifle or fixed bayonet? Every time I'd been on the firing range my bullets had landed up on someone else's target, and my flaccid lunging at straw dummies had made my instructor raise his eyes heavenward and bid me, 'Go and make the tea, Casey', with awful resignation. I feared the worst.

Then I heard the posting officer announce: 'Williams, K. C. to the Royal Engineers, Survey Section.' I could hardly believe my good fortune. The other conscripts congratulated me ('You've got a cushy number, Casey') and when they all piled onto huge lorries departing in comradely unison, I left alone on a 15 cwt truck, feeling strangely desolate and sad. I was sorry to be parting from these temporary friends; adversity had made them valuable acquaintances and there had been

13

many kind exchanges. They had admired my lettering and I had printed their names and numbers on kitbags and cases, in bold black marking ink. In return I got my webbing blancoed, my rifle cleaned and my bed made up. Most of them were Geordies, an accent that brings back affectionate memories to this day. They'd given me my first taste of communal living, loosened my inhibitions and taught me a truth about vulnerability. It went something like this: 'If you put out a hand and it's spat on, don't tuck it under the other arm for the rest of your life, or you'll end up disabled. Wipe your palm and put it out again: there's a chance that someone will grasp it.'

Chapter Two

My new life in the army began in Ruabon in Denbighshire. The truck dumped me at the bottom of a tree-lined avenue which led to the Survey Training Centre. With my kitbag slung over my shoulder, I started walking up the long drive. I was full of worried preconceptions and the dread of starting all over again with strangers. I kept looking out of the corner of my eye towards the red flash on my shoulder, announcing Royal Engineers. I still hadn't got used to it. Halfway up the road, I saw an officer approaching and I saluted smartly.

'Morning, Sapper!' came the greeting as he passed, and the title sounded strange after all the weeks of being called Private. I said the new word aloud to myself over and over again. I decided that I liked it.

At the end of the drive, I found a huge mansion in which the REs were housed. I met the Sergeant Draughtsman who showed me to a desk and talked in a leisurely fashion about the sort of work they did. It was all very gentle and pleasant.

The sapper working at the next table chatted amiably about the print world and it transpired he had a friend at Stanfords.

'Dear old Edward. Is he still there?'

'Yes,' I replied delightedly. 'He's head of the litho department.'

We were on common ground. I was back at the drawing office and, in a sense, I was home again.

Having satisfied Ruabon with my qualifications I was transferred to a hutted encampment at Ruislip where there followed a series of posting to RE survey stations where we printed army maps. Apart from wearing uniform it was a life comparable to my civilian apprenticeship: there was a minimum amount of military discipline, even brass buttons no longer required polishing since we were issued with plastic substitutes. I was surrounded by skilful craftsmen and cultivated, easy-going superiors. The war seemed very far away.

I had frequent leave passes. It was easy to hitch-hike home to London – the uniform always engaged the sympathy of motorists – and I would swagger about in it showing off and dropping heavy hints about secret military intelligence work on which I was engaged. People narrowed their eyes and nodded when I told them, 'You understand of course . . . I'm not allowed to discuss it,' and I was regarded with a new respect. At the local pub I wasn't allowed to pay for a drink. I downed ginger wine freely and smoked other people's cigarettes with ludicrous self-importance.

The even tenor of this comfortable existence was rudely shattered when I suddenly got an overseas posting. I practically stammered with surprise when I saw my name on the army order paper. I asked another sapper who was drafted, 'Where d'you think they'll send us?'

'Search me, could be anywhere.'

'I hope it's Europe.'

'Why?'

'I'd hate to get mixed up in the Japanese campaign; they sound perfectly horrible. Besides I can't stand the heat.'

It was 1945 and many of us were being posted abroad. 'I expect it will be Europe,' said my companion, and I persuaded myself that he was right. On the 12th of April I embarked on a troopship at Greenock; on the 17th the convoy was assembled and we sailed with an escort of naval destroyers into the open sea.

The weather gradually became warmer. On the sixth day someone said we were passing Gibraltar and soon we were at Port Said. Obviously we weren't intended for Europe at all and the schoolboy German I'd culled at Stanley Central was going to be useless. On the 29th we entered the Suez Canal. All the way, Egyptians lining the banks offered goods for sale to the troops. When one of then held up a hookah a soldier from the deck shouted, 'Up your pipe' – and the pedlar repeated it gleefully, 'Yes, up your pipe.'

Apart from accommodation the voyage proved quite enjoyable. Other ranks were stowed on their decks in crowded conditions and the propinquity of perspiring humanity caused frayed tempers and outbursts of aggression. At night there was a rush for the boxes containing the sleeping gear. If you were lucky enough to find a hammock and a place to sling it, there was a chance of reasonable repose; otherwise you laid a blanket on the mess table, and if that was occupied, you slept on the floor.

It was a relief to escape to the open deck and fresh air. I stayed up there as much as I could. I didn't care for the food but managed to subsist on snacks from the Naafi canteen where I also purchased endless tins of effervescent liver salts. I had to return to the mess deck to dissolve them, and my companions watched in horror. I was warned that I'd get the runs if I kept downing all that fizz, but the heat made me continually thirsty and their predictions were never realised; the drinking had no ill-effect whatsoever.

By the 7th of May the ship tied up in Bombay and lumbering lorries conveyed us to a transit camp at Kalyan. I *hated* Kalyan. We arrived late at night in darkness and confusion and I never understood the geography of the place. If I ever ventured very far away from the tent it always took me ages to find it again; the heat made me torpid, mosquitoes droned with maddening regularity, and it was here that I first incurred the wrath of military discipline.

I was given night sentry duty guarding the armoury. There was a lot of talk from the adjutant about the importance of this task: 'This requires stringent vigilance, it's probably the most important site in the entire transit camp. You lads had better be on your toes. You'll be given two-hour turns.'

At about midnight I was completing the first half of the patrol when I met the sentry coming from the opposite direction. We were supposed to report 'All's well', or something to that effect, then turn and retrace our steps. This soldier did nothing of the kind. He rested his rifle on the ground and grumbled, 'Bleeding creepy, ain't it!'

I readily agreed. 'Yes, awful. The heat makes everything stick to you. I'm covered in this anti-mosquito stuff but it's no use. I still get bitten.'

'Smoking puts 'em off,' he said, fumbling in his tunic pockets.

'Does it?' I enquired interestedly.

'Why don't you rest that thing on the ground,' he gestured toward my rifle which was still shouldered.

Obediently I did so, and he offered me a cigarette from a battered pack, deftly lighting it with his hands expertly cupped round the match. I inhaled the smoke with satisfaction and remarked, 'Yes, it does keep those bloody mozzies away.'

'I must have a pee,' he said disconcertingly and turned, retreating a few paces. Suddenly there were footsteps behind me and a voice loud in my ear demanded: 'Are you smoking, soldier?'

I turned, astonished and surprised, with the cigarette poised in my raised hand. Denial was useless. 'Er – yes,' I admitted, adding a belated 'sir', when I saw the pips on his shoulder.

He called to the other sentry: 'You smoking as well?'

'No, sir,' came the reply as the soldier saluted with one hand and buttoned his fly with the other. He told me afterwards, 'I swallowed the fag. Soon as I heard him coming. Destroyed all the evidence, see.'

I had no such *savoir faire*. I was caught, literally red-handed. 'Someone else will relieve you,' the Duty Officer told me curtly, 'and then you'll report to the sergeant of the guard. You're on a charge. Dereliction of duty.'

Minutes later I was in the guardroom cell, feeling like a criminal. A corporal brought me a mug of cocoa. 'What d'you have to go and do a stupid thing like that for?' he asked.

'It was only a fag,' I returned lamely. 'It would have been out in five minutes. It was so late I never dreamed an officer would turn up.'

'He's very hot on the armoury guard, always checks. You're in the cart. Smoking on duty; it's worse than jankers. Could mean the glasshouse.'

'Glasshouse?' I echoed, and he relented.

'Well, probably not if there's nothing on your crime sheet.'

I grasped at this straw. 'There isn't,' I replied hastily. 'I've never been in any trouble before.'

Then the sergeant of the guard appeared and motioned the corporal out of the cell. 'What the hell have you been up to?'

'I just had this cigarette,' I bumbled. 'It was to calm my nerves. The heat was getting me down, the mosquitoes were all round. I thought the smoke would put them off . . .'

'And the officer caught you at it?'

'Yes.'

'And you admitted it?'

'I had no option. I was holding the cigarette in my hand.'

'Did you say anything else?'

'No.'

He sat on the bunk beside me. 'All right. Now, we've got to decide on your story. You'll be up in front of the CO tomorrow. He'll ask if you've got anything to say for yourself.'

'What can I say? I just had a cigarette to calm my nerves,' I repeated.

He seized on this. 'That's it. Listen, you say you felt nervous.

It was dark. You got frightened; you had a smoke to steady yourself. Got any history of nervousness?'

'I used to sleepwalk as a child.' He looked sceptical but I pressed on. 'They said that was due to nerves. I was worried about this school play I was acting in . . .'

'You'd better act tomorrow,' he said fervently, 'and it had better convince the CO. I'll back you up. I'll say you looked tired and edgy when you came on duty, and you'd better look the part. You've only been out here a week, and with any luck you'll swing it.' He rose and turned at the door, adding kindly, 'Now you'd better try and get some sleep.'

Oblivion was not forthcoming. I rehearsed a stammering speech of nervousness and desperately tried to compose an explanation for my invidious behaviour. If ever a performance was called for, it was now.

In the morning I was quick-marched between the escort and brought before the CO, my cap was humiliatingly snatched from my head and the charge read out. It sounded damning.

'Do you realize the seriousness of this offence?' asked the officer, and I nodded mutely, forcing the tears from reddened eyes.

He looked pained. 'Have you anything to say for yourself?' I did a lot of lip-trembling and stuttering before bursting into an impassioned account of panic on a hot night in a strange new climate, of imagined fears in the darkness, and the attempt to recover composure through nicotine. I ended with a weeping declaration of heat malaise and a plea of nervous irresponsibility. 'I wasn't myself,' I cried and begged forgiveness. By this time the tears were flowing in abundance.

The CO cleared his throat embarrassedly. 'This man is obviously ill,' he began, and the sergeant of the guard came in on cue. 'I noticed when he came on duty, sir. Very pale and drawn, sir. Didn't look at all well.'

'Quite so,' he replied. 'I shall dismiss the charge. Take this man to the sick-bay and inform the MO.'

My cap was returned and the sergeant ushered me out.

'You were bloody good,' he conceded. 'Nearly convinced me,' and before I could answer he added, 'You'd better keep it up 'cos now you'll have to convince the MO as well.'

The performance lasted all day. I wept and raved in the sick-bay with such consummate skill that I even began to believe it myself. The doctor nodded understandingly and prescribed sedation. I was put to bed between cool sheets, under a mosquito net and the curtain descended. There was no applause, but my crime sheet remained unblemished.

I exchanged the torpid heat of Kalyan for the verdant freshness of Dehra Dun, high in the foothills of the Himalayas, three days' train journey away. This was my introduction to a very different kind of India; a region of lush grassland against a backdrop of purple mountains which glowed red at sunset and twinkled after dark with a thousand lights from village townships. The REs were housed there in a fine colonial building which was every bit as grand as Ruabon but the printing presses were identical – offset litho – and I was back to the same kind of work as before.

Life returned to normal. There was a sticky moment the second week when I visited the MO with a skin complaint. He looked up from my papers and remarked, 'So you had a spot of bother down in Kalyan, Williams?'

'I was never any good with a rifle,' I admitted, thinking that the sentry incident had been reported after all. 'I'm useless at combat duty.'

'That's not my department. I'm concerned with your health. It appears that excessive heat renders you prone to nervous disorders.'

'Oh yes, that's true. I used to sleepwalk as a child.'

'Really. Where were you brought up?'

'Er – London.'

'Shouldn't have thought that was particularly hot.'

'We were over the bakery.'

'But it says here your father had a hairdressing shop.'

'We moved to those premises later.'

'I see. Well you'd better stay in the shade, Williams. We don't want you getting neurotic from sunstroke. I'll give you calamine for this inflammation in your crotch. We call it dhobi rash. Don't let the bearer use so much starch in your laundry, or better still, do your own washing.'

I was hobbling painfully back to my quarters reflecting that there was little point in having Indian bearers and dhobis if it resulted in urticaria, when a CSM stopped me.

'Why are you mincing round like that, Sapper?'

I poured out my tale of woe about the nettle rash. 'My crotch is all red and stinging and the skin is aflame. The

20

doctor's given me calamine but I should be in hospital. My feet are bad as well. These army boots are too stiff, they hurt my instep. I can only move with difficulty.'

He eyed me distastefully. 'Stop feeling sorry for yourself. A soldier doesn't reveal his feelings. March properly.'

I moved off stiffly. He called after me, 'Walk like a man.'

If I could, I thought, I wouldn't need calamine, and returned to the barrack room complaining loudly about the inhumanity of service life.

My room-mates listened with wry amusement. 'I should never have been graded A1,' I lamented. 'I had to be sent to a Harley Street specialist. He said I should be B2.'

'What's that stand for?' asked a wag – 'brain deficiency?'

I removed my clothes and applied the lotion gingerly. 'Don't sneer at sickness,' I rebuked him. 'This specialist diagnosed anaemia: that's why I'm pale.'

'Yes. Pale pink with all that calamine. Keep that up and you'll match the carnations. You could go AWOL in Kew Gardens, they'd never find you in the flower beds!'

There was spluttering laughter from the others, but I pretended indifference. I pulled my pyjamas carefully over my legs and got into bed. 'You are incorrigible,' I said witheringly, and pulled up the sheet.

'You're not going to bed at this hour, are you?' they asked incredulously. 'Yes,' I returned shortly.

'But we're all going to the pictures. *The Dough Girls* is on at the local.'

'I'm far too ill,' I told them. 'I wouldn't get up for Rudolph Valentino.'

The ensuing silence was so profound that I wondered what was the cause. I raised myself on one elbow and looked round the room. They were gazing in awe at the CSM who was standing in the doorway holding a parcel in his arms. He saw me blinking with surprise and came towards the bed.

'You the one with the dhobi rash?'

I nodded.

He dropped the bundle on my bed. 'These tunics and slacks are made of poplin khaki. Very soft. They should fit you all right and won't give you any skin trouble. And there's a pair of boots as well, made out of Indian leather. Better for your feet.'

I sat upright in the bed. 'Thank you, sar'nt major.'

'That's all right. See you on parade in the morning.'

As soon as he'd gone I was out of the bed, trying on my new finery. My room-mates crowded round, fingering the material, heavily mocking: 'Well, who's sergeant's pet then? Who's the crawler? Who can't wear ordinary uniforms like the rest of us?'

'It's my skin,' I explained, donning the tunic. 'It's very sensitive.'

'Oh we know, we know you're delicate.'

I pulled on the boots; unlike the ordinary issue, they were as soft as kid. 'Hmm, these are lovely,' I murmured appreciatively and walked up and down like a mannequin.

'Thought you were ill,' said the wag derisively. 'What are you getting all dolled up for?'

'The pictures, of course,' I replied. 'I'm going with you to *The Dough Girls*.'

I'd always had a fear of being stationed near any fighting area in the Japanese campaign. Working in the RE survey branch made it highly unlikely, but there were mobile map reproduction sections which moved in ten-ton trucks with drawing boards and printing presses and they could go practically anywhere. There was always the chance of danger. The idea of actually seeing these almond-eyed enemies made me quail. Whether the fear was instilled by propaganda films or stories heard from ex-prisoners of war, I don't know. Certainly the things I learned were horrifying. Veterans from Burma recounted ghastly experiences of torture and brutality and when I saw some of the resulting physical disablements they filled me with dread. It was comforting, at least, to be told in the relative safety of Northern India that I wouldn't see any combat because the war would be over before the year was out.

But I was never totally reassured until the fateful events of Hiroshima and Nagasaki caused the Japanese surrender in August 1945. It was in Dehra Dun that I heard the news and my feeling of relief was intense. It was really over at last. Everything was going to be different. I can still remember the recoil from wartime attitudes among soldiers. Sentiments like 'Churchill was all right for the war but we want another man for the peace' were often expressed and when the radio announced his political defeat and the election of Clement Attlee, there was no great feeling of surprise. Just the satisfied

22

sense of a proper denouement. The memory of an inspired leader whose grave oratory had once stirred our hearts quickly receded. It was something that was fine at the time, but the time was past. Now he should go. I had no idea of the vision that was to go with him.

The cessation of hostilities brought about a rundown in the Royal Engineers' survey section and many men became redundant. I was sent to Ceylon, where I served with the 62 Map Reproduction Section in Kurunegala until the maps were no longer required and the unit was disbanded.

It was in Kurunegala that an incident occurred which engraved itself upon my memory. The unit was in *bashas* – huts made of rush matting – in a coconut grove, and at the centre of the buildings was the CO's office and the British other ranks' mess. The Indian other ranks had their mess in their own barrack block. One day, the CO, Captain Hardman, took the BORs swimming and they all set off in two large trucks, leaving me, since I didn't care for exercise, to look after the camp as Duty NCO. At this time I was a lance corporal.

It was a hot day and during the afternoon I left the office and went to my hut where I undressed and lay on the bed, pulling down the mosquito net to have a snooze. After a while I woke to the sound of a radio blaring nearby. To my knowledge the only wireless in the camp was the one the BORs had sub-scribed to pay for out of their own pockets and it was housed in their mess, but they were all out of the camp on the swim-ming trip, so who could be using it? I rose from the charpoy, knotted a towel round my waist and walked to the mess. To my amazement, the entire Indian contingent was all crammed into the building listening to our radio. I pushed through the throng and switched off the set.

'This is a BOR mess,' I told them, 'and you are trespassing – now all of you get out!'

They rose resentfully and some surged towards me menac-ingly, but a subadar, whom I'd not noticed in the crowd, quietened them and told them in Urdu to leave the room. As he departed he gave me a long look and I wished I'd been wearing something more substantial than a towel and my identity discs.

I returned to the *basha* and went back to sleep in the warm and now silent afternoon. It must have been about an hour later when I woke to find the CO at my bedside shaking my shoulder and asking, 'What on earth went on in the BOR's mess while I was away?'

I told him I'd found Indians using our radio and that I'd put a stop to it. 'I told them all to get out.'

'Yes, well the trouble is they were listening to a broadcast from Delhi about the imminent declaration of Indian independence. They're about to get self-government and all this racial discrimination will become an anachronism. At the moment race relations are at a tricky stage and we must tread very carefully. Apparently you insulted their subadar by not even addressing him properly. He's called Subadar Sahib you know.'

'I didn't even see him till it was practically all over. I just told 'em all to shove off.'

'Well, they've been to see me full of grievances about the incident and they are indignant about the way you treated their officer. I think you should go and apologise to him.'

'All right,' I agreed. 'I'll go over and tell him it was a mistake.'

I rose and pulled on my khaki shorts.

'No,' said the CO, 'put on trousers and gaiters, wear your tunic and belt. Do it properly. You can't slop on to a parade ground like that.'

'Parade ground?' I echoed.

'Of course. He will line up his men to hear your apology – after all, you insulted him in front of them all, so you'll have to undo the damage in the same way. I'll be back in ten minutes to take you over there.'

The other soldiers in the hut helped me into uniform, one even lent me a freshly blancoed belt. I rehearsed what I was going to say and eventually I made my way with Captain Hardman to the Indian barrack square where the IORs were assembled with their subadar at the head. He called them to attention as we marched up and they watched the spectacle of this erstwhile arrogant lance-corporal delivering a humble speech of contrition. I saluted smartly and said loudly, 'Subadar Sahib, I behaved in a stupid and discourteous manner. I acted on the spur of the moment without realizing the gravity of the occasion. I hope you will overlook this unhappy business and accept my sincere apologies.'

I saluted again, expecting a formal reply, but to my surprise,

24

this Sikh officer took me in his arms and embraced me as his men cheered and then he said, 'You have spoken well, come and eat with us.'

My OC beamed his approval, and later on I found myself eating unaccustomed food with this friendly and forgiving man among a throng of smiling Indian faces.

'I expected you to return my salute and dismiss me,' I told him, 'not invite me to dinner.'

'Why not?' he asked. 'Isn't it written in your book – forgive us our trespasses as we forgive them that trespass against us?'

I nodded agreement as he said the words, but even as I did so I realized I had never taken them in before. It was ironic that a Sikh should tell me the meaning of a prayer I'd recited from childhood. From that moment on I was to re-examine not only the Lord's Prayer but a hundred other things I'd hitherto taken for granted. Someone with another creed had taught me the value of my own and I had learned another lesson on that day as well; where there is reciprocity racial barriers become irrelevant – what matters are the human affections that bind all mankind.

It wasn't long after that, in the same camp at Kurunegala, that we held an impromptu concert at which my impersonations won vigorous applause. The Quartermaster Sergeant – who had written the scripts and put the show together – told me I should take up entertaining professionally. At that stage I had no such ambition, but when an area order announced that soldiers with a preference for alternative regiments could apply for transfers I persuaded the CO to sign my application for CSE which was a newly formed organisation to succeed ENSA. It was called Combined Services Entertainments because it drew on talent from the Army, Navy and the RAF, to provide diversion for the forces. Its base in South-East Asia was Singapore, and after various vicissitudes, I arrived there from Colombo on the SS *Cameronia* on the 31st of August 1946.

Transport awaited me at the dockside where a taciturn young captain stood by a staff car.

'Are you for CSE?'

I saluted smartly. 'Yes sir.'

'Thought so,' he replied, opening the car door.'Get in.'

We drove to Neesoon where the unit was housed. On the

way I asked the officer, 'Are there many entertainers there, sir?'

'Loads.'

'I suppose they're mostly variety, singers and dancers, and all that. I do impersonations – hope they haven't got a lot who do that.'

'They've got everything except performing seals.'

I began to laugh but he turned and gazed at me so mournfully that it froze on my lips. 'They'll come,' he assured me, 'don't you worry. Bouncing balls and all.'

This weird prenotion sent my imagination reeling. I began to wonder what I'd let myself in for.

The CSE offices were housed in Neesoon transit camp and it was all oddly inappropriate. In the middle of a huge army barracks, accommodation was provided for an assortment of performers, musicians, writers and designers, who possessed little or no regard for military discipline or protocol; though they were servicemen and sometimes wore uniform, their interests and activities were totally alien to regimental procedure, and this dichotomy aroused the antagonism which invariably exists between the conventional and the eccentric. Officers and NCOs drilling troops on the parade ground didn't relish the sight of actors in casual shirts and silk cravats swanning around the perimeter in animated conversation; six o'clock reveille was not observed by itinerant thespians who performed at night and rose late. Long-haired flamboyancy contrasted strangely with martial stiffness and there were dark mutterings about 'these arty-crafty CSE fairies' in their midst. It was a paradoxical situation which gave rise to all sorts of anomalies. The garrison theatre was known as 'The Gaiety' and it was there that the auditioning took place.

I waited nervously with a motley throng of aspiring performers. They included would-be conjurors, tap-dancers, singers, acrobats, musicians and heaven knows what else. A brisk and a languid voice could be heard alternately calling out from the stalls, asking questions and then frequently using the initials 'RTU'. When a towering Scotsman from the Cameron Highlanders ended his turn with the bagpipes, the languid tones cried out, 'Very good, very good, but your eyes are like gimlets, can you overcome that with cosmetics?'

'What?'

'Can you make-up?'

'No.'

'We'll have to teach you then.'

'Not me thanks. I want no make-up on my face.'

'They all wear make-up in the shows.'

'Then I'll not be in any shows.'

'Then what did you audition for?'

'To play my pipes, not powder my nose.'

'Very well then, you can go. RTU.'

And he tramped disgustedly off the stage while the sergeant ticked the name on a list in the wings, echoing the letters RTU.

'What does RTU stand for, sergeant?' I asked.

'Return to unit, dear. It's the army version of we'll let you know – don't call us, we'll call you. And don't call me sergeant, call me Terry.'

I was surprised at this unexpected familiarity from an NCO.

'Do many of them get RTU?'

'Yes, many are called but few are chosen. What do you do?'

'Impressions. I can do Winston Churchill and Nellie Wallace.'

'I should think you're the only one who does.'

'Eh?'

'Nothing, dear – go on, you're next.'

In the middle of my audition the languid voice moaned, 'Oh dear, oh dear.' When I finished, the brisk tones declared 'RTU' and I returned, humiliated, to the sergeant in the wings.

'What on earth am I going to do?'

'Rejoin your old mob, love.'

'It's disbanded.'

'What crowd were you with?'

'RE Survey. I was a draughtsman.'

'Oh, they want posters done for the shows. Can you draw posters?'

'Well, yes,' I said uneasily. 'But I came here to act.'

'Half a loaf's better than nothing, dear – hang on till the break – I'll tell the Old Man you can do posters.'

And so I was taken on the unit strength as a poster designer. But it was through this unlikely avenue that I finally got into a show. I went with note-pad and pencil to the theatre where a production was being rehearsed. I had to get the cast list and ascertain the nature of the billing. The director suddenly asked me, 'Before we do that, could you stand in and read for me? I've an actor down with malaria and there's no understudy.'

I jumped at the chance. I walked onto the stage and was handed a marked script. It was the role of a detective in an interrogation scene. I played it with steely determination. At the finish, the director complimented me. 'You're really very good . . . bit young for the part, but you could wear a moustache . . .' Where had I heard that before? Never mind, the Mary Ward Settlement was a long way away. This time the spirit gum did work and the sick actor didn't return, and I ended up playing the detective in a play called *Seven Keys to Baldpate* at the Victoria Theatre in Singapore.

The opening night was chaotic. The troops were restless and impatient with our creaky old thriller. One of the characters had to remonstrate, 'You've searched all of us but what about her?' indicating a seductive creature in a low-cut gown. My reply was, 'Don't worry, if she's got anything on her I'll get it.'

Straightaway a heckler bawled, 'After you with the crumpet!' The girl's following line, 'I've nothing to hide,' got a rousing 'You could have fooled us,' and the ensuing catcalls and ribaldry killed this scene stone dead. The distracted players forgot their lines, an overzealous prompter leaned too far forward and fell onto the stage, script and all, causing more hilarity. I had handcuffed an actor who couldn't be released because I'd left the keys at Neesoon, fifteen miles away from Singapore, and the curtain descended on derisive applause. Incredibly the play ran for two weeks, but admittedly the houses were not overfull.

It was backstage during this production that an aesthetic twenty-year-old called Stanley Baxter with a bulky kitbag pushed through the stage door and asked in a soft Scots accent, 'Is this the headquarters of CSE?' He said he'd flown from Burma to join us.

'No, this is one of the dates we're playing,' I told him. 'The HQ is at Neesoon; we go back on the lorry at midnight. I'll get you a complimentary seat and you can watch the show and come back with us afterwards.' He thanked me profusely and left for the auditorium.

Stanley returned with us to Neesoon and an empty room was found for him in a recently vacated block next to the CSE billets. He asked me why the walls bore such curious stains. I explained: 'Native troops were living here, and there were tribal customs: slitting the throats of sheep and goats in sacrifi-

28

cial rites, you know the sort of thing, the blood splashes everywhere.'

He reproached me afterwards for causing him a sleepless night by conjuring up such a nauseous picture, but the accommodation was not the only reason for his misgivings on arriving at Neesoon. He reported to the CSE office next day and stood waiting to be seen by an officer who was seated at a desk, looking adoringly up at a young RAF sergeant who was standing stiffly to attention before him and loudly demanding, 'Permission to return to unit, sir!'

'Don't be silly, Brian, how can you leave after all that has happened?'

'Permission to return to unit, sir?'

'Don't keep calling me "Sir". It was Christian names last night. What about the dinner at Raffles? What about the silk shirts you liked so much?'

'Permission to return to . . .'

'Oh don't keep on, Brian. We'll talk about it tonight. Dismiss.'

The sergeant saluted, turned and marched off. Stanley took his place in front of the desk but the officer's head remained turned as he watched the retreating back and murmured endearments. Stanley had to announce himself twice before the reverie was dispelled.

He told me afterwards of his amazement. 'I've never heard anything like it in an army set-up!'

'That's one of the producers,' I said. 'Brian wants to leave his show; he was asking him to reconsider.'

'Sounded more like a proposal. What sort of show does he produce?'

'Revues, plays, musicals, all kinds of things. For his latest one they're flying a soprano out from London specially, but there's a rumour the troops will boycott the show.'

'Why?'

'Cos the ENSA shows were free but CSE is charging four-pence. The lads don't want to pay.'

When the show in question was staged at the Gaiety Theatre, Stanley said he didn't blame them. The opening number, 'You've Done Something To My Heart', had the leading lady twirling coquettishly before a chorus of male singers who had to *la-la* in descant to her song. Her red velvet dress was unsuitable for the hot climate and she had foolishly eaten melon grown in infected water. It became obvious at the dress rehearsal that she was in some distress when her performance was marred by loud eructation and she complained of stomach pains.

The MO was sent for and diagnosed dysentery, but she stoutly maintained that the show must go on and insisted on appearing. She struggled valiantly at the beginning and when her voice grew faint the chorus loudly compensated, at least until the end of the first verse when she rushed to a portable commode in the wings. The singers were then left to *la-la* without her. They made a ragged attempt to fill in and started the line 'Some strange something in my heart' but she shot back on for 'When you're there there's something in the air', words which acquired an unfortunate ambiguity. One cynic said the show should have been re-titled 'The Lady Vanishes' for she staggered on and off several times before disappearing altogether, leaving a hapless chorus to finish the reprise alone. The show never recovered from this ignominious start and it became the subject of risible comment in the mess.

All the performers in CSE were automatically promoted to sergeant; they enjoyed the privileges of twin-bedded rooms instead of dormitories, and were served by Malayan bearers in their own mess. It was a source of irritation that only officers were allowed to produce shows, and another sergeant, Peter Nichols, felt sure that we could get together and write something and put it on ourselves. Stanley Baxter agreed: 'Anything would be better than that rubbish at the Gaiety.' Someone else mentioned that there were some bods at HQ who had formed their own theatre group and put on plays. He said he knew one of them and would arrange a meeting.

He did. And John Schlesinger came to Neesoon and told us about the Singapore Stage Club, where all kinds of talent were encouraged and direction wasn't dependent on officer status. John suggested that we organise a discussion, a sort of whole-day symposium where we could work something out. He said there was a rest camp on the coast. 'I can fix up transport and we could all go out there for the day.'

The 26th of May 1947 was Whit Monday and we set off early in a station wagon with our bathing costumes, a copy of Gordon Craig's *Art of Theatre* and high hopes of a stimulating day by the sea. On the way there was a lot of lively conversation about the sort of shows which *should* be devised and produced by other ranks. Stanley was full of ideas for

30

spectacular openings and story lines while John talked enthusiastically about how they could be staged.

There was also considerable argument about our map reading and we only found the rest camp after taking a lot of wrong turnings. We need not have bothered. A faded signboard reading 'Leave Centre' hung neglectedly at the entrance, and we drove unbelievingly into a fenced area containing two ancient Nissen huts built on cracked concrete with weeds sprouting through the gaps. There was no sign of life.

We got out of the wagon and walked round the huts, past some decaying wooden latrines, to where the ground sloped towards the sea. The water lapped the shore sluggishly; there was oil slick all over it.

Our spirits sank to zero as we stood indecisively surveying the desolation. 'There must be someone about,' said John desperately. 'After all, it's an official rest camp.' I said, 'It looks like a death camp.'

We retraced our steps and found between the two huts a solitary member of the Army Catering Corps. He was sitting on an upturned bucket peeling potatoes and throwing them into a dixie with a plopping sound.

'Is this the leave camp?' we asked.

'Yeah, but there's only me here. It's the bank holiday, see.'

'But surely that's the time when everyone comes?'

'No. They go into Singapore. That's where the life is.'

There was precious little life here. We returned to the transport dejectedly and drove back to Neesoon where we ended up in the New London café eating egg sandwiches and complaining bitterly about logistics in South-East Asia Command.

The next theatrical event at Neesoon was provided by a new show, largely civilian, which came out from England, starring the improbably named Barri Chat, whose arrival caused quite a stir.

A group of staff officers were disbanding after a conference outside HQ, when Chat leapt out of a jeep, performed three pirouettes before a slack-jawed brigadier, tapped him on the shoulder, crying, 'Tell your mother we're here, dear. Put the kettle on,' and disappeared through the swing doors in a cloud of perfume.

He was followed by a supporting cast shouting sibilant greetings and an irate danseuse demanding the loo.

When an aide explained to the astounded officers that they

31

were a stage troupe sent out from London, the brigadier said the city was damned lucky to be rid of them and predicted dire consequences for the colony.

But the troops were delighted. Barri Chat devised satirical dance routines which were sharply observed and very funny; he also enjoyed great success as a female impersonator and won cheering applause from service audiences every time he appeared. He took bows with great panache, smiling archly and calling out, 'Thank you lads! Thank you. See you at the stage door. There's more round the back!' And the invitation seldom went unheeded.

His dressing room was packed after the show and his north country accent overladen with stage locution could always be heard welcoming the abashed and awkward visitor. 'Come in, dear, don't be shy – think of me as your sister!' When a crony quipped – 'Like the one in Cinderella!' – Barri retorted tartly, 'Don't bite your tongue, dear, you'll get blood poisoning!' He always got his laughs and his patter was well rehearsed. Banter between friends provoked mirth and that cut the ice. 'Give the lads a beer,' he'd tell them, 'while I get the slap on.'

At the end of a show when most actors were removing the make-up Barri was putting another lot on. He always had a bronze matt complexion under his blond upswept hair and boasted, 'I never shave dear, never. Pull all the hairs out with tweezers in a magnifying mirror, and rub in the cream. Face like a baby's bum, dear. You'd never *guess* my age. We must keep the illusion. Let's face it, lovies, it's life, it's the theatre!'

This last sentence was one he continually iterated, and it soon became a catchphrase. People copied his accent and mannerisms. The Chat idiosyncracies symbolised gay show-biz abandon and soon there was a band of imitators following in his wake.

The stories told of his blithe disregard for authority were legion. To ensure that civilian entertainers had decent accommodation they were given honorary officer status and it was as Captain Chat that he boarded a troopship for the tour of South-East Asia. It sailed from Singapore with Barri ensconced in the top bunk of a double cabin, but in the night the ship stopped at Port Swettenham to let another passenger come aboard. He was a grizzled colonel, a veteran of the Burma campaign, and was stowed in the berth underneath. In the morning he woke to find face powder cascading down from above, and leaned out of bed to see the other occupant liberally applying the *poudre rachel* and humming gaily. There was hoarse protestation, and the hair-netted Chat called down, 'You might as well get used to this, dear. I do it every morning.' His fellow-traveller had no intention of getting used to it and, pausing only to knot a towel round his waist, he rushed off, remonstrating, 'There's a woman in my cabin.'

A surprised OC Troops was told about the curious circumstances of the colonel's awakening, the concert party escorting NCO was sent for and an explanation demanded.

'Are you aware of these morning rituals?'

'Professional performers often practise their make-up at seven in the morning. These players are perfectionists.'

'But he's a captain.'

'Rank means nothing to artistes, they live in another world.'

The Colonel demanded another cabin, and Captain Chat enjoyed sole occupancy for the rest of the voyage.

'We thespians need the privacy, dear,' he confided afterwards. 'Let's face it, the mask must be maintained. It's life, lovey – it's the theatre.'

It was nothing to do with the theatre as far as the Army was concerned, and the emulation of such feminine frivolity produced alarmed reaction at the CSE offices. The CO paraded the unit and inveighed against this unbecoming behaviour: 'You may be artistes but you are in the army. You'll get your hair cut and try to look like soldiers.'

'Get the madam,' was whispered from the back row.

'I heard that remark!' he barked angrily. 'Now cut it out or there'll be CB (Confined to Barracks) for everyone. You've been asking for trouble and you're going to get it. I'm bringing in a sergeant major from the DLIs to knock some discipline into this shower! Your feet won't touch the ground!'

From all we'd heard about the Durham Light Infantry and their fiercesome marching pace, his threat sounded all too real. There were some feeble attempts at laughing it off when we were dismissed but it was a subdued unit by the time the new CSM arrived.

I'd been rehearsing a play called *Not So Much The Heat* – Stanley Baxter and Peter Nichols were in the cast too – and we were looking forward to performing at last when we were suddenly told that there were complications over copyright and the project was cancelled. Instead we were all put into a revue entitled *At Your Service* and the opening number ran into trouble straightaway. We appeared in coloured uniforms singing a lyric which began 'We're boys of the service'.

The CO objected: 'Far too sibilant, sounds like a load of pansies. Change it to something more masculine.'

The same line-up reappeared singing 'We're men of the Service' in stentorian tones.

He pronounced himself satisfied: 'That's more like it – sounds like soldiers.'

We thought there was very little difference, but the delivery didn't last long and it was soon much the same as before.

The revue went on the road, with its complement of songs, sketches and dances. Peter Nichols wrote and performed a humorous monologue; Stanley had a spot as a kilted Scotsman; Rae Hammond was the conjuror. I did impressions and Les Wilson portrayed a very funny Goon-like character. I particularly remember Les because of his extraordinary ability to improvise. Proper stages were not always available, and we often performed under makeshift conditions. Once on tour we worked on a verandah platform surrounded by a deep monsoon ditch, with the troops sitting on the other side. Les sang 'Goodnight Pretty Maiden' for his finale, and on the line 'I come from the hills and the valleys below' he jumped into the monsoon ditch and continued singing with only his head visible, moving along the ridge and slowly out of sight. The comic effect was enormously enhanced and this involuntary variation made the cast laugh as much as the audience.

We toured Malaya going as far north as Penang and Butterworth and we returned to Singapore via Taiping and Kuala Lumpur.

Back at Neesoon we were told of the discipline now being imposed by the new sergeant major; many of the old liberties had been restricted, pukka parades were held. There were endless inspections and a lot of petty impositions.

'You'll have to wear proper boots and gaiters,' I was told. 'Those sandals and flowered ankle socks will have to go! If he sees them, you'll be for it!'

Everyone was frightened at the prospect of incurring his wrath and we waited to see if the lightning would strike any of us. It didn't. The sergeant major committed suicide by taking poison. There were wild rumours about his motives. Some talked of a 'double life' and alleged 'woman trouble' and

34

others hinted at embezzlement and fraud, but nobody seemed to know the truth.

The OC paraded the unit. 'Now look here, the sergeant major's killed himself. The man's more trouble dead than he was alive; someone's got to bury him. Volunteers stand forward for pall bearers!'

No one stepped forward. There was little love felt for the deceased and even less for the task of carrying his coffin. A burial party was detailed and several actors staggered with their awkward load to the graveside. Their clumsiness resulted in a very sloppy interment. The padre hastily instructed them to remove the Union Jack from the coffin since suicides received no honours, and the burial party found their rifles superfluous for the same reason. No shots were to be fired over the grave. There was confusion throughout. With pall-bearers on each side of the grave, the order for the march-off should have been 'Left file right turn, Right file left turn', but it was never spoken. The man who should have said it was in the coffin. Rain poured down to the discomfort of everyone and after the padre's embarrassed withdrawal the grave party drifted away, resentful, wet and grumbling.

I only heard reports of this bizarre incident – I wasn't there. My diary for that day reads: 'Went into Singapore, lunched at Ciro's. Taxi to Botanical Gardens for the afternoon, then on to the Rex Cinema to see *Talk of the Town* which was very enjoyable. Pegasus Club for dinner after and on to the studios where Roy played the piano for a broadcast. Another taxi back to Neesoon.' It doesn't smack of mourning, but it doesn't sound like a typical soldier's day-out either.

At Your Service was sent off touring again and we embarked on the SS *Empress of Scotland* on the 4th of September 1947 for Hong Kong. We were billeted at the China Fleet Club and performed at the theatre there as well as playing to various units in Kowloon and the New Territories areas. For some dates we produced a cabaret version of the show and revised the running order because Peter Nichols became ill and was taken to the military hospital. Stanley and I visited his bedside, taking a box of chocolate éclairs, but the nurse told us he was on a diet and wasn't allowed to eat them. To our chagrin the gift was confiscated.

Peter was eager for news and we had much to tell him. We

had broadcast excerpts from the show on Hong Kong radio and this had led to our being asked to work on the ZBW Forces network. There was to be a dramatic reconstruction of Nelson's Death, with Stanley and me playing the leading roles. The programme was to be narrated by an admiral of the fleet. It was all very exciting and we did the usual actors' embroidery. Think of what this could lead to: broadcasting experience out here might well mean overtures from the BBC in London.

When the event took place we were invited by the admiral to have drinks aboard his flagship. A chauffeur-driven car flying his pennant took us from the studio to the dockyard, where the guard presented arms, and we were taken by launch to a cruiser. In the wardroom a smiling lieutenant served us with pink gins and everything was warmly hospitable.

We were wearing civilian garb and somebody asked, 'Do you live in the colony?'

'No,' we replied. 'We're touring with CSE.'

'What's that?'

'Army entertainments.'

'You're military then?'

'Yes.'

'What is your rank?'

'Sergeants.'

There was a polite 'Oh really', and within minutes we were relieved of our drinks, ushered out of the wardroom, bundled over the side and sent back to the shore. This time there was no admiral's pennant flying and we were despatched without ceremony. Loping miserably through the dockyard, Stanley said it was no way to treat incomparable artistes and at the gates the sentries didn't present arms. In fact one of them blew a distinct raspberry. Our glory had been short-lived.

The company embarked on the SS *Devonshire* on the 25th of October 1947 to return to Singapore, and when we arrived there, they went ashore. I stayed on board, however, because I was due for demobilisation, and continued the voyage to Liverpool without them. In order to forget my loneliness, I flung myself into work on a ship's concert, rehearsing daily with all sorts of volunteer players, producing sketches, production numbers, and compèring.

A sergeant PT instructor, Ted Durant, joined us, performing a brilliant clown act which involved balancing on a table and

36

three chairs. By the time the ship was out of the Mediterranean she was rolling heavily and some nights it looked like touch and go whether he'd stay up in the air or crash, but his counterpoise was unerring and he never fell. Only at the end of the voyage, when Ted admitted that he used to be with Bertram Mills I realize where he had acquired such extraordinary skill.

We did the show twice daily on the promenade deck with makeshift rafts and bunting for a stage. As the weather got colder the troops were overcoated and gloved, so the clapping was enthusiastic but muffled, and our voices got hoarser and hoarser as we tried to be audible against sea and wind. It was worth it because we got the laughs and the applause but I bitterly regretted not indenting for a greatcoat in Hong Kong for by the time we got to Liverpool on the 2nd of December I was so cold that my goose pimples seemed to have become permanent.

Two days later at Aldershot I was formally discharged from the army and took the train to Waterloo. I got a taxi at the station which drove me along familiar roads and streets where I had walked so often in the past. The sight of war-torn London, sandbagged doorways and battered buildings was strangely moving. By the time we got to Kingsway I was weeping.

There were more tears when I was reunited with Louisa and Charlie. We sat drinking endless cups of tea and I recounted the events of the last six weeks. There'd been no mail since Hong Kong so there was a lot of catching up to do. They told me all the family news. Pat had married an Australian and gone to live in Sydney. Grandma Williams had moved to Leigh Street, Cousin Ronnie was engaged; it was all happening!

That night we celebrated in the local and I was greeted by lots of old faces: 'Let's have a look at yer! Very smart in your sergeant's uniform, I must say. How did you win the war?'

'I spilled my blood for you,' I cried, 'sharpening pencils in the drawing office.'

There was obligatory laughter. Everyone did a turn: Gran sang 'Grace Darling' and we all joined in the chorus. I went to bed very tired in the early hours of the morning. I was back in my own room, a civilian again after three and a half years.

Chapter Three

At the beginning of 1948 I returned to the drawing office. Stanfords had been taken over by George Philip & Son Ltd, and now I commuted by tube to Acton every day. The building was so cold I had to keep my overcoat on. I started off diligently enough and tried to interest myself in the work but my heart wasn't in it.

Stanley Baxter came down from Glasgow, and his visit altered everything. He too had been demobbed and was in London for an audition for the Young Vic which was run by Michel Saint-Denis. Stanley visited me at my home in Marchmont Street, where I waxed nostalgic for the old days ... 'In a way I wish I was still acting.'

'Well, what on earth are you doing as a draughtsman?'

'It's my old job and my father thinks there's no security in a theatrical career.'

'*Security*? You don't take up a profession like an insurance policy. You've got talent and you enjoy acting. You don't enjoy maps.'

'No, but I don't really know how to get into the theatre.'

'Write letters. Write to every repertory theatre in the country. Tell then you've had experience, mention CSE, say you're willing to be a stage manager and do small parts. No good sitting on your arse moping about the past. Do something constructive about your future!'

By the time he returned to Scotland, I was fired with enthusiasm. I sent letters to every company in *Spotlight*, placed an advert in *The Stage* and handed in my notice at Acton. I don't think they were particularly surprised.

I had interview after interview and all of them were barren affairs. One agent asserted that I hadn't got the height for a juvenile, and a lot of people told me I lacked the necessary experience. A would-be confidant also said, 'You'll never get a job dressed like that.' This last was the cruellest blow for I thought my clothes were very swish. I went around in a loud, checked, belted overcoat and wore a clip-on bow-tie with changeable paper collars. I thought I looked like the cat's whiskers. Alas, potential employers did not.

Just when I was beginning to despair of my chances, three opportunities appeared at once. They were all offers from repertory theatres, and I chose the one furthest away from London thinking my errors should be rumbled remotely.

On the 29th of April 1948 I got the Cornish Riviera Express from Paddington and a week later I opened with the Newquay Players as Ninian, the young son, in *The First Mrs Fraser*, the sort of drawing-room comedy that flourished in repertory theatres at that time. I wrote about the first night in my diary: 'I did very well, got loads of laughs.' The amount of merriment evoked was my only yardstick. With my background it was hardly surprising. Probably I would have continued in that vein, playing light comedy, for the rest of my stay there, had the advent of a new director not changed all that. Richard West arrived and brought new stimulus and abundant nervous energy to the company, the play policy was changed, acting styles challenged and conventional casting got severely jolted.

Under his aegis we performed Strindberg, Chekhov, Wilde, Bridie, Sartre and Shaw, and his principal concern was with clarifying and highlighting dialetic argument. He had a gift for encapsulating a characterisation in a meaningful phrase, and, despite his unusual mannerisms, he created the uninhibited atmosphere which is essential for good direction. His tall figure, neck craned forward and long arms whirling, would bound over the footlights from the stalls to demonstrate some movement or interpretation. 'You must whack it up!' he'd cry, apropos of cue response. Our half-heartedness always got short shrift: 'Convince yourself first, and then you'll convince me.' When one actor bridled, and burst out indignantly, 'How dare you be so rude!' Richard told him firmly, 'Get *that* quality into your acting.' An hirsute actress showed great pique when she was told she ought to get a shave.

But his amiability and infectious good humour always achieved a rapprochement. 'We can't have these Celtic twilights, unless they're theatrically exciting,' he said. 'Otherwise vent your grievances and get it over.' And we generally did. His praise was as unstinting as his censure.

He cast me as Napoleon in Shaw's *Man of Destiny*, but on the opening night, in the scene with the inn-keeper, I got the lines wrong. Instead of 'Are you not moved by action and victory?' I said, 'Are you not moved by viction and actory?' Afterwards I wailed about spoiling the speech, but he dismissed my misgivings. 'It was all right because you did not acknowledge it and falter. You kept going and the attention was held; conviction always convinces.' It was advice which was to stand me in good stead.

Richard West inspired loyalty in a small group of actors and after the Newquay season he endeavoured to keep them together at other theatres. In places as far apart as Stratford Bow, Salisbury and York, he managed to find parts for actors he admired, and when he became assistant director to Clifford Evans at the Grand, Swansea, I was one of his three 'loyals' in the company.

My companions were Annette Kerr and John Hussey, and we had digs near Mumbles. The landlady's guest book was full of references to 'delicious lemon pie' which so intrigued us that we foolishly asked about the much-praised dessert. 'Oh, they all love my lemon pie', the landlady said. 'I will make it for you tonight, you can have it when you get back from the show.' We were completely taken aback when it was presented; it was quite unlike anything we'd envisaged. It consisted of a whole unpeeled lemon entirely encased in dough covered with glutinous yellow sauce. It was quite revolting. John and I hurriedly emptied our plates out of the window but Annette thought such riddance too risky. 'She might find them under the plants,' she said fearfully and, wrapping hers in newspaper, she fled with it to the lavatory. In her absence the landlady returned. 'I can see you enjoyed it,' she smiled. 'All your plates are empty.' 'Quite delicious,' we lied, talking loudly to cover the noise of endless cistern flushing from upstairs, and she departed satisfied. Annette returned very red in the face. 'I pulled and pulled that chain but it kept coming back again, like some bloated spectre. Oh it was horrible. Why on earth did all those people write about "delicious lemon pie" in her book?' John supplied the answer: 'One of those endless practical jokes. Somebody was once so appalled by that pudding they thought the experience should be passed on!'

It was during this season at the Grand Theatre, Swansea, that I saw some of the most adroit skill in physical movement on any stage. Clifford Evans was directing a scene from Sartre's *Crime Passionel* which was so full of people that the door through which the leading character approached was obscured. The actor called out from over their heads: 'How can I make an entrance with everyone standing in front of me?' Clifford replied from the stalls, 'Walk!' The man obeyed. As he proceeded, the others naturally made way, and by the time he arrived centre stage there was a clear lane behind him, like a swathe cut through a field of ripened corn. The effect was dramatic, the importance of the character enhanced, and a star entrance created with insouciance. This was characteristic of Clifford's direction and sometimes it seemed amazingly offhand. At the dress rehearsal I asked him, 'What about the shooting? We've only read the scene, we've never plotted it!' and he simply said, 'Don't worry, Kenneth, it will play itself.' And it did, with astonishing success. One sees in retrospect that it was the result of strategy, an amalgam of psychological encouragement and imaginative expertise, but at the time it seemed effortless. Clifford Evans employed the art which conceals art.

There were many talented people in the company, including Rachel Roberts and Wilfred Brambell, and when Clifford staged *The Seagull* Richard Burton played Konstantin. I am never likely to forget it because I was his understudy. When I arrived at the theatre for the midweek matinée the stage manager buttonholed me immediately: 'You'll have to go on. Richard Burton is ill. Go up to his dressing room and get the costume.' I couldn't believe it. Richard ill? He was as strong as an ox. It must be some elaborate hoax to frighten me. I ran up the stairs with my heart thumping. Richard was lying on a divan in his room; he certainly looked pale but I still wasn't sure.

'Are you really ill?' I asked anxiously.

'It's food poisoning', he told me. 'The doctor thinks it's ptomaine. Must've been something I ate last night. I've been in pain ever since.'

'But you *must* go on,' I explained. 'I couldn't possibly play Konstantin.'

He looked surprised. 'Why ever not?'

'I'm not right for it.'

'Of course you are.'

'No I'm not. I couldn't do it. You'll have to. I certainly can't.'

'You must.'

I cried desperately, 'I don't know it!'

He sat up. 'Are you serious?'

'Yes, I never bothered to learn the lines, you always seemed so fit, I thought it would never arise. I don't know a line.'

He rose groggily to his feet and held on to the dressing table, looking at the ashen image of his face in the mirror.

'If you go on I'll give you my week's money,' I told him.

'How much is that?'

'Seven pounds.'

He smiled wanly. 'It wouldn't cover my expenses. Help me on with the costume and listen: there is one way I may get through this. Go next door to the pub and ask for their draught special. It might just do the trick.'

I needed no second bidding. I rushed off to secure the libation as if it were some miraculous elixir. It certainly worked. The recrimination scene with his mother mounted to a dramatic crescendo and there was appreciative applause on his exit. He was exultant in the wings and declaimed the words of a popular song, 'If you're ever up a tree, send for me,' so fervently that a harrassed stage manager hissed, 'Be quiet! You can be heard on stage!' Richard muttered to me, 'It's the boiled egg', a private joke about the man's baldness. We were barely suppressing our mirth when the leading lady came off stage and saw us. 'If you chattered a little less, the audience might enjoy it a little more,' she said icily, passing in a silken rustle of skirts to the dressing room. The abashed silence was broken only by a loud burp and she paused momentarily and turned enquiringly. Every face looked innocent and no hand covered the lips. She resumed her progress. Richard said afterwards that it was simply the result of the draught special, but it sounded to me very much like a riposte.

It was at Swansea, too, that I played the Dauphin in Shaw's *Saint Joan* opposite Hermione Hannen and I can still remember the moving intensity of her appeal to the Inquisitor. There was immense contrast in her performance; as the soldierly Joan in chain mail and armour, her ringing tones were those of a young commander, but in the trial sequence there was a gamin pathos about this young girl caught up in machinations which she was powerless to control.

Shavian anecdotes abound, but Clifford Evans, Hermione's husband, told me a delightful one during the play. He was in a company doing *Saint Joan* in New Zealand and in order to get from one theatre to another they had to catch a train which necessitated shortening the performance. They therefore cabled GBS asking if they could leave out the last scene.

Promptly they received the reply: 'Permission to cut epilogue granted, provided cast perform it on train.' Clifford said that the company dutifully obeyed the instructions, reciting their lines in the railway carriage as they rocketed along.

After the Swansea season I worked in various repertory theatres at Guildford, Worthing and Bromley. In 1951, during the Festival of Britain, I returned to Wales for Clifford Evans's production of *Land Of My Fathers* in Cardiff. I played several parts in this, including John Penry, the Welsh martyr, who was beheaded for his beliefs.

On the opening night, when we came to the execution scene, I mounted the scaffold, the rope was placed round my neck, and just before the lights dimmed, I made the sign of the cross with my hand. It wasn't rehearsed, I did it instinctively. Several newspaper critics mentioned it disapprovingly in their reviews, asking what on earth a Protestant was doing making such a Catholic gesture. However, on the following Sunday there was a broadcast by a distinguished Welsh scholar who said how interesting it was that the portrayal of Penry saw him return to the custom of his fathers at the moment of death and that the actor was to be congratulated on making such a subtle point. I was delighted with this vindication.

So often there is no refuting adverse criticism. With the exception of a few intrepid performers, most actors hold that it is inadvisable and unethical to reply to critics, and they suffer their houndings in silence, but in fact there are no rules about it. There are just as many bad critics as there are bad actors and they are the rule rather than the exception. The good actor and the good critic both have something in common: they should be entertaining. It's amazing how often one finds the cliché, 'I never read the critics', in articles about performers. All the actors I know are interested in anything that's been written about them. I have never met anyone who was indifferent to their publicity. Every time I have seen praise for my work in the newspaper or a magazine I've cut it out and preserved it and when I have read anything disagreeable I've always tried to get rid of it as quickly as possible. Flattering descriptions of my acting are stored away and I remark upon the satisfying nature of printed praise; any rude references are thrown into the waste paper basket and then I talk of today's newspaper being tomorrow's fish and chip wrapper!

*   *   *

43

In 1951, before going to Cardiff for the Festival of Wales, I was in several productions at Guildford Rep where Lawrence Payne directed a season. I played Maudlyn to his Richard of Bordeaux. In the same production Peter Nichols, my old chum from Singapore days, played Mowbray, so I remember that play as our reunion.

But the most memorable aspect of the Guildford season was that Peter Eade, a new young London agent, came to watch my work. He'd just started in Personal Management and, at Richard West's suggestion, I'd written to ask him to represent me. He came backstage after the show, a dapper young man with a military bearing, only three years my senior. Nervously I awaited his verdict, but he only talked about generalities in the communal dressing room and not until we were on the train back to London did he start discussing my work.

It was something of a bombshell for me. 'Your consonants are overdone and the vowels are too clipped,' he told me. 'There's a great danger in such mannered speech: the form gets in the way of the content, you see. The audience stops listening to what's being said and starts thinking about how it's being said. You'll have to watch it.'

Outwardly agreeing, I was inwardly furious. No one had ever spoken so directly of my shortcomings. Nevertheless I needed an agent, and it was better to have an outspoken one than a sycophant, so I swallowed my pride and listened to his advice.

Peter Eade was good for me. He took me under his wing and I became one of a small group of actors which included Nora Swinburne, Esmond Knight, Joan Sims and Ronnie Barker. Peter's philosophy was 'small is beautiful' and he only represented a few people in whom he detected a talent he liked. Once he had taken them on, he did all he could to nurture their aspirations. When he had asked me on the train which actress I liked most I'd told him of my admiration for Rachel Roberts and he had agreed to meet her. At that time Rachel was working as an usherette at the Ideal Home Exhibition and she telephoned me. 'I haven't got a smart dress for this interview with Peter Eade. I mean, the only thing I've got is this velvet number I wear at the Exhibition and that doesn't belong to me, it's hired. Shall I keep it after work and go and meet him in that?'

'Yes, that'll be fine,' I cried encouragingly.

On a very hot summer day an even hotter Rachel Roberts sallied forth to meet her first manager. It was the beginning of a relationship that reached its climax in 1964 when Peter arranged her contract for *Maggie May* at the Adelphi at a salary that was higher than anything ever before paid to a musical leading lady.

But in 1951 this sort of star billing would have seemed a pipe dream to both of us. We were making our first tentative steps and there was to be a lot of preliminary work before we got any chances in the West End.

By the end of 1951 I had managed to move a rung up the ladder because I had joined Richard West at York and the company interchanged with Scarborough, so productions were fortnightly with more time for rehearsals. It was during this period that Pat Smith, who was casting director for the film producer Herbert Wilcox, expressed interest in my work. Peter Eade wrote and told me she had liked my performance in a comedy called *Wilderness of Monkeys* at York and had suggested a meeting when I returned to London. Herbert's next film was to be *Trent's Last Case* starring Michael Wilding and Margaret Lockwood. The thought of getting a small part alongside such glamorous names left me goggle-eyed. But there was more! Douglas Allen was directing an adaptation of H. G. Wells' *The Wonderful Visit* for BBC Television and was looking for someone to play the Angel.

I returned to London full of excitement and anticipation. Perhaps 1952 was going to be the turning-point for me. I was interviewed by Douglas Allen in January and asked to read some of the dialogue. It seemed to please him but he expressed reservations about my hair. 'It should be long and curly,' he said, 'in the Botticelli fashion, to match the costume. Yours is rather short. We'll have to see about a wig.' I was sent to the perukier and fitted with a mass of golden curls. The wig was strangely synthetic and someone simpered that I looked just like Harpo Marx.

At the time the BBC produced their television drama at Alexandra Palace and everything was live. The sets were built as near to each show as possible, dressers stood by with your next costume, you changed, and then ran from set to set desperately trying to remember what the new scene involved. At the beginning of the play I wore huge swans' wings but as the Angel became more worldly, these shrank and shrank till,

45

at the last, only ducks' feathers were sprouting from the shoulders. All this entailed wearing different harnesses and fitting the costume over them.

The transmission on the 3rd of February 1952 was a great success. There were so many congratulatory letters and phone calls that those who hadn't seen it decided to watch the live repeat which was then customary and which we were supposed to perform on the 7th of February. On the 6th, however, the BBC announced the death of George VI, the cancellation of all programmes, and the substitution of requiem music. *The Wonderful Visit* was never seen again.

Ordinarily this might have depressed me, but I still had the prospect of the interview with Mr Wilcox, and in the meantime Michael Harald – with whom I'd worked at York – wanted me to play the lead in *Before You Die* by Zygmont Yablovski. It was about a youth sentenced to death for a crime of passion and was staged at a tiny fringe theatre called The Chepstow at Notting Hill Gate. My old friends John Hussey and Michael Hitchman were both playing in it as well, so rehearsals were friendly and uninhibited.

On the 26th of February 1952 a sparse audience attended our opening night but the following day I was delighted to find myself mentioned in *The Times* as having given an 'emotionally explosive' performance. I thought that a good notice like this would boost the box office at the Chepstow but, alas, our attendances dwindled nightly. On the fourth evening the stage manager came into the communal dressing room and said, 'There's only one old lady out front, she's sitting there on her own with a bag of buns. Shall I make a speech from the stage saying the performance is cancelled?' 'Just go and give the old girl her money back,' John Hussey told him, swiftly removing his make-up, and suggested to the rest of us that we go to the pictures to see Tracy and Hepburn in *Adam's Rib*. We needed no further bidding.

With the TV repeat cancelled, and now the Chepstow performance cancelled as well, I was becoming hardened to adversity, so by the time it came to meeting Herbert Wilcox I was ready for anything, including disappointment. It certainly looked foredoomed because he was looking for someone to play the gardener, an elderly rustic, who finds the murdered body in *Trent's Last Case*. Herbert said, 'You're far too young for the role as it's written, but try reading it as a youngster;

46

play it as an eager and garrulous innocent: that may pay dividends in the court scene when the Judge has to check you.' I did it all wide-eyed with a Welsh accent and he nodded, satisfied. 'That's fine. You start on Monday at Shepperton Studios.'

The meeting lasted less than ten minutes but during that time he put me at ease and filled me with confidence. He did so on the set as well. Whenever you talked to Herbert you felt he gave you his entire attention. He was forthright, unfailingly kind, and seemed to remember everything, even correcting a continuity girl over the position of an ornament on the set.

When I went to the studios at Shepperton for the first time, they were shooting part of the courtroom scene where Margaret Lockwood stood, being cross-examined, in the witness box. There was a diatribe from the prosecuting counsel accusing her of complicity in her husband's death at the end of which she cried out 'No'. Seconds later, Herbert Wilcox called 'Cut!' and the cameras stopped and the actress relaxed. The director told her, 'Lovely take, you were perfect!' An assistant ordered, 'Get Miss Lockwood's tea', Herbert said solicitously, 'Put your slippers on, dear,' and there were murmurs of admiration all round the set.

I was surprised. In the theatre it would need an entire scene to evoke that reaction and considerably more time, but here, with two close-up shots, dramatic tension was encapsulated in minutes, culminating in the final passionate protest, 'No!' If one got slippers and tea after saying 'no', I thought, what must one get at the end of a speech! But then, I knew nothing of cinema technique and had no idea how much incompetent acting cost a producer. Margaret Lockwood was a star whom everyone called professional, and in *Trent's Last Case* she was playing with the equally expert Michael Wilding and Orson Welles.

When the film was eventually released, Peter Eade took me to the première and I experienced the weird sensation of watching myself alongside these celebrated names, shrinking at the comparison of standards. Peter was comforting, however: 'You've acquitted yourself admirably,' he said. 'Not bad at all for your first try.' I was even more gratified when I read C. A. Lejeune's notice for the picture: she referred to me as an 'interesting new "Welsh find".' That was true as far as ancestry went. My mother was a Morgan and my father a Williams.

47

The names mean morning and bright helmets – they seemed good auguries for my burgeoning acting career.

I can't remember how much I was paid in the film, but it was certainly higher than anything I was used to and I frittered it away in an uncharacteristic bout of theatre-going, restaurants and bookshops, and there were trips to Hepworths to replenish my wardrobe. I spent the money so rapidly that I was forced to work again very quickly.

This time it was Salisbury Repertory Theatre and I opened with a favourite role of mine, Bastien in *By Candlelight* by Siegfried Geyer. Since I got lots of laughs during the run, it all started going to my head and I began to develop a comic persona which wasn't always appropriate for the production.

My second play there was *School For Scandal* and, in rehearsal, I sailed on in my part as Benjamin Backbite. But before I could get under way, Guy Verney, who was directing, called out, 'Go back and make that entrance again – try coming on as an actor in a company and *not* as a star!' I can still remember the shock of hearing such sharp criticism from the stalls but it couldn't have delayed me overmuch because I walked down to the footlights and said, 'I don't take that kind of cheap contumely from you or anyone else,' and walked off the stage. I was only persuaded to return after an apology and even then I complained, 'You're rude in public and sorry in private.'

The incident is significant. What that director deplored in my work was something which other critics were to seize upon again and again. It's the difference between performing for oneself, and acting as part of an ensemble. But of course it's not as simple as that. The subjugation of self in the attempt to realize a playwright's vision is difficult for the man who lives on ego and, for an actor, the solution to the problem can be a long time coming. Speaking to others, looking at others, reacting to others, picking up cues cleanly, not staring at the fourth wall: all this is the give-and-take essential for ensemble theatre, and creates the water in which a company can swim. Only because of the water can the ocean itself accommodate such a variety of creatures. If the tide suddenly recedes some very peculiar monstrosities can be found marooned on the beach.

By September I was back in London. Peter Eade told me that Herbert Wilcox had remembered me, that he was producing a

48

film of *The Beggar's Opera* with Laurence Olivier as MacHeath, and that he wanted me to meet the director, Peter Brook, for the part of Jack.

I went down to Shepperton Studios, full of apprehension, clutching a few sheets of paper comprising the scene between MacHeath and the pot-boy at the inn where the hero is hiding. I had to wait until the day's shooting was over and then found myself facing both the director and Sir Laurence. I read the scene rather haltingly and my accent was criticised: 'He's supposed to be cockney, you know.' 'But I *am* a cockney', I protested. 'I was born in the Caledonian Road.' They didn't seemed convinced.

I returned home on the train resigned to defeat, thinking the part would go to someone else. Next day, however, Peter rang to tell me I'd got the role and that I was to have a costume fitting 'for a period pot-boy'.

At the costumiers I was duly attired in waistcoat and breeches and looked rather like a junior footman. But when I arrived on the set there was as much disapproval for the costume as there had been for my accent. 'No, no, it's far too smart,' said Sir Laurence, and Peter Brook agreed. 'Yes, he's a pot-boy in a hostelry, not an attendant at Chatsworth. Take the waistcoat away.' The wardrobe people obliged. 'And dirty the the shirt down.' The garment was trampled in dirt and liberally stained, and I was produced again. 'No, it's still too smart. Tear the shirt and dirty the breeches and stockings.' The clothing was torn to tatters, my face daubed with dirt and eventually they seemed reluctantly satisfied.

This inauspicious beginning, coupled with my awe for Sir Laurence, created inhibitions which I never managed to overcome, and I was bad in the role. The filming was spread over several weeks and I dreaded every day. I didn't like being on the set and I didn't like being in the communal dressing room. I spent most of the time alone and since I also looked extremely dirty and unpleasant I suppose it was understandable that the other actors weren't over-eager for my company, and didn't wish to go to lunch with me. I was relieved when the job was finished.

There was also a sting in the tail. Some time afterwards I was asked by an acquaintance if I knew that my voice had been taken off the soundtrack for that film. When I expressed bewildered ignorance, he told me he'd overheard an actor in a bar saying he'd had to go down to Shepperton and dub all my dialogue because it was unsatisfactory. At first I thought it was all invention but then I went to Peter and asked if he knew anything about it. Were people really allowed to remove your voice from a screen performance and substitute someone else's? Would they do such a thing to me without even informing me and explaining my inadequacies? Peter was soothing. I wasn't to worry about it, he would check with Shepperton. He did and it was all true. I remember the humiliation vividly and I was fearful about the general reaction when the film was shown. What on earth would people say when they heard me speak? I needn't have worried. The film was withdrawn before completing one week in the cinema and by that time I was rehearsing for another nightmare of a job.

This was *Peter Pan* at the Scala Theatre: the building has since vanished and the site is now the home of Channel 4 in Charlotte Street. The play starred Brenda Bruce and James Donald. The rights to *Peter Pan* are controlled by Great Ormond Street Children's Hospital and the director looked as if he needed a little treatment himself. He was an elderly eccentric called Cecil King, whose hand-rolled cigarettes continually fell in unsightly bits about his person, as his dribbling dissolved the glue. He kept calling Brenda Bruce 'Miss Lockwood' – she had played it the year before – and hectored the Lost Boys about alleged misdemeanours in the wings. 'Your talking and giggling is ruining Miss Lockwood's performance! Do you hear?' He also affirmed that all the original moves and business of his production had been approved by the author. 'Before he died Sir James Barrie begged me, "Oh Cecil", he said, "don't let them alter my lovely play".' James Donald left abruptly before the end of the run and I didn't blame him. At first I found this whimsical concoction merely risible: after weeks of performing it I became nauseated. One of the actors told me that Cecil used to go to the back of the stalls to start the applause in case the spectators didn't react to Peter Pan's cry, 'Do you believe in fairies. If you believe, clap your hands!' I can understand Cecil's misgivings. Direct appeals to an audience are often hazardous but for resuscitating a *peri* they're well-nigh embarrassing.

The whole experience was even more miserable on tour. When I couldn't get into theatrical digs, I stayed in cheap commercial hotels where the rooms were cold and I invariably lacked the right coin for the gas meter. In one such place in Norwich, I returned from the performance to find several boarders chatting in the lounge; they told me they had seen the play and the conversation turned on actors in general. One of them said, 'Of course they're all queers, aren't they?' and began a dissertation about the corrupting influence of homosexuals. It was so unexpected and so aggressive that I didn't do much to gainsay him. I went to the kitchen, where we were allowed to make tea, and to my surprise he joined me in preparing cups and saucers. 'Hope my little outburst didn't offend you, but I had to talk like that in front of my mates. I always run down the poofs in company 'cos it diverts attention from myself. I'm queer you see . . . but I expect you saw through all that, didn't you?'

In fact I had seen through nothing. I had assumed his censure was genuine. It was only one of many arguments about deviants that I was to go on hearing over the years. Lines like 'I can't stand queers' are as daft as 'I can't stand heterosexuals,' but people will go on saying them. Whether it is sexual, religious or racial, discrimination will occur in one way or another in most societies, and eradicating efforts are futile because the prejudice is born of ignorance. Bernard Shaw wrote that the only thing to do about ignorance is to enlighten it, and a lot of idealists think that education can achieve that enlightenment. Legislators think that laws can do it, and trendsetters think that fashion can do it. They are wrong because they start from a false premise. They're like the doctor who once told me that smoking cigarettes would shorten my life; he made the erroneous assumption that I craved longevity.

I certainly needed a few cigarettes to get through the tour of *Peter Pan* and by the time I arrived back in London I was determined that my next job should be as far removed from the cloying sentimentality of Barrie as possible.

Most of my work in the theatre had so far been in weekly or fortnightly repertory and the idea of working in a company where four weeks were spent on a production was luxury indeed, so when Douglas Seale of Birmingham Rep came to London seeking actors for *Henry VI* I was anxious to meet and impress him. He gave me an interview at the Arts Theatre Club. 'We shall be the first company to perform the play – parts one, two, and three – in its entirety, since Benson,' he assured me, and after an appraising glance he said that I might be suitable for the part of Lord Saye. 'Actually,' I swiftly interjected, 'I heard you wanted someone for Rutland, the boy who's murdered in the first act.' Already I was envisaging myself removing the make-up, getting excused the curtain and leaving the theatre earlier than the others. That's what a tour of *Peter Pan* does for you.

'How old are you?'

'Twenty-seven,' I replied, 'but I can play seventeens and seventies. Nothing in between, if you see what I mean.'

He said he did and continued to peruse his cast list. I pulled my legs up on the seat of the chair and tucked them under my behind. This will enhance the juvenile effect, I thought, and started to bite my nails. In the long silence that followed I could feel the blood pumping through me loud as a drum.

'I've always had trouble over Rutland,' he said eventually. I didn't know how to react to this so I just murmured sympathetically, pushed my lips forward and looked as if the profundity of the whole thing was killing me.

The meeting ended inconclusively. He rose, offering his hand, thanked me for coming and said he'd let me know after seeing the other applicants. I left thinking it would come to nothing. My scepticism, however, was not justified because shortly afterwards Peter Eade telephoned to say they wanted me to go up to Birmingham to rehearse on May the 18th – they were offering me Burgundy in Part One, Hume and Smith in Part Two and Rutland in Part Three. I accepted immediately.

Luckily I knew someone else who was joining the company for this production – Frederick Treves, with whom I'd shared a dressing room at Newquay – and we travelled up to Birmingham together. He had worked there before so I bombarded him with questions – what was the company like, when did they rehearse, was the director easy to work with? Freddie understood my nervousness, and answered my questions patiently. 'You'll probably find them a bit cliquey,' he mused, 'but that's natural in a provincial arty theatre – I think they need a little fresh air! Don't worry. We shall stir 'em up a bit!' He winked and laughed and I began to feel more confident.

I found lodgings in Edgbaston with a delightful old lady called Mrs Parkinson. She was at great pains to inform me that she 'never took people from the door' and during the subsequent interview she frequently addressed a portrait of her dead husband glaring from the wall. 'He knows what goes on,' she told me. 'He talks to me, even now: you can have the room and breakfast for three pounds a week.' I accepted and told her I was rehearsing with Birmingham Rep. 'Oh, I've put up actors from the Rep before,' she smiled. 'I've had Godfrey Kenton and Vivienne Bennett under this very roof.'

I looked suitably impressed.

'What play are you doing?' she asked and I told her it was *Henry VI*. 'Oh,' she cried, 'that's funny. That's what Godfrey Kenton was doing when he stayed here sixteen years ago.'

I frowned. This was ridiculous. Mr Seale's words at the Arts Theatre Club came back to me distinctly. This was the first time the play had been performed since Benson.

'You must be mistaken,' I said, '*Henry VI* hasn't been acted in our lifetime.'

Mrs Parkinson knitted her brows and then laughed shortly. 'Course not, it wasn't *Henry VI*, it was *1066 And All That!* Mind you they sound the same don't they!'

I remember walking to the first rehearsal thinking they very nearly did.

There was a read-through of the play at 10.30 am on the Monday and we all took our places in the assembled circle of chairs. Douglas Seale arranged his papers at the centre table and then looked up. 'I'm always nervous on these occasions,' he began. There was indulgent laughter from the actors. He continued in a louder tone, 'Now a word about the three parts of this play. They don't call for any subtleties in acting. The characters are mostly a lot of gangsters and thugs. They want to be played broadly and big. Their success depends on the amount of vigour and zest with which the lines are banged over . . .'

After a while in this vein the players began to recite their lines, but boredom set in halfway through the morning. Few actors enjoy sitting on chairs and saying the lines of a dramatist; those who do enjoy it are seldom good at acting and those who don't usually are. People quietly stole away – ostensibly to go to the lavatory, but in fact they stood outside the pass door smoking and gossiping. A pale young man offered me a cigarette and said, 'All I hope is that I'm left out of those ghastly battle scenes. It's such a small stage, and everyone charges around shouting the odds hurling their swords about in the most abandoned fashion; you get cuts all over the place. You're *covered* with sticking plaster!'

'Well of course,' deprecated another actor. 'All the fight scenes should be produced symbolically. No audience believes in people shouting "Miscreant" and "fie at thee" at each other, and a lot of tinny noises.'

We were joined by an elderly character actor who said, 'I've nothing to say now till the end of the play so I thought I'd come out here. It's much cooler, isn't it?' We murmured agreement. 'I think I'm going to enjoy this piece, you know,' he continued. 'I like old Dougie's methods. Of course I don't think he's an actor's producer, but he knows his lighting. There's no one can say he doesn't.'

'Judging from my costume,' said the pale young man, 'he'd better keep it dark. It's the most hideous bit of old blanket you've ever seen. I honestly feel you can't act well in a bad costume. I mean, it's so off-putting. No good saying anything to Dougie about it. He always gives you that old line about it looking good from the front. I feel like saying what about the back? . . . I *mean* . . . I've had tights that don't even cover my bum properly.'

When I crept back on stage to see if it was getting near my entrance there was a lengthy discussion ensuing about motivation. The Duchess of Gloucester got as far as saying to the Duke: 'Why droops my lord like over-ripened corn . . .' when she stopped and asked, 'Why does she say "why droops my lord"?' Douglas replied, 'You find him looking dejected and you ask why.' 'Yes,' she said, 'I see that but isn't there a deeper motive? Isn't she egging him on? I mean she's the bitch really, isn't she? She has all the ambition: she wants to take the throne from Henry and Margaret and she's putting the idea into his head.'

'Yes,' rejoined the director, 'it's along those lines.' The Duchess suddenly seemed enlightened. 'Of course,' she cried. 'It's really a sort of Lady Macbeth thing, isn't it?' The director agreed doubtfully and the Duke helpfully interposed, 'Yes, it's she who puts the poison in his ear.'

'No dear, that's *Hamlet*,' said the Duchess. 'I'm talking about *Macbeth*.' Whereupon the director told her, 'Yes. It's a sort of *Macbeth*, but it's better than *Macbeth*. You see, Macbeth is a whole play but it's all here in one scene!'

They all seemed delighted with this reasoning, and started to play the scene all over again. I sometimes wondered during rehearsals if the play would ever get staged at all, but it all went according to schedule and opened to such enthusiastic reviews that the company was invited to transfer the production from Birmingham to the Old Vic in London. So it transpired that I was seen by Michael Benthall who was artistic director there. He was sufficiently impressed by my Rutland to offer me Prince Henry in *King John* and I actually rehearsed with the Old Vic Company – which was headed by Richard Burton and Claire Bloom. I was with them for over a week before I suddenly recanted and asked to be released from my contract.

Michael Benthall remonstrated with me on the stairs of the theatre. 'Do you really want to leave the Old Vic? It will be one of the most fashionable companies in London. It is the Burton–Bloom season. Why do you want to go?'

I muttered something about not wanting to be tied down.

'Tied down!' he echoed, 'we're performing Shakespeare, not Sacher Masoch.'

The reference to masochism made me smile, and it was Michael's good humour that ensured that I left without rancour. I resumed my search for work. This was the 22nd of July 1953 and my diary records the unease I felt about taking such a step: 'Can't help wondering if I have done the right thing; my savings don't amount to much and I've given up a year's security.' Auditions during August for various parts came to nothing and in September I went to the Players Theatre, thinking to eschew straight acting and try for revue. I was seen by Johnny Heawood who said I sang well but that he wanted someone who could dance, too. Alas, I had to admit to having no talent in this sphere. Perhaps it's connected with being sinistral but the fact is, I have no physical co-ordination; my feet can start waltzing 'one-two-three' etc., but invariably they will stray into 'one-two-three-four'.

The days of inactivity began to depress me, but just as I started searching the job-vacancy columns in the papers, thinking of trying for some other kind of work, Peter Eade sent me to Pinewood to meet the film producer, George Brown, who was casting for a film called *The Seekers*. It seemed to me pointless and I thought that, like all the other interviews I'd had recently, nothing would come of it. But on the 22nd of September I was asked to go for a second interview with him. This time he was with the director of the film, Ken Annakin,

55

and they asked me to take a screen test. On the appointed day at Pinewood I was made-up and costumed at 8.30 am and then waited with the other actors untill 11 am when I was called on to the set.

I had to play a scene where I lay dying – speared by an assegai – saying halting words of contrition. I thought I played it well but I had met all the other aspirants for the role and knew they were good, too, so it wouldn't be simply a question of talent, but of who *looked* right in the part and who would fit with the rest of the cast.

I was on tenterhooks for days. On the 29th of September, Peter Eade telephoned. 'You've got the part in the film. You're to play Wishart in *The Seekers*. It stars Jack Hawkins and Glynis Johns.' I said, 'Oh that's a relief, I'm broke, could you lend me ten pounds?' He kindly agreed. Then I got the bill for my advertisement in *Spotlight*, the actors' directory, for £6.15s, so my funds were quickly depleted.

My first work on the film involved night shooting. We were supposed to be firing muskets from dug-outs during a rainstorm. The water eventually filled the trenches, my clothes got soaked and within a few days I was shivering and sneezing with a nasty cold. I was never happy in this picture and felt little affection for anyone in it except for Norman Mitchell, an actor I've always enjoyed meeting since. Norman's cheerful disposition and his hilarious derision of pretension transformed some of the dreariest days for me – I always think of him with gratitude. It wasn't only the fun he created, it was the encouragement he gave. I felt alien on the set, I knew no one. But he ceaselessly exhorted me, 'Don't let 'em get you down', reminding me that nothing was for ever and that I'd be able to smile in retrospect.

Of course he was right, and in later years when we worked together in that same studio, in the different atmosphere of a *Carry On*, I marvelled at the contrast of being on a friendly set surrounded by amiable people and a director with that gift of rapport, creating ease rather than apprehension.

Chapter Four

The year 1954 started badly. There were countless auditions which were all fruitless and my days were so empty that Charlie suggested I help him with the decorating. This started me on a flurry of activity and when the dining room had been repapered I made endless trips to the Elephant & Castle where obliging timber merchants sawed the right lengths of wood for me to build shelves in the bedroom to house all my books.

Quite out of the blue, John Hussey, who was working very successfully in South Africa, wrote to me suggesting I join the company out there. So in April I spoke to Peter Eade about leaving England. He was against it. He thought it would be culturally debilitating and bad for my career. 'Even if you were a success you'd only be a big fish in a small pond', he said, and he dissuaded me from going. Luckily I then had a telephone call from Peter Ashby Bailey with whom I'd worked at Newquay. He told me he'd started a repertory company in Bridgwater and he offered me character roles in his opening season there.

By the 1st of May I was in digs at 59 Victoria Road, Bridgwater, where a delightful lady, with a Persian cat called Smokey, provided bed and board at four pounds a week. Peter Ashby Bailey had gathered together an interesting company which included James Beck (who was later to achieve great success as the 'flash-Harry' character in *Dad's Army*), the leading lady Beryl Hardy, the leading man James Roose Evans, and the assistant stage manager, a clever young actor called Mark Kingston. On the 10th of May I opened with them in *Traveller's Joy* and wrote in my diary, 'Haven't been on the stage for nearly a year; felt like an amateur and probably looked like one,' but before the week was out I was getting back into my stride, and was beginning to enjoy it. Then the Town Hall (which we used as a theatre) was suddenly denied us because it was to be used for Polling Day.

Peter Ashby Bailey was undaunted and set off in search of other venues. A few days later he hired a van to take us all to perform at Tonevale, a vast mental hospital some miles away. It was a disconcerting experience. In the middle of one of my speeches, a group of spectators rose in a body and began lustily singing 'Rock of Ages Cleft for Me.' (I was told afterwards that the hall was used for church services and as I looked quite like the vicar, they thought it was the cue for hymns.) Apart from this unnerving moment our comedy was received in respectful silence and I thought normality had been restored until it came to the National Anthem when they all walked out. 'Anti-Royalists, I suppose,' muttered Roose Evans.

Roose Evans showed me some delightful walks in the surrounding villages outside Bridgwater, which was then a sleepy, unspoiled market town, and we used to stroll to Durleigh and Wembdon along quite country roads. On one such jaunt, the pair of us became so absorbed in conversation that we lost all track of time, till I suddenly became aware of a church clock striking 7 pm.

'The curtain goes up at 7.30,' I cried to Roose Evans and he immediately became practical. 'Don't worry, we shall stop the first vehicle that comes along.'

He stood with arms outstretched in the middle of the road and a big car, with a driver in dungarees and a blind Alsatian beside him, halted before us. Once our predicament was explained, he reversed his motor and drove us both back to Bridgwater, depositing us at the Town Hall with ten minutes to spare. He refused our offer of payment but waved us off with good wishes for the performance. It remains one of my fondest memories to this day.

I left Bridgwater in July and returned to London to rehearse for Douglas Allen who was producing Shaw's *Misalliance* for BBC Television. I was playing Bentley and Lord Summerhays was played by Maurice Colborne whom I liked and admired – as a playwright as well as an actor. He had that delightful combination of humour and authority which he used as lightly as a Leslie Howard, and it was a pleasure to work with him. We rehearsed at the old Stoll Theatre in Kingsway and I brought along a copy of his play *Charles the King* and asked Maurice to sign it. There was a fine portrait in the frontispiece of Barry Jones in the title role, with the Van Dyck beard falling on to cavalier lace, and since Barry had played the lead in my last television play, *The Wonderful Visit*, I felt I was truly among friends again.

Misalliance was transmitted on the 27th of July and the very next day I was offered another Shavian juvenile. This time it was the Dauphin in *Saint Joan* which John Fernald was directing at The Arts with Siobhan McKenna. The first rehearsal was on the 27th of August. I purchased a Chinese lacquered penbox for my room and took to keeping a bottle of lime juice and a carafe of water on the bedside table, and I bought a new gramophone adding Flagstad singing Grieg songs to my collection of records. With my parents away on holiday I had the house to myself and I decided to make an heroic effort for Louisa by doing all the washing. I put everything in the copper and ran it through the wringer. All my mother's dresses shrank horribly: 'stick to acting and leave the laundry to me', she told me firmly afterwards. I have done so to this day.

I persuaded my father to make my hair very short for the part in *Saint Joan*. I'd seen portraits of the King and I wanted to look as authentic as possible. Siobhan was so impressed by the cut that she came to Marchmont Street and had her hair cropped as well. My father liked her because she was so un-actressy. She never wore any make-up and she had a fine fresh complexion and an impish sense of humour which always seemed to be bubbling just below the surface. She once took me to a restaurant favoured by the Irish, where the waiter serving aperitifs in the bar turned up again in the dining room to take our order. A surprised Siobhan asked, 'Are you doubling?' and he said, 'No, Tipperary', and we both giggled over the pun.

In the play the elderly Frank Royd, as the Archbishop, had to reprove Joan, saying, 'You stand alone – with your own impiety . . .' etc and one night it went hopelessly wrong. Frank muttered, 'Er – you're on your own you are,' and then turned and asked the prompt corner, 'Oh what's the line?' Siobhan's mouth began to tremble, Frank walked to the side of the stage, got a very loud reminder, thanked the prompter and said to the audience, 'You must bear with us, this is a very difficult piece you know,' and then continued to Joan with great aplomb, 'You stand alone'. By this time the line was doubly appropriate because everyone else had turned upstage to hide their amusement and he was reproving a solitary and broadly grinning Saint Joan.

In the Epilogue to the play I used a heavily ageing make-up and a querulous old man's voice and to my astonishment this led to a call from the BBC asking me to join the radio programme, *Hancock's Half-Hour*. I was interviewed at the

Aeolian Hall by the producer, Denis Main Wilson, who told me he'd been very impressed with my vocal characterisation in *Saint Joan*, and offered me character roles in the radio series which had made Tony Hancock so famous. Denis showed me a script describing an old and shaky baronet who had let his stately home to Hancock, and who arrived back to find the place in a terrible mess. He had to cry out, 'Oh there's jelly all over my Rembrandt.' I knew I could make this funny. The writers were Ray Galton and Alan Simpson; their facility for comic characters and amusing lines makes me smile to this day. One episode where Hancock entered a dance competition is still fresh in my mind, with his triumphant assertion, 'My feet'll be going round like helicopter blades.'

The cast of *Hancock's Half-Hour* varied over the years, but the stalwarts were Hattie Jacques, Sid James and Bill Kerr. Hattie's ample figure and jokes about her size were taken for granted. At one rehearsal her lines called for her to talk about serving spotted dick, cabinet pudding and roly-poly for sweet. Hancock had to refer to her greediness, and she had to say, 'No, I eat like a bird,' and then Hancock replied, 'I know. A gannet.' We all laughed at rehearsal till an unsmiling Hattie asked, 'Do we have to have these sort of jokes in the script?' I suddenly realized how sensitive she was about allusions to weight.

Alan and Ray slanted her scenes differently after that. Indeed they would tirelessly rewrite in order to accommodate all their actors, and this was no small contribution to the success of their series. They created for Tony the superb character of a dreamy optimist battling against adversity, surrounded by figures of fun who bounced against him with delightful comic effect.

On the 18th of December 1954, when we were recording two programmes before Christmas, the pipeline to Broadcasting House was suddenly lost and we had to fill in for twenty minutes with impromptu dialogue. Tony stood centre-stage declaiming a monologue, 'It's a funny old world we live in,' while the rest of us ran on with interruption gags. Bill Kerr came on and said, 'I got a pound of meat from Smithfield for only a shilling', and Tony asked, 'Was it mutton?' and got the ready reply, 'No, rotten'. Then Sid James came on quizzing him with 'What's got four legs and flies?' and Tony said, 'I don't know, what's got four legs and flies', and Sid exited shouting, 'The corporation dustcart'. Then I had to come on prancing round the stage pretending I was throwing dust. Tony asked what I was doing. I had to tell him I was sprinkling woofle dust to kill the wild elephants. When he protested that there were no wild elephants my line was, 'No, and this isn't real woofle dust.' In the event he stood watching my balletic mime in silence. Eventually I whispered in a desperate aside, 'Ask me what I am,' 'Don't worry, we all know what you are,' he said, and got the biggest laugh of the evening.

By April 1955, *Saint Joan* had transferred to the St Martin's Theatre and I found myself recording *Hancock's Half-Hour* at the old Camden Theatre with someone else in the title role! Tony was indisposed and his part was played by Harry Secombe. I wrote in my diary: 'He's like a thoroughbred horse when it comes to the laughs – taking every fence with consummate skill and great style: he kept the pace of the show bubbling throughout and the success of the evening was largely due to him.' He did this for every episode till Hancock's return in May and I think it's been one of the best-kept secrets of BBC Radio. As a performer at the microphone Harry showed all the versatility which had made his work in *The Goon Show* so hilarious. His energy and enthusiasm infected everyone and the show never had a better atmosphere. He got laughs where I thought they didn't exist and nothing was sacred: when the very dignified BBC announcer at the centre-stage microphone said, 'This is the BBC Home Service,' he cried out in a high falsetto, 'And serve you right!' The audience were laughing before the show began.

Even before *Saint Joan* finished its run on the 28th of May 1955, I was already rehearsing for another production. Earlier in the month I had read for Orson Welles who was staging his own adaptation of Melville's *Moby Dick*. 'I could use someone of your versatility in the company,' he told me, making me feel very pleased with myself. I was to play Elijah, the carpenter, the old Bedford sailor and several other parts, including a look-out who had to keep shouting excitedly, 'She blows! A great white spout!'

It was during these rehearsals that I met Gordon Jackson who played Ishmael. He says that during the morning break I went up to him with outstretched hand, and said, 'I'm Kenneth Williams, the only one in the cast worth knowing, let's go and have coffee together,' but for the life of me I can't remember such vainglory! My diary does record my instant liking for Gordon and his work. His opening line was 'Call me Ishmael . . .' and Orson shouted from the stalls, 'And if a man answers, hang up'. But Gordon struggled on, repressing his giggles, and we have been friends ever since.

Moby Dick was an open-stage production with no scenery, consequently the actors were seen as soon as they entered the pass door. Orson achieved his effects by lighting and stage grouping. In the chapel sequence, where he played Father Mapple, he stood holding a chair back for the pulpit with a multi-coloured spotlight casting the glow of a stained-glass window over the scene. It was economical and practical. When Orson spoke the lines, 'O Lord, I have striven to be thine', he was both vulnerable and moving. He used the stage area for the deck of the whaling ship *Pequod* and the auditorium was the sea. We lowered a rostrum as a symbolic boat into the front stalls when it came to the encounter with the whale. Orson was playing Captain Ahab and told me, 'You will be Fool to my Lear; kneel in the prow and I can tell my playing positions by standing above you for the harpoon throwing.' This was where he cried out, 'That whale – I'll have his blood!' It was all right rehearsing such a scene in an empty theatre, but on the night, with a packed house, it was a different matter. Sailors were clambering into the stalls trying to lower the boat into the central gangway while well-dressed spectators shrank in their seats from the proximity of burly perspiration. One lady's box of chocolates got squashed on her lap, and she protested loudly; and the spectators in the circle completely lost sight of the cast. They rose in their seats to extend their view, provoking cries of 'Sit down' from those seated behind. Orson, with his hand raised for the harpoon, was roaring 'Shut up' to the audience between his vengeful curses to the whale, and we eventually returned to the stage amidst considerable confusion.

In the interval I used to lie full-length on the dressing-room floor. The unaccustomed exercise had exhausted me and the continuity of the play was baffling because Orson frequently changed the scenes. One night I was playing the carpenter and during a long speech about carving Ahab a false leg made from ivory, Orson suddenly leant over my kneeling figure and muttered 'Get off'. I rose muttering a lame ad lib, 'God bless you, Captain', and backed away into the wings with the scene unfinished. As there was no set, we had been instructed that when we exited, we were to stand still at the side of the stage, and I was frozen in this position next to Joan Plowright who was playing Pip the cabin boy. 'What happened?' she whispered and out of the side of my mouth I replied, 'He told me to get off'. She looked heavenward: 'What about your speech?' 'It's cut', I whispered. At this point she realized it was her scene which followed the now absent carpenter episode. She rushed on saying her line, 'O Captain put thy hand in mine, the black and white together . . .' with such incoherent haste that Orson was quite taken aback, but Joan rattled on with the speed of a gatling gun about white being black and black becoming white, till it sounded like a high-speed detergent commercial.

Afterwards I went to Orson's dressing room and asked why he had cut the dialogue so drastically. 'You bored me,' he said shortly, and if there's a snappy answer to that I haven't found it. He was just as unpredictable to those outside the cast. I remember seeing a young man who bore an uncanny resemblance to a famous film star on the stage one day. I asked him if he was Dirk Bogarde and he replied, 'No, I'm his brother Gareth.' He went on to explain that he'd been appointed personal assistant to Orson. 'Then don't stay here,' I warned him, 'the last one left after only a week, and the one before that wasn't much longer.' Gareth was assuring me he knew how to handle temperament when Orson appeared expostulating, 'Why haven't you found me somewhere to live?' and dismissed him before he had time to reply. Gareth went the way of all the others.

Orson could change in a moment from thunderous denunciation to a humorous chuckle over a remembered incident, and his anecdotes always enlivened rehearsals. I remember him once making the comparison between the generosity of American pronunciation and what he called the pinched, snobbish vowel sounds of the English. I argued with him about this, citing the example of Gielgud, and he admitted that I had chosen a notable exception. Later on at rehearsals I was arguing with him again, this time about positions, when he suddenly roared: 'Not since Ruth Chatterton left high-society drama has anyone in the theatre been so damned difficult as you!' At which point I collapsed laughing and so did everyone else.

Moby Dick finished its run at the Duke of York's Theatre on

9th July and I went to the Isle of Wight and stayed with John Hussey's mother, Nell, for a holiday in Shanklin. I was on the beach there paddling in the water one day when frenzied calling from the promenade informed me of an important telephone call, and I ran back to the house. It was Peter Eade on the line. 'Orson Welles wants you back in London for this film he's making of *Moby Dick*.' There had been talk of such a project but I'd never believed anything would come of it. I asked where he was filming it and received the improbable answer, 'Hackney Empire'.

Within hours I was on the train back to Waterloo and the next day I started work on the film with, amongst others, Gordon Jackson again and Christopher Lee. It was to be a film of the play and from the outset Orson was at loggerheads with the lighting cameraman who vainly protested that theatrical arc lamps were insufficient for filming. 'You're not Rembrandt painting with light,' he was told. 'Shoot the scene'. When the rushes revealed stygian gloom, it had to be filmed all over again. The reels are still stored in Orson's archives.

Gordon used to bring his guitar to the theatre and I would sit in the dressing room listening to him playing the music from *Le Jeux Interdit*, utterly rapt. 'You must be fed up with it,' he'd say as I kept asking him to play it again. It wasn't the only music to which he introduced me. Before I met Gordon my favourite composer had been Schumann, but Gordon gave me the *German Requiem*, then the *Four Serious Songs*, and that began my passion for Brahms which has lasted ever since. I used to spend absorbing evenings with Gordon and his wife, Rona, at their flat in Mulberry Close, Chelsea. Their drawing room was dominated by a grand piano and Gordon would encourage me to sing or he would play something I had not heard before, and I often didn't return home till the early hours.

It was to Gordon that I took the music when I had to do a singing audition for Sandy Wilson's musical play *The Buccaneer*. The part was the boy editor of a children's paper, something between Kingsley Martin and Clifton Webb, but with a young voice. 'I'll never be accepted,' I said. 'I can't sound like a boy. It should be sung treble really and I'll never get up another octave.' 'Don't bother about sounding young', Gordon reassured me, 'just sing it naturally.' In the event I sang it baritone, there were a few giggles in the stalls, and I felt

I'd died a death. I went afterwards to St Giles' churchyard, and sat among the tombstones, wondering how I'd ever thought I could carry it off. Gordon was right, though, I did get it, and after a month's rehearsal *The Buccaneer* opened in Brighton and Southsea and then at the Lyric, Hammersmith, on the 8th of September 1955. The critics were enthusiastic, the audience enjoyed us and everything seemed set fair.

Then I caught a heavy cold and my voice was reduced to a croak. Billy Chappell was directing the play and he came backstage with John Perry who was presenting it for H. M. Tennent. They said I should see an ENT man without delay and on the 14th of October I went to meet the brilliant laryngologist, John Musgrove. His manner was urbane, suavely diplomatic and decisive. If he said something would take thirty hours to cure, it always proved to be true. He liked actors and would discuss their foibles animatedly until, with disconcerting brusqueness, he would suddenly extend a hand and one was politely but firmly ushered into Wimpole Street. I lauded his abilities to all my friends. Stanley Baxter once went to him on my advice when he had difficulty swallowing. He told me afterwards, 'He took this enormous medical dictionary from the bookcase and showed me an entry, *globus hystericus*, which described my symptoms as "a psychosomatic condition usually occurring in pregnant women". We had a giggle over that, and I was starting to enjoy his company when he simply bade me goodbye, and left me on the landing – it was an extraordinaty volte face; but my complaint had disappeared.'

Meanwhile *The Buccaneer* played to very good business. Christmas came and went, and by February 1956, Tennents belatedly decided to transfer it to the West End. On my thirtieth birthday, the 22nd of February, we opened at the Apollo Theatre, but the box office plummeted and we closed on the 17th of March. I had little time to reflect on the failure of such a short run because I was busy with several things: searching for a place to live, rehearsing and performing most Sundays with the *Hancock's Half-Hour* team and also preparing to play Maxime in *Hotel Paradiso*, which Peter Glenville had asked me to do. The cast was headed by Alec Guinness and included Martita Hunt, Frank Pettingell, Irene Worth and Douglas Byng. It was in the midst of rehearsing this that I also left the parental home and took possession of my first flat at

817 Endsleigh Court. The key money, or 'fixtures and fittings' price, was £800 – extortionate, I thought, since the stuff was so dreadful. I had to clear it all out and start afresh. After paying that bill I was left with £94 in the bank. I wasn't worried about insolvency, though: *Hancock's Half-Hour* was bringing in £3 a week plus repeat fees of half again, and I was about to open in *Hotel Paradiso*.

We rehearsed at various London theatres and, since we were the two youngest members of the company, I saw a lot of Billie Whitelaw who was playing the saucy French maid. I don't think either of us were very happy in this Feydeau farce. Peter Glenville exhorted me to play it 'Byronically', instructing me to 'let the voice ring out like a trumpet', but I was floundering in uncharted waters, and I confided my confusion to Billie at rehearsals. She heard me out with infinite patience, admitted her own misgivings, and proved to be a sympathetic mentor. It was a coincidence that she lived across the road from my newly acquired flat and the first time we walked home together she surprised me by saying, 'I'll just pop in here', and disappeared into St Pancras Church. Later I was to learn that this was her way of retreating and finding relief from the nervous tension of the day.

The production toured for three weeks before the London opening and I lodged again with Mrs Parkinson in Edgbaston for the first week at the Alexandra Theatre in Birmingham. We rehearsed Sunday and Monday and it opened on Tuesday the 10th of April 1956.

Peter Eade came up to see it, said encouraging things to me afterwards and took me to supper. I told him my doubts apropos of characterisation and he asked, 'Do you remember what you first thought when you read the role? Go back to *that* – do it with style and conviction.' On Wednesday and Thursday I thought I was improving somewhat but by Friday there was a bombshell. Frank Pettingell announced he was unhappy in the play and was leaving. We had to start rehearsing all over again with his replacement, D. A. Clark Smith,

I adored Frank; he was an imposing figure, striding about in a travelling coat invariably armed with books. He once told me, 'I've got so many books in the house they have to be stacked on the landing. The floor is sagging under the weight. The architect says I've got to reinforce the timber joists or the bedroom floor will give way'.

'What's below?' I asked.

'The dining room,' laughed Frank. 'I'll be able to read and eat in bed.'

I was crestfallen at the news of his departure but the rest of the cast remained intact and the following week we played and rehearsed in Glasgow. Stanley met me at the station and I was very impressed with his motor car. By now he was a rising star in the world of comedy and this was only one sign of the attendant affluence. He drove me to the new home he had found with his wife Moira and we had dinner, revolving many memories.

After the performance on the 17th April, Alec Guinness asked Billie and me to dine with him at the opulent restaurant, Mal Maison. We were both very impressed. The grandeur of the establishment contrasted starkly with our digs and the food was superb. A few tables away Martita Hunt was merrily entertaining other guests and ever and anon their gusts of laughter could be heard across the deeply carpeted dining room. Our table was quiet, however, presided over by a grave host who offered us three different brands of cigarette: 'Turkish, Egyptian or Virginia?' Billie and I struggled embarrassedly over the vast menu and the pauses in conversation lengthened. Suddenly she launched into an hysterically enthusiastic account of *Picture Post*. 'They have a fascinating article this week on this Dutch community in Staines. It's flourished there for years and they've managed to preserve their own cultural traditions, even costumes! All the women wear Dutch caps.' She'd hardly observed the full stop before adding hastily, 'On their heads, I mean.' Alec smiled unperturbed, and mercifully ordered for us.

Later as I stole through the long corridors and out into the night I remember thinking how luxuriously stars lived and what a diverting time they had. I didn't realise then how much dutiful kindness was involved in entertaining members of a company; actors can prove quite a handful. Alec always seemed to find time for everyone and they can't all have been as delightful as Billie and me!

After a further week at Newcastle we returned to London where at the dress rehearsal I was delighted to see Frank Pettingell back in the cast. He'd had second thoughts and decided to rejoin us. Everyone greeted him with affection and I felt that this was a portent of success. We opened at the Winter

Garden Theatre in Drury Lane and I wrote in my diary: 'Fabulous opening night, terrific reception. Alec sent me champagne.'

Next day I was at the Westminster Ophthalmic Hospital being treated for an eye concretion and because I couldn't afford to pay decorators I found myself painting my 'studio' flat with one eye bandaged. I was only allowed to remove the dressing for the evening performance. Nevertheless I had transformed my abode in a week from dreary brown to dazzling white. I had a large alcove for which my Aunt Daisy made curtains to hide the single bed and I purchased a cane chair from Heals. When it was all finished I sat drinking endless cups of coffee and smoking cigarettes gazing contentedly at my achievements.

During stage breaks at the Winter Garden I sat in the dressing room reading with my feet up on the dressing table and the chair inclined backwards, and in this position I was so entranced by my book, Marguerite Yourcenar's *Hadrian*, that I developed a bad back. I also used to undo the fly buttons on my very tight trousers and unfasten the high starch collar. Both activities led to trouble. One night I was so absorbed in the book that I was almost late for my entrance. I rushed down to the stage and came on to play the scene in which I virtually blackmailed my uncle. I remember thinking it very odd that Alec had changed his moves and kept trying to stand in front of me, later even edging me behind a potted palm. When we came off I asked him, 'Why?' 'Your flies were open,' he said. To my horror I found I had indeed failed to dress properly before making the entrance. I apologised profusely but he simply said, 'Always remember before going on stage, wipe your nose and check your flies.' I've done so ever since.

It was the other star of the company, Martita Hunt, who helped me over the second mishap. My bad reading posture had resulted in appalling backache; during the run I consulted doctors, physiotherapists, masseurs and orthopaedic surgeons, all to no avail. When I bemoaned my fate at their hands, Martita told me I'd been wasting my time and she packed me off to see her favourite osteopath, Johnny Johnson. Although he had three goes at it, he was finally successful where everyone else had failed. I admired him because, like John Musgrove, he made no false promises, his treatment was quickly effective, and he understood actors.

I certainly needed to be fit because I was doing the play at night, the radio series with Tony Hancock during the day, and I was also rehearsing a comedy sketch with Zsa Zsa Gabor for the *Night of A Hundred Stars* at the Palladium – which was formerly called *Summer Stars* until Noël Coward remarked, 'Some are stars and some are not'. This took place at midnight on the 28th of June 1956. Afterwards I wrote in my diary: 'The double act with Zsa Zsa went very well indeed – we got all our laughs nicely.' The next night at the Winter Garden in the darkness of the wings, Alex Guinness suddenly hissed at me 'Zsa Zsa Gabor to you too!' before sailing on to the stage. It made me laugh so much I nearly missed my entrance.

The summer was hot and airless so I was glad for the cool of September but on the 20th I noted that Alec was looking exhausted, and I arrived at the theatre the next day to find that he was indisposed and that his understudy, John Salew, would be appearing in his place. The difference in performance was off-putting for audience and cast alike but we got by for two nights until out star returned. When this happened, John Salew complained to me, 'I've just passed Alec at the stage door and do you know he never said a word about my going on for him. He didn't say anything about my stepping into the breach and I flatter myself I gave a very creditable performance. But he said nothing.'

'He said nothing?' I echoed.

'Not a dicky bird, simply ignored my performance.'

Privately I thought that was the best thing anyone could do about his performance, but aloud I said, 'Well it's no good brooding. Do something about it.'

'There's nothing I can do.'

'Rubbish, of course there is, you can go along and tell him how disappointed you were about him not mentioning your stepping in at a moment's notice; you could say even a small acknowledgement would have been gratifying under the circumstances.'

'Do you think I should?'

'Of course.'

'All right, I will.'

He departed, full of resolution and I shot round the dressing rooms telling everyone how slighted he felt.

Frank Pettingell was appalled. 'And you've put him up to going to Alec and complaining?'

'Yes,' I cried gleefully, 'isn't it a riot?'

'No, it's nothing of the kind. You know Alec has to prepare an elaborate make-up. You know he doesn't like to be disturbed before the play – you're incorrigible.'

Soon the lugubrious understudy was back. 'Well, I told him. I knocked on the door and he was in the middle of making up. I said "I'm sorry to barge in like this but I've gone on for you the last two nights, and given a very competent performance, if I say so myself, and I would have thought you might have mentioned it. After all a word of thanks can be very encouraging." '

'What did he say?'

'Oh he said something about being remiss and having other things on his mind.'

At this point Alec Guinness's dresser appeared and gave John a large parcel which he hastily opened. He found several bottles of whisky lying in a row and a note in immaculate copper plate, inscribed, 'With my belated thanks, Alec.'

I eyed the contents enviously. 'Well, you've done very well out of that,' I told him. 'What a lovely present.'

But he looked doubtful. 'No, you see I'm not a whisky man, I'm a gin man.'

'Oh,' I said, 'in that case you must take it back. He wouldn't want you to have a present you don't enjoy.'

'You don't think it would look churlish?'

'Heavens no, he'd much rather know you'd got something you liked!'

'Yes, all right then. I'll take it back to him.'

He grabbed the unwrapped package and returned to Alec's room. Again I went round telling the others about my machinations.

Douglas Byng looked shocked. 'Telling people to return presents! No good can come of it.'

But John Salew returned with his bottles of gin pronouncing himself entirely satisfied with the course of events, in spite of my reminders that but for me he wouldn't have had any bottles at all.

Hotel Paradiso finished its run on the 3rd of November 1956, not because of bad business but because of Alec's commitment to play in the film *Bridge On The River Kwai*. I started rehearsals for a radio production of H. G. Wells's *The Man Who Could Work Miracles*. Tony Hancock had agreed

70

to play the lead because people had been advising him to eschew variety and concentrate on straight acting, and Wells was a writer he admired. When I had visited Tony in the London Clinic during one of his slimming bouts I found Wells's *Outline of History* lying on his bed, and we talked at length about theories of historical inevitability, the Malthusian doctrine and the decline of great civilizations. Tony always returned to the same themes – 'What is the purpose of human existence?' and 'Is there a discernible pattern in human progress?' Again and again he held that such imponderables were unanswerable and when I ventured to suggest that only faith would explain apparent meaninglessness, he rejected that on the grounds that it was unprovable. 'Our reasoning must be answered by reason,' he would say. 'Men want a rational answer, not mystery and magic.' He was married to Cicely then and I remember the nights at their flat in Hyde Park Gate where she would wearily announce that she was going to bed, leaving the two of us arguing into the early hours with the wreckage of empty wine bottles and overflowing ash trays all round us.

Once, as Tony was walking back with me across the Park as dawn was approaching, he suddenly stood stock still and said, 'All this money I'm getting – it makes me feel guilty', and went on to talk of the huge fees he was being offered. I made some rejoinder about the rewards of top billing, star status deserving its reward, but he only shook his head and talked about popularity being ephemeral. 'You can't trust it, Kenny,' he insisted.

In the event his sally into straight acting was something of a disappointment. After the performance I wrote, 'Tony didn't come up at the end; perhaps because he didn't believe in what he was saying. If he can't totally identify with a role, he doesn't seem to be able to perform it. He's convinced that True to Life should be the same as True to Art, and it isn't.'

I spent Christmas with Louisa and Charlie at Aunt Daisy's house in Rainham, Essex, where we had turkey and Christmas pudding and sang all the old songs. My Uncle Clifford drove us back to London where the adorable Hattie Jacques presided genially over a splendidly theatrical New Year's Eve party and I wrote in my diary that 1956 had been a most satisfying year in the theatre, that I'd managed to set aside £400 in the building society and that at last I'd found the privacy of a home of my own.

At the start of 1957 I was still doing *Hancock's Half-Hour* every week and in February I was offered the role of Kite in Mervyn Peake's Gothic comedy *The Wit To Woo*. I had a friend in the cast because Wensley Pithey was playing the father and I'd worked with him in *Moby Dick*. Colin Douglas and Zena Walker played the lovers. It was produced by Peter Wood and because he told me I was talented I thought he was the most discerning director I'd ever met.

Kite was a slithering, fawning, hypocritical servant in the play who had amusing asides to the audience and acted sometimes as the chorus. Peter had him appear unexpectedly from behind a screen, through a window, and at one point even out of a grandfather clock. At one rehearsal I sat chatting with the author in the stalls and commented on his passion for certain words in the script: 'You use plum quite a lot.' 'Yes,' he enthused, 'I love the sound of plum and rum and dumb and sum and mum and bum.' He said the last word with such lingering relish that I couldn't stop laughing. From then on I knew he was not only a funny writer, but also an amusing companion. He had a great flair for making you feel like an old friend and conversation flowed easily.

We opened to mixed reviews at the Art's Theatre on the 12th of March. The fact that the play didn't transfer to a larger theatre was disappointing, but fortunately I was almost immediately distracted by rehearsals for the first BBC Television production of *Hancock's Half-Hour*. By then the radio series had become so popular that Galton and Simpson had written a television version.

In the first programme, one scene involved a yodelling competition in the Tyrol. Tony represented East Cheam, and I had to maintain, 'I've got the biggest yodel in West Dulwich.' We were attired in lederhosen and bragged about our vocal prowess until a truce was declared with me saying, 'Come on, let's do little fingers – no, stop messing about, let's do little fingers,' and this childish ritual was then enacted.

In another sketch we had to share a room in an overcrowded hotel managed by Richard Wattis. John Vere played the part of a clerical guest, a bishop who mistakenly received Hancock's morning paper every day. Tony got the *Church Times* and the bishop got a comic. It was apt casting for John Vere. He looked loftily academic and affected such grand disdain that when he was deflated the result was wonderfully funny. His look of dismay, followed by a rueful 'Charming', punctuated a scene perfectly.

This was the first of a series of six shows, and looking it up in my diary I was surprised to find that the BBC transmitted these programmes live. Today most comparable comedy material on television is recorded and edited.

I remember talking to Tony about the success of the Tyrolean piece a few weeks afterwards and he nodded agreement. 'Yes, it went very well on the whole but there were complaints from some people; they thought it was a bit poofy.'

I was astounded. 'Poofy? Why on earth should they think that?'

'Oh, it's the two men in one room, and us doing the little fingers bit.'

I was still full of disbelief. 'But little fingers is a children's formula for pax.'

'Yes, but they read these things into it, two blokes holding hands, you know.'

I found it hard to accept. The authors and the actors intended to give no such impression; some spectators simply chose to interpret the scene in this way. I think this was the first time I got worried about the inferences that could be made about acting. I suppose I must have been very green in those days because when I heard the joke about the bad golf player excusing himself to his skilled partner with the line, 'I'm sorry, but I'm a country member,' I never understood the laugh which greeted the tag line, 'I'll remember.' This is why I initially failed to grasp the import of Malvolio's lines in the letter scene – 'This is my lady's hand: these be her very C's, her U's and her T's; and thus makes she her great P's.' (I still find it delightful that in the Temple edition of Shakespeare there is a note about it saying, 'This joke can be explained to the actor by any common sailor.')

I did the last of the Hancock's television programmes on the 10th of June, playing a half-deaf dodderer with an ear-trumpet. I did my stock version of a funny old man and I thought I was rather good, but Tony said he disliked stereotype characters. 'Once established in a series you have to have them every week and that interrupts the story-line.' He made no secret of the fact that he didn't like my 'snide' character, a nasal cockney who invariably had the line 'No, stop messing about.' 'It may get laughs,' he said, 'but it's just a funny voice, it's not true to life.' Nevertheless the scriptwriters kept putting it in and the audiences continued to laugh.

In the 1950s London had a lot of tiny fringe theatres and there was one in Villiers Street called The Watergate; it was here that I'd seen a young actress called Maggie Smith, with riveting eyes and an original approach to comedy. She was in a revue called *Oxford Eight* and soon afterwards she was spirited off to America for the revue *New Faces*. By July 1957 she was back in London and Michael Codron, the producer, asked me to join her in a revue written by Bamber Gascoigne called *Share My Lettuce*. Michael had seen the undergraduate production of this at Cambridge and thought it witty and fresh. He took me to lunch and described how he envisaged restaging it, with me linking it and taking part in the sketches.

Michael had an engaging manner and a delightful sense of irony but when engrossed he could be silently enigmatic. I told him that some people thought his conversational pauses were designed to make them talk too much. 'Nothing so profound,' he replied 'it's generally because I've nothing to say.'

He had plenty to say about the planning of this revue which rehearsed for three weeks and opened on the 5th of August 1957 at the Theatre Royal, Brighton. There was endless trouble over the running order with Michael making changes again and again and demanding more material from the author. At one point he asked for something poignant to contrast with another sketch and Bamber came up with 'Wallflower Waltz'. This was a charming song which was sung by the girls who were left languishing while the men danced with long pieces of chiffon which descended from the flies. Initially I wasn't in it because I couldn't dance but eventually they settled for my inadequate footwork in order to make up the number of men in the scene.

The first night in London was at the Lyric, Hammersmith, on the 21st of August and all went well until we came to the 'Wallflower Waltz'. All the pieces of chiffon floated down from the flies but my bit got stuck on a spot-bar and never appeared. I ran round the other waltzing men trying to take their lengths of material but they wouldn't be budged and

74

there was a ripple of amusement from the audience. The girls kept up their sad lament and I got more desperate, crying out 'I haven't got a bit,' pulling and shoving the dancers and trying vainly to grab their pieces of chiffon. By this time there was so much laughter you couldn't hear the song at all; what was intended as a plaintive musical sequence had become a comedy number. At the end of the performance Michael came backstage and announced, 'Your chiffon must *never* come down: that's how I want it played every night,' and thereafter 'Wallflower Waltz' became a surefire laugh in the show.

Maggie Smith's comedy was a continual fascination for me. In one scene she played a society hostess inventing Party Games, singing, 'Here's a pencil and pad and you won't find it bad these are games that we all of us know. Pass 'em on as you write 'em and ad infinitum it's just Party Games that make a good party go.' All the while she fiddled with a rope of beads, first twirling them round her neck and then, amazingly, round her waist. Just as they seemed to be heading for her ankles, she deftly altered their course and the beads ended up round her neck again. She finished the song looking as immaculate as when she'd started. She had the knack of appearing to keep great tension under control and her panicky asides were just as effective offstage as they were on. In Fortnum's lingerie section she was once aghast at the prices. 'Seven guineas for a bra!' she complained, 'Cheaper to have your tits off!' and departed leaving the opulent salon full of gigglers.

Share My Lettuce became very fashionable. On the night of the 7th of September Terence Rattigan came backstage and was very complimentary. That seemed to set the seal of approval on us as firmly as the Royal Warrant and two weeks later we transferred to the Comedy Theatre in the West End.

The dressing-room windows overlooked an open space across which I could talk to Maggie, and I remember one night she called out, 'What's in this bottle of stuff you've given me for my eyes?'

'It's a balm to soothe the pupils,' I told her. 'Some sort of alkaline solution. Why?'

'W-e-ll,' she called back, elongating the vowel disapprovingly, 'I just spilled a drop of it on the window sill and it's gone clean through the paint.' I can recall my involuntary alarm and the subsequent laughter as if it were yesterday.

*   *   *

By October 1957 I was doing the pilot radio series for *Beyond Our Ken* with Kenneth Horne, filming with Richard Wattis at Elstree Studios in a series called *Dick and the Duchess*, and also doing the revue every night. Something had to give and on the 23rd of October I overslept and arrived at the theatre just in time to see the audience streaming out. Because of my absence the show had been cancelled.

Telephones began to ring almost immediately and within half an hour, reporters were at the stage door. The company manager suggested that I told them that I had gone to the country and got caught in a traffic jam and someone else suggested saying that my car had broken down, but Michael Codron arrived and said simply, 'Tell them the truth,' and that's what I did. Next day, my sleeping through a performance was headlines on the front page of the *Guardian* and the *Express*, second page in the *Mail*, *Herald*, *Sketch*, *Telegraph* and *Times*, and the BBC television news asked me to appear at 6.25 pm to describe it all. By this time it didn't smack of negligence: it was practically heroic.

During the evening show at the theatre, there was a solemn ceremony in the interval when a famous watch company presented me with a huge alarm clock in front of a cheering audience. I made a speech, there was a party backstage, and it appeared that my tardiness had given the show a great fillip.

Share My Lettuce flourished through the rest of the year, at Christmas there was talk of yet another transfer, and on the 29th of January 1958, with Maggie remarking 'This must be the longest tour in town', we had our third London opening at the Garrick Theatre.

It was here that I misbehaved in more ways than one and incurred Maggie's wrath. There was a sketch in the show where four men stood selling newspapers; one, two and three cried, 'Star,' 'News,' and 'Standard' respectively and I called out 'Figaro'; then we shouted the virtues of our papers, each of us attempting to drown the others till Maggie appeared. Dressed in a slinky black mackintosh, she walked sexily across the stage and as she passed the vendors one by one, they fell silent. When she was almost at the proscenium arch, the first man asked, 'Paper, lady?' and she exited saying, 'No thank you, dearie, I won't be needing any paper.' It always got a big laugh and there was an immediate stage black-out.

One night I didn't stay mute when she passed me, I sang

76

'Figaro' basso profundo and then continued with 'When you're a barber . . . Figaro, Figaro,' etc. Of course Maggie couldn't say her line and after a momentary hesitation, she simply walked off stage, the electrics didn't get their cue, the blackout was late, and my choral efforts, while raising an initial titter, ruined the end of the scene.

During the interval an irate Maggie came into my dressing room demanding an explanation. I was sitting at the make-up bench doing my face and she perched herself on it between me and the wash basin, flicking cigarette ash into the bowl while she talked.

'Why did you put in all that operatic stuff?'

'I thought it was a funny idea.'

'It ruined my tag line.'

'I had this urge to do something new.'

'You need to rehearse something new.'

'I know, but I just couldn't wait.'

Maggie suddenly leant over the sink and asked, 'Have you been peeing in here?'

I started a stammering denial, reddened and faltered.

'Hmm,' she said. 'I suppose you couldn't wait for that either?' Then we both started laughing, and a potential row over a foolish ad lib had an entirely happy ending.

It was during the run at the Garrick that Peter Eade told me that the film producer Peter Rogers and his director Gerald Thomas had seen the show, liked my work and were offering me a part in their latest picture. 'It's called *Carry On Sergeant*. It's about a set of recruits conscripted for the army.'

'Is it a good part?' I asked.

'It's a sort of toffee-nosed intellectual who resents authority.'

'Oh that does sound rather me, doesn't it?'

'Yes it does, but I should tell you that they're not offering much money.'

'Well I'm getting twenty pounds a week in the theatre so anything else I earn is supplementary, isn't it?'

'You could say that.'

'How much are they offering?'

'Over a four to five week period you would make about £800.'

I whistled soundlessly. Eight hundred pounds in 1958 seemed astronomical to me and I didn't hesitate. I told Peter to tell them I'd do it.

The film was shot at Pinewood Studios and the army locations were at the Queen's Barracks at Stoughton in Surrey. We were meticulously drilled by sergeant majors and it reminded me of my earlier days with the Border Regiment in Carlisle. It was as if nothing had changed: drilling and marching, rifle and bayonet practice, and that sadistic invention, the assault course. The actors in my squad included Charles Hawtrey, Terence Longdon, Kenneth Connor and Bob Monkhouse. The sergeant was William Hartnell and the CO was played with absent-minded dottiness by Eric Barker.

The weather in April was warm and sunny and the conditions perfect for filming. I was up every morning at 6 o'clock, out by 7 and made-up and uniformed by 8. We exercised, climbed trees, swung on ropes across rivers, and marched till the blisters appeared and unused muscles began to ache. There were rumbles of protest. 'Might as well be in the real army, the pay is just as bad!' complained one actor nursing a bunion. But Kenneth Connor would chuckle and say, 'Yes, but it's better than working,' and endlessly assured us that we were on the crest of a wave – and time proved him to be absolutely right.

Gerald Thomas directed the film and during the kitting-out sequence an over-large beret was plonked on my head and I was supposed to be pushed unceremoniously out of camera by the quartermaster. In fact, when we shot the scene, I couldn't resist a touch of John Vere; as I was crowned by the hat I dropped the chin sardonically and said, 'Charming', and then walked away. Gerald reproved me. 'You weren't supposed to say anything there, you were practically on the edge of the frame.' But he allowed it to stay in the picture and it got a nice laugh.

It was this kind of indulgent direction which made Gerald so popular with actors. Once, when considering the photographs of two players for a role, he unhesitatingly pointed to one and said, 'Get him'. The casting director remarked, 'They're both good.' Gerald replied, 'I know, but I've chosen the one who's most amiable on the set.' A happy working atmosphere certainly contributed enormously to the success of the films which he and Peter Rogers made together.

This was the first *Carry On* picture and it was made on a shoestring budget with the simple formula of a good story and a good team. I had no idea then that it was to be the start of a series.

78

On the 6th of May 1958 I returned from filming to find a cast meeting in one of the dressing rooms at the Garrick. A despondent Michael Codron told us that the bus strike that was then on in town was killing the business and he was reluctantly obliged to take *Share My Lettuce* off on the 17th. In spite of the transport troubles, there was a wonderful last-night house – not mad or hysterical, just people properly enjoying themselves. I made a speech at the end which was wryly sad and shamelessly sentimental.

The end of the revue didn't leave me totally idle for I was still doing *Hancock's Half-Hour* every week, albeit in a steadily worsening atmosphere. At the Paris Studios in Lower Regent Street where we did the recordings, there was a disturbing moment in rehearsal when Tony made his feelings plain. I was in the midst of my 'snide' speech crying, 'Oh no, stop messing about,' when he suddenly exploded, 'I don't want that voice in this show.' He turned to the writers and asked them why they'd put that character in again when he'd told them he didn't want it in.

Alan Simpson and Ray Galton were both embarrassed. They pointed out that the script required a laugh at that particular point, that this was a tried and trusted formula, and that radio audiences enjoyed a catchphrase. But Tony was adamant. 'It's a gimmick – a funny voice – it's cartoon stuff. It's not true to life and I don't want it in the show.' The atmosphere was hardly conducive to comedy and I longed to dissolve. I suppose I should have asked the BBC to cancel my contract; certainly I would like to have left there and then, but something held me back.

Hancock was at great pains to say that it was nothing personal, that it wasn't me he was getting at, which was supposed to placate me, but I didn't see then and I don't see now that you can divorce the actor from his work. Tony's endless analysis of the scripts and the characters was becoming destructive, but I stuck it out and ostensibly everything continued amicably to the end of the series in June.

At that point just when I was becoming disillusioned with radio comedy, Kenneth Horne telephoned from out of the blue: 'Hello chum, remember that pilot show we did last year? The BBC want to do it and we start on the 18th of June. Can you make it?' I never said 'yes' more joyfully to any engagement. It was the beginning of a long and fruitful relationship.

79

Kenneth Horne always deprecated his talents ('No chum, I can't *act*, just call me Peg, something you can hang the show on') and certainly the cast of *Beyond Our Ken* orbited round this genial anchorman with a comical success that won enormous popularity. The scriptwriters, Barry Took and Eric Merriman, created a host of characters: Betty Marsden did everything from cockney cleaners to sibilant spies, Pat Lancaster trilled '20s songs, Bill Pertwee rendered valiant choruses about the Yeomen of England, Hugh Paddick was wonderfully laconic, à la Noël Coward, and he and I together frequently depicted decadent dilettantes. The Fraser Hayes Four provided the musical interludes and the producer was Jaques Brown. He was always urging us to 'Keep it clean – precious rather than poofy' and to 'Lift the words off the page'. His personality suggested something between a *maître d' hôtel* and a vicar and he would beam and twinkle benevolently with the players and the technicians alike, tailoring the show with precision and style. On-stage Kenneth Horne introduced funny diary items every week, which he told us 'came from my Salvation Army lass who writes to me', and off-stage he showered us all with presents – socks for the men, for instance, and mittens for the ladies – and gave us sumptuous lunches at the Spanish Club in Cavendish Square. No one could have headed a cast and steered it with greater skill than this establishment figure who presided over the show with urbane charm and elegance.

He always wore a formal blue suit with a fresh carnation. He would stand centre-stage before a performance smiling at the audience, saying things like, 'For those of you who are not familiar with the studios, remember the Ladies is on the right and the Gents on the left. No, I'm sorry, the Gents is on the right and the Ladies is . . . oh, what does it matter! You'll make a lot of new friends!'

The rehearsals were light-hearted but thorough and if there was a hint of bad humour K.H. would always intervene with a conciliatory gesture. No one poured oil on troubled waters more tactfully than he did. He nursed wounded egos and encouraged experiment with one single objective: to make the whole team a success.

Once when I was ill, he went out of his way to visit my flat, putting the details of a recuperative holiday through my letter-box and departing without saying a word. And all this from a man who was a husband, a father, the chairman of two large companies, a writer and a remarkable entertainer.

August found me reacquainted with Billie Whitelaw when I played in her Granada TV series *Time Out For Peggy*. I had the part of a moony young man who composed doggerel for greeting cards. I stood at a lectern declaiming, 'May this day be bright for you and may the sky be always blue, may your fairest dreams come true, may your love come smiling through,' and though the audiences laughed at my fictitious verses they were not that far from the real thing which they purchased every day.

We rehearsed the show in London and then got the train to Manchester where it was televised, returning on the night sleeper to London. There wasn't much sleeping, though, because we used to sit drinking gin in Billie's berth and talking through the night.

I followed that, still in August, with a BBC television play, *The Noble Spaniard* which starred Margaret Rutherford who I can see in my mind's eye now, with her knitting bag at rehearsals. 'Pains,' she would say. 'It is all a question of taking pains,' and when it came to the performance she was as delightfully eccentric as always.

In October I was immediately into rehearsals for another television programme, this time at Chelsea, for Granada, when I played the Dauphin again to Siobhan McKenna's Saint Joan; and at the beginning of November it was back to Manchester for another episode of *Time Out For Peggy* before starting my second film with Gerald Thomas and Peter Rogers, *Carry On Nurse*.

This entailed my first screen love-scene and since tender and emotional acting was never my forte I was relieved on seeing the rushes to find that I had carried it off all right. The success was really ensured by my partner, Jill Ireland: she played the role with such vulnerable attractiveness that we couldn't fail. Even so I was particularly gratified when Peter Rogers congratulated me afterwards. Gerald was always encouraging but Peter seldom gave unqualified praise. When he wasn't enthusiastic about a scene he could be disconcertingly frank. Once when an actor complained, 'I should have more funny lines – I'm a comedian', he retorted, 'Your secret is safe with me,' and exited amid a gaggle of giggles.

81

Artistes often had to be comforted by Gerald. 'Take no notice, that's just Peter's way, don't worry, he'll ask you back again,' and of course he always did. From the earliest days Peter saw the potential for a long-lasting comedy-film team, undreamt of by the rest of us.

Before *Carry On Nurse* was finished I was rehearsing what was, for me, a new departure in the theatre: the musical *Cinderella* with a score by Richard Rodgers and Oscar Hammerstein II. I played one of the Ugly Sisters and I was apprehensive about appearing in female apparel but the director Freddie Carpenter allayed my fears. 'Don't worry about it, Kenneth, the costumes will be outlandish and funny, grotesque rather than feminine,' and they were. One gown was covered in tiny lamps which were wired up to an enormous battery slung over my posterior under the skirt. At a given moment, the stage lights dimmed, my dress lit up like a Christmas tree, and the other ugly sister lifted me up so that I literally blazed over the ballroom scene. The actor capable of this kind of acrobatic skill had to be very strong indeed and Freddie Carpenter cast for this role my old chum from troopship days, the Army PT instructor, Ted Durant.

It was a doubly happy reunion for me because again my fears about drag were quietened. Ted and I made a vigorous pair; where he was big and bullying, I was sharp and aggressive, discussing Cinderella's arrival at the Palace by crying out, 'My dear, her eyes are so far apart I think I shall have to take a taxi.' Kenneth Tynan in *The Observer* gave me a complimentary mention, noting that some of Mrs Patrick Campbell's lines had been purloined for pantomime, and Harold Hobson wrote in *The Sunday Times*: 'This is the best thing of its kind I've seen.' Freddie Carpenter broke with tradition by having a male principal boy, Bruce Trent, playing Prince Charming and he and Yana made a splendidly romantic couple. Jimmy Edwards was a genial King, getting huge laughs with his array of trumpets, and my old friend from *Beyond Our Ken*, Betty Marsden, was a grandly dramatic Fairy Godmother. But the ovation of the evening always went to Buttons: when Tommy Steele came bounding on at the curtain I have never heard such deafening cheers. At first I thought it was because of a particularly enthusiastic opening-night audience but it lasted throughout the run and his energetic enthusiasm never seemed to flag. Certainly mine did. I went moaning to Betty Marsden

82

about the exhausting nature of performing twice nightly and she straightaway gave me the remedy: 'In between shows prepare a bed in the dressing room with proper sheets and pillows, take off the make-up and wash, put on pyjamas, tuck yourself in and go to sleep. Even if it's only ten minutes, you'll get up psychologically and physically refreshed and ready for the next performance.' I obeyed her instructions implicitly and they worked admirably.

Cinderella opened on the 18th of December 1958 at the Coliseum and on the 29th I wrote in my diary, 'Noël Coward came to my dressing room after the performance. He said, "You were wonderful, such a dreadfully vulgar walk." I protested, "I wish you'd seen it earlier, they've cut a lot of my dialogue."

"My dear, put it all back. Gradually."

"Oh, d'you think I should?"

"If I know you, you will."'

There was bad news on the domestic front at the beginning of 1959 when I learnt that my father's hairdressing business was floundering. Louisa had told me how customers had drifted away as assistants had left but it was Charlie who revealed to me that he'd become hopelessly enmeshed with the Inland Revenue. He blamed the accountants. He said they had always prepared his figures and he assumed they were therefore responsible, but of course he had signed the returns and ultimately he had to answer for them.

The upshot was an alarming demand for tax going back several years and, by the time the dust had settled, Charlie was bankrupt. The shop and the house had to go, and I quickly found my parents a modest flat in nearby Judd Street. I had it decorated and carpeted for them to move into at the end of January.

It was a blow from which Charlie never really recovered. His personality had hitherto been confident, even dogmatic, and though outwardly he seemed cheerfully resigned to the new *modus vivendi*, he now began to drift aimlessly between the local pub and the betting shop. I failed to see the danger signs probably because my own living conditions were deteriorating as well. Traffic and noisy neighbours were combining to make Endsleigh Court intolerable and I too began to think of finding somewhere else to live.

However, I'd barely got Louisa and Charlie settled in to their new abode before I was starting a new radio series of *Beyond Our Ken* as well as doing the pantomime, and in early March I started work at Pinewood for my third film with Gerald and Peter. This time it was *Carry On Teacher*, and a newcomer to the team was Ted Ray as the headmaster. I remember how we all sat in a circle of chairs on the set listening to Ted telling story after story with astonishing expertise. He had a mind for jokes like a file index and he vocalised characters so that you were entertained all the way to the tag-line. That's the sure art of story-telling. The ones who can't do it are the ones who leave you thinking, 'Oh get to the end, for heaven's sake.'

The rest of us may not have possessed Ted's vast repertoire but we all had some entertaining stories. In one tea-break Charles Hawtrey told us about his first thriller in the West End. His elderly mother had accompanied him on the set, and she was listening so intently to him that a lit cigarette dropped from her lips into her handbag where it began to smoulder. Seeing the danger, Joan Sims cried out, 'Charlie, your mum's bag! It's on fire!' Charles hardly paused before emptying his cup of tea into the reticule which Mrs Hawtrey then snapped firmly shut. Charles resumed the conversation, the sodden handbag was forgotten, and he went triumphantly on to the denouement. It was a typical incident as far as actors are concerned. With the narrative underway they bitterly resent any impediment to the climax.

It was a very happy company and it is a testament to the camaraderie of the *Carry Ons* that at the end of the film the cast got together to give Peter Rogers and Gerald Thomas a special thank-you dinner at an hotel in Harrow. It was all planned very carefully. Leslie Phillips was deputed to purchase special cuff-links for the two honoured guests and Ted Ray gave the speech – a long tribute entirely in verse – which was afterwards presented as an illuminated address. Having over-stayed our welcome in the hotel we then repaired with great hilarity to the nearby home of Kenneth Connor where we continued singing and carousing into the night.

Cinderella completed its run at the Coliseum in April and I continued with *Beyond Our Ken* which was steadily gaining in popularity. I was surprised to be asked back for the new *Hancock's Half-Hour* series in June because after the inquest

84

of the year before I'd not expected to return. I was dismayed to find that Hattie Jacques had been dropped from the cast and that my own contributions had been reduced to a trickle. I only did four episodes before I asked the producer, Tom Ronald, to rescind my contract. I said I felt I was extraneous, that as I was in another radio show I thought it would be better if I went. He agreed and on the 7th of June 1959 I performed with Tony Hancock for the last time.

There is always something sad about a parting of the ways, but my gloom was mitigated by a sense of relief. Though Tony had said in rehearsals that he didn't like my characterizations in the show, I think he didn't like *me* in the show. In the early days he had not criticised my style of performing: it was only in this later period, when popularity had built the kind of laughter which he felt was disproportionate, that he objected. In fact, the audience was responding to what the writers had created: I was putting flesh on their comic ideas. Ray Galton and Alan Simpson wrote the sort of scripts which enhanced the comedy as well as the performer. All the stuff about comedians who can be funny reading the telephone directory is rubbish: they need material as much as a tailor needs cloth. And the actor facing the audience without a good script is as hapless as a rifleman without bullets. I don't think Tony Hancock ever understood how much he depended on his writers. Later on, when he jettisoned not only performers but authors as well, it was like a yachtsman dismissing his crew and then getting rid of the boat-builder.

Ever since the production of *Share My Lettuce* Michael Codron had spoken of his desire to mount another revue and we had had several preliminary meetings and discussions about the form it would take. He had collected a lot of material from authors and composers, ranging from Harold Pinter and John Law to Lionel Bart and Sandy Wilson, and he was particularly enthusiastic about a new young writer and performer, just emerging from university, called Peter Cook. I read several of his sketches and thought his zany humour could be easily shaped to my style. Michael engaged Paddy Stone to direct and choreograph the show and found a singular new comedienne in Fenella Fielding.

The rest of the company was assembled and we started rehearsing *Pieces of Eight* on the 4th of August 1959, touring for three weeks before the opening at the Apollo Theatre on the 23rd of September. At the beginning of the show the cast sang a mock revivalist chorus, 'We've got to help each other! Hallelujah!', ending with arms raised heavenward. Whereupon I descended on a Kirby flying ballet wire as an angelic cherub. I was hoisted into the flies before the curtain rose and waited up there before being lowered on cue. The leather harness was suspended under my crotch and I felt as if I was being perpetually goosed. After a time they rigged up a trapeze for me to stand on, and I couldn't understand why my hands became covered in an angry rash, till the doctor analysed my allergy as manilla and thereafter the ropes were bandaged. Even so, it was all distinctly uncomfortable.

I had some good comedy spots in the revue and, significantly, the two biggest laughs were due to Peter Cook. He wrote a sketch about an egomaniac in a railway carriage holding a cardboard box and iterating: 'I've got a viper in 'ere; it's not an asp,' to an impatient and bored fellow-traveller. There was a comparable manic character in another scene called Arthur Grangely, who ranted and moaned, 'If only I'd had the *flesh*! I could have been the fattest man in all the world!' with Fenella echoing his lament. Audiences found the two of us wailing in descant wildly funny and both items became firm favourites throughout the run.

Finally exasperated by the noise, I left Endsleigh Court and moved into Alexandra Mansions where my old friend John Hussey, now back from South Africa, let me have his spare bedroom. The quiet was bliss after the place I had vacated. On the first morning I told him of my relief but grumbled about his toothpaste: 'I don't know how you can use that stuff. It tastes vile.'

'What toothpaste?' he asked.

'The red and white tube in the bathroom,' I replied.

He looked pained. 'That's my haemorrhoidal ointment,' he said, and I practically choked over the coffee.

Nevertheless it led to an enlightening conversation because I confided my fears about pains in my nether regions and he advised me to consult a specialist. 'Doctors are no good, they'll simply tell you to use bran or prescribe laxative, you need someone who's dramatic. See a surgeon.'

I telephoned my friend John Musgrove and asked him to recommend someone; within twenty-four hours I had an appointment with a rectal surgeon, Mr Desmond Mulvaney. After examining me he said, 'Ideally you should be treated in hospital, but since you're appearing nightly in the theatre that's not possible. I suggest we try rectal injections, say one a week, and see how the condition progresses.' I nodded dumbly and was thankful that I was in no position to see the hypodermic. I felt it, though. I remember the painful walk home from Harley Street as if it were yesterday.

The treatment continued all through November and on the 9th I started filming *Carry On Constable* at Pinewood. It wasn't possible to forget the bum because one of the earliest scenes involved the team as policemen in the shower baths, so we all had to take our clothes off. Joan Sims, as a woman police constable, had to enter inadvertently and all the men then had to run naked out of the room. The cameraman asked the director to peer through the viewfinder. 'You can't shoot it like this, Gerry – take a look!' Gerald Thomas inclined for the scrutiny and murmured agreement. He straightened up and said, 'The bums are all flaring. You'll have to get them made-up.' A murmur of disbelief ran through the set. 'Make-up on the bums, Gerald?' asked Leslie Phillips. 'Are you joking?'

'No,' said Gerald shortly, and instructed the make-up men to put us all on trestle tables so that the wet white could be applied more easily. Leslie was incredulous. 'I say, this really is a bit much,' he said to the rest of us. 'Don't you think we should make a stand?' Not the happiest choice of words considering our embarrassment.

Kenneth Connor made light of it. 'Look, Leslie, these films are on the way up, audiences are up, the takings are up, so get your bum made up.' Charles Hawtrey only wanted to know if the body make-up matched his face. 'Is it the *poudre rachel*?' he asked, trying to view his rear. A make-up man complained bitterly, 'I've done Margaret Lockwood, and I've done Jean Kent and I've done some of the best faces in the business, but I never thought I'd end up doing a bum.'

After that the cameraman re-examined the shot and said that the bodies were now an acceptable colour. White flesh was no longer flaring at the lens, and we tried rehearsing over again. Joan Sims collapsed with laughter every time she entered. 'Oh, those sad little behinds', she kept saying. Gerald told me later that it had taken longer to shoot the scene than anything else in the picture. 'But it was worth it,' he smiled. 'It will get one of the biggest laughs in the film.'

And it did.

Chapter Five

Pieces of Eight did good business throughout 1960 and in May Michael Codron was already planning the sequel for 1961. Somehow I found the time to organise my domestic life a little better. I was only a temporary guest in John Hussey's apartment so I spent my spare moments flat-hunting in all kinds of neighbourhoods. I eventually settled on Park West in Edgware Road. This time I had two very spacious rooms – which looked even more spacious because they were bare but for my bed and the desk.

It didn't matter. With only the show to worry about at night I had most days free to do the necessary things like buying carpets and light fittings, purchasing cooker and fridge and all the household articles I needed. I got three chairs in Heals in Tottenham Court Road which were covered in an oatmeal tweed fabric and I trudged all over the place to find a matching material for the curtains.

When they were hung I asked Gordon Jackson over for his approval, keeping him well away from the window, because when he'd visited my bachelor pad in Endsleigh Court he had stood too near the curtains and his cigarette had set them alight. I was furious but Gordon had just stood there laughing, saying 'Don't worry, I'll pay for another pair.' Anyway this time he pronounced Park West an improvement on my last home and complimented me on the décor. 'Very clean-looking and frugal but it will be even nicer when you've got some pictures on the walls.' These were eventually provided by two young painters, the Avery twins, Wilfred and Sam. I had a framed drawing by each of them. Peter Nichols had introduced me to the Averys, and it was through them that I met playwright Robert Bolt.

What endeared me immediately to Robert was his instinctive sympathy for the actor. Early on in our acquaintanceship someone reproved me for embroidering a story: 'That isn't how it happened and you know it, Kenneth. The man was slightly unsteady and the woman's blouse had come awry, but the way you tell it she was doing a striptease and he was dead drunk.' Robert came to my rescue: 'It does sound better as

Kenneth describes it.' But the protester continued, 'It's not true, he's a liar.' 'Yes', said Bob, 'but a liar in search of the truth.'

After that he became an oracle for me and I used to pour out all kinds of confidences to him. I told him I thought my sense of inferiority was what made for the superiority of my performance and that only in acting did I feel the desire to share. 'I don't want to share in Life – I can hardly bear to lend a book to someone, let alone live with them. People go on and on about their need for an emotional attachment but I can't understand this compulsion. I am thirty-four and I have never known physical love.'

Instead of the reply I usually got about being abnormal and frigid, Bob simply said, 'It is more important to like than to love,' and I wrote that in my diary with approval.

In those days I turned more and more to friends and became less and less interested in work. The injections were continuing but the pain was not diminishing and I needed all the sympathy I could get. Stanley Baxter had moved down from Scotland; he and Moira had a house in Bewdley Street where I always found a sympathetic ear. He told me that however dispirited I felt I should never forget that pain, like everything else in this life, always passes. Moira offered herbal concoctions which seemed to me to be improbable remedies. Once when I went up to see her with a nascent boil, she suggested treating it with root of marigold, and handed me some brown, sticky, unctuous stuff in a wax box. When I got home I applied it just to humour her, though I really thought it was a load of quackery. The next day the boil had shrivelled to half the size and thereafter I only had to cope with a pimple. I told Moira I'd been staggered by such rapid results but she wasn't the least surprised. 'Herbs are the basis of all medicine,' she said, taking no notice of Stanley flitting in and out of the room, doing a mock Barbara Mullen, crying, 'All right, Doctor Finlay – I shall be with you in a jiffy – coming, Doctor Finlay.'

I completed another series of *Beyond Our Ken* during the summer and continued playing nightly at the Apollo but the rectal problem became steadily worse and when I saw Mr Mulvaney in the autumn he told me I would have to go into hospital.

So when *Pieces of Eight* finished a year's run at the end of

90

October I went into the St John and St Elizabeth for the operation. Mr Mulvaney said afterwards that it was completely successful, and a glass of sherry was solemnly borne into my room for us to celebrate. In early November I spent a few recuperative days in Brighton before returning to London.

A bombshell awaited me when I came back. Louisa and Charlie were in a panic: the rent of their flat had been doubled and this, plus the rates, meant they couldn't afford to go on living there. I made a quick decision. During the revue I had saved assiduously and I now had enough money put aside to buy them a long leasehold apartment with low outgoings in which they could manage comfortably. With the help of several estate agents and a hired motor car, I took my parents around various locations and they ultimately settled on a garden flat in Brunswick Gardens in Kensington. But by the time we'd bought carpets, curtains and some new furniture, my capital had disappeared and my bank balance looked alarmingly low.

But Gerald Thomas and Peter Rogers came to my aid. They gave me a part in *Carry On Regardless* and at the end of November I started filming at Pinewood again with the old team. In December we were on location at Windsor where the owners of a lovely Georgian house had lent their premises for a shot of me coming out of the front door holding the hand of a smartly suited chimpanzee called Yoki. Gerald was outside with the camera crew and on the call 'Action' I was to open the door, and the two of us had to toddle down the steps and walk into the street. I was standing in the hallway holding Yoki's hand and waiting for the cue, when he suddenly broke away from me, picked up an iron doorstop and began smashing the framed prints which lined the walls. I was so taken aback at the suddenness of his actions that I just stood there, frozen with horror, watching the devastation. By the time I managed to restrain him, damaged pictures and broken glass were all over the floor and the lady of the house gazed in shock at the destruction.

Then I heard 'Action' and proceeded with Yoki out of the door, closing it quickly behind me to hide the havoc he'd wreaked. Once the shot was taken Gerald asked, 'Why were you so long coming out? I called you several times – were you larking about in there?'

I said, 'No but Yoki was,' and told him about the accident.

91

He went immediately to apologise to a distraught owner, and to assure her that restitution would be swiftly forthcoming.

Shooting a film on location always attracts bystanders and *Carry On Regardless* was no exception. Kenneth Connor was rehearsing a long walk towards camera when a small child ran up to him with an autograph book: 'Would you sign for me please?' Kenneth told him, 'Later on son, not now, I'm being directed,' whereupon the child asked, 'Oh, are you lost?' making Kenneth burst into laughter.

In the same picture I got the giggles myself when we did the sequence with Stanley Unwin. His extraordinary gobble-degook delighted me. He played a property developer who talked of building sumptuous apartments fit for a king. This came out as 'Luckshe flabberblock dangly chandelery, Harry the Acres and Kathering of Arabolde.' The dialogue always flowed trippingly on cue, and when I said to Gerald, 'Marvellous the way he knows his lines,' he replied, 'Certainly nobody else does.'

The sequel which Michael Codron produced for *Pieces of Eight* was entitled *One Over the Eight* but rehearsals in January 1961 were less than happy as far as I was concerned. I thought the material was thin and the content generally inferior to our first revue, but I certainly liked the cast. Sheila Hancock was our leading comedienne; there was strong support from Lance Percival and Lynda Baron, and our dancers were Terry Theobald and Sheila O'Neil. Paddy Stone was directing again but suggesting ideas with which I was in fundamental disagreement.

The opening was a dance-mime with members of the cast playing instruments and mine was a triangle that fell to bits. I didn't like it and wanted an opening chorus, but that was considered old hat. I moaned a lot to Sheila Hancock, 'They're not interested in my ideas; why employ a comedian and then not listen to him!' I was shouting most of this from the pillion of her Vespa while she drove me home, but I don't think she heard much through her crash helmet.

Touring began at Stratford-on-Avon where everyone's spirits were low, followed by two weeks at Brighton where morale went up a bit, then Liverpool where it went down again. Golders Green was encouraging, then came Blackpool – Siberia for intimate revue – where we sank to zero.

First formal portrait.

Class I at Manchester Street Infants School. I am third from the left in the
front row.

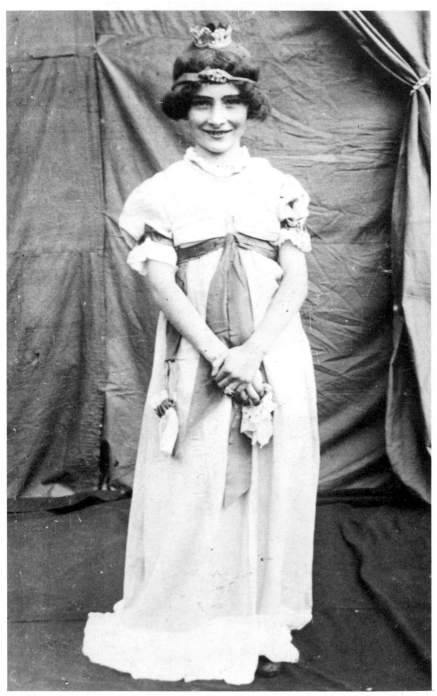

First stage role (in the school play) as Princess Angelica in Thackeray's *The Rose and the Ring*.

Aged about 14, taken during the wartime evacuation to Bicester.

Hiding the brim of my sea-cadet hat to seem as authentic as my uniformed sister, 1942.

L: K.W. *R:* Stan Walker and fellow-conscripts at Hereford P.D.C. 1944.

My sister Pat and me, 1944.

Charles and Louisa on the Isle of Wight ferry, about 1950.

L–R: Wilfrid Brambell, Rachel Roberts, William Moore, K.W., in Sartre's
Crime Passionel, Grand Theatre Swansea, 1950.

As Jack the pot boy, with Laurence Olivier as Macheath, in the film *The Beggar's Opera*, 1952.

As the Dauphin in *St Joan* with Siobhan McKenna, Arts Theatre, 1954.

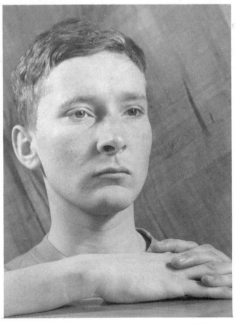

Portrait by John Schlesinger, c. 1954.

With Tony in the BBC TV series of *Hancock's Half Hour*, 1957.

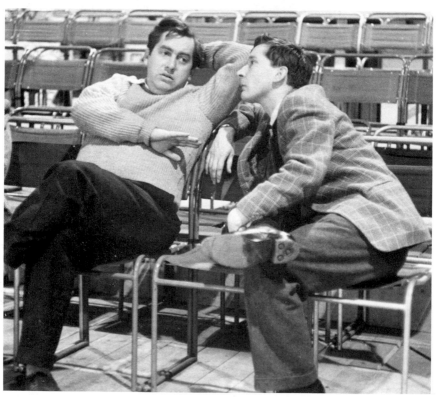

With Tony at rehearsals for the same series.

We opened in London on the 5th of April at the Duke of York's. I noted in my diary on the 6th: 'Press reviews are all unfavourable,' but on the 7th, 'Very good house to play to. Rachel Roberts out front. She came round after and was aggressively complimentary saying we were to ignore the critics whom she dismissed with some very rude epithets. Actor George Rose added support by bringing several fans with him and producer Peter Bridge was full of encouragement. It is extraordinary how sheer loyalty and fellow-feeling can make for extravagant praise from actors. It's one of the heartwarming things about our profession, the way it inspires a deep and not quite explicable devotion.'

In spite of the adverse comments in the press, the business flourished, and soon I was back in the old pattern of performing at the theatre in the evening and filming during the day. On the 10th of April I was back at Pinewood where Gerald was directing *Raising The Wind*. It was about a group of music students and I was playing an arrogant upstart who fancied himself as a conductor. In one of the scenes I had to rehearse an entire symphony orchestra and for the first time in my life I felt quite awestruck when I stood on the podium facing this array of seasoned musicians. I had to get terribly worked up conducting the 'William Tell Overture', and the climax came when the entire platform gave way and I fell beneath the stage in the wreckage. I've never been physically adroit and I was apprehensive about the fall, but in the event I sank beneath the broken wood and splinters and emerged unscathed.

Gerald had planned the 'accident' very carefully because he didn't want a repeat of the time when, in *Carry On Regardless*, I had had to jump from a rostrum and, instead of landing neatly, had hurtled to the ground catching my groin on a nail in the process. Venting some loud obscenities, I started to remove my trousers. Gerald reproved me, 'Please Kenneth, there are ladies on the set!'

'I don't care if there are duchesses,' I screamed. 'Look at the blood!' I pointed to a disappointingly small cut on my leg.

He took me to an elderly nursing sister in the Medical Room and she applied some soothing antiseptic cream and gave me liquid sedation. I was laid upon a couch and told to relax, then my leg muscles were massaged. It went on and on. Gerald kept peering round the door and asking, 'Are you ready for the next shot?' But each time the nurse rejected any such suggestions.

93

'He's had a shock: he must rest', and I didn't get back for ages. There were dark mutterings from the second assistant about malingering. When I did return to the set I affected a limp, complained of concussion and generally milked it until Gerald mollified me with a glass of chilled Lyena. There's no doubt about it, I was indulged all right. That day I wrote in my diary, 'If only all the professional work would be with Gerald and Peter.'

On the 1st of May Noël Coward came to see *One Over the Eight* and it was a tonic for the entire company. 'You have another success,' he told me.

I said, 'You wouldn't think so from the notices.'

'Some notices aren't to be noticed.'

'They were very bad.'

'And your business is very good.'

I nodded agreement. 'Yes, it's funny.'

'You make it funny, my dear. Everything you do is authentic. I can't imagine it being done by anybody else.'

His radiant enthusiasm was infectious and I went home feeling elated.

The confidence evaporated next day when I had to go to the BBC for *Desert Island Discs* with Roy Plomley. He filled me with inhibition and the whole thing became turgid and phlegmatic. It was like a prison release to escape into the open air at the finish. Stanley Baxter heard it and I anxiously enquired how it came over. 'Oh very well,' he assured me, 'except for the luxury article. I thought you went a bit over the top there.'

'Why?'

'Asking for one of the greatest nudes in the world.'

'It's the God-like head I admire.'

'Hmm. I thought it was a bit much.'

I'd asked for Michaelangelo's 'David'.

Since I'd been in Park West Stanley had taken to visiting me there, changing in my flat and then going down in the lift to the swimming pool. I even went myself on some occasions, though I don't care for exercise. A lot of my friends came to swim at the block. It became very popular and eventually the management made a ruling: all guests would have to pay. That took the gilt off the gingerbread, but I still enjoyed living there. I found the area very inviting, I liked the closeness of Hyde Park and I liked the wideness of the Edgware Road. The ambience was totally different from Bloomsbury and it felt as if I was on holiday.

94

Looking through my records of those days it appears a halcyon period. I was reading Newman on the efficacy of religion ('When the church shows her proper gifts she flourishes, when she uses them she declines'); I was discovering Philip Larkin's poetry ('1914' still remains one of my favourites); and the books that most impressed me were J. R. Ackerley's *We Think the World of You* and Eric Bentley's *In Search of Theatre*.

Peter Eade, however, must have fancied that my career was getting into something of a rut about this time because he asked me to consider two future ventures in the theatre, which I declined, and then he insisted on my going to meet the American film director Hal Roach. 'He's asked to see you and you must go – he's one of the veteran Hollywood names, he directed Laurel and Hardy, he's something of a legend. He's over here to make a new picture, you really should go.'

So in July I went with him to meet this tubby, jovial little man who launched into a long description of the film he was going to make. 'There's a funny scene for you, where you're sitting on this freshly painted lavatory seat and the cistern overflows and the water shoots all over your legs, then you get up and we have a long shot of you running away with the lavatory seat stuck to your behind!' He stopped to laugh uproariously, 'Can you imagine, a lavatory seat stuck to your behind! I can tell you I am going to make you a comedian like a Kaye or a Lewis or a Chaplin with this film.'

I felt like saying, 'I hope it keeps fine for you,' but in reality I smiled and nodded acquiescence. When we left I told Peter I didn't think it was 'me' and, to my surprise, he wholeheartedly agreed.

Another series of *Beyond Our Ken* came round in the autumn and in October Peter and Gerald offered me the role of Halfpenny in *Twice Round the Daffodils*, a change from their usual *Carry Ons*, which they were shooting at Pinewood. I started work there in November with Juliet Mills, Ronald Lewis, Donald Houston, Donald Sinden, and Andrew Ray. The story was set in a hospital and I spent much of the time in bed.

I was doing the show in the theatre at night and rising very early to get to the studios by 8 am so I suppose it was natural that I should feel tired, but the warmth of the bedclothes lulled me into such frequent stupors that it became a standing joke on the set. One day Gerald casually took a photograph from his script case, which depicted me lying somnolent in the bed, holding a banana with a rude notice tied round my neck. He asked, 'Do you remember that?' and I had to confess I didn't. I had slept so soundly I never knew the picture had been taken.

Lance Percival, who was in the revue with me at the Duke of York's, was also in the film, and we spent a lot of spare time rehearsing a sketch for a CND show which we performed with Sheila Hancock on Sunday the 17th of December at St Pancras Town Hall. It was a disaster. The sketch was called 'Buy British' and was one of the Peter Cook items from *Pieces of Eight*. I played a Blimp-character who kept expostulating 'Filthy foreign muck' every time the waiter suggested an exotic dish, and I got more and more vituperative about every nation in turn, and kept asking, 'Why can't we have something English?' In the end I rejected all the food and settled for a cup of tea, 'You can't go wrong with a cup of tea', and my companion (Sheila Hancock) echoed that, 'Oh yes, a lovely cup of tea', whereupon the waiter asked, 'Indian or China?', and there was supposed to be a black-out. On this night there was no black-out. The lights stayed on, obstinately illuminating our predicament. I began to ad lib wildly, 'Tea is English! Tea is grown on the Cotswold Hills.' Lance Percival as the waiter, affected polite interest but I could see his lips starting to tremble. I struggled on, 'My old grandmother was out there picking the tea leaves on the Cotswold Hills and making the blackberry wine.' I turned for help to Sheila. 'You remember her, don't you, my old grandmother?' She said, 'Who could forget her, silly old cow,' which got the most enormous laugh. Then thankfully someone lowered the curtain and our embarrassment was over. When we came offstage I asked Sheila, 'What on earth possessed you – what made you call my gran a silly old cow? It was very rude.' She said, 'I was desperate. I didn't know what you were talking about . . . I just said the first thing that came into my head. It wasn't personal – why?'

'She lives near here,' I told her. 'I just hope she wasn't out front.'

Sheila looked quite stricken but she needn't have bothered, the CND show was teetotal and my gran wouldn't attend any entertainment where there wasn't a bar.

By December Kenneth Connor was rehearsing my role in

96

One Over the Eight and he took over at the Duke of York's when I left the show in January 1962. Almost immediately after that I was thrust into another busy period. I was back at Pinewood filming *Carry On Cruising*, I was finishing another lot of *Beyond Our Ken* broadcasts, and then Peter Eade sent me the script of a double bill by Peter Shaffer called *The Private Ear* and *The Public Eye* which was to be presented by H. M. Tennent, and he told me that Binkie Beaumont was very keen for me to do it because he thought it was high time I got back to some straight acting. This pleased me, but I was disappointed to find that the character I was offered – Christoforou – only appeared in the second half. I told Peter I didn't fancy spending half the evening in the dressing room. He disagreed. 'The size of the role isn't important, it's what you do with it that matters.' I read it again and was struck by the writing of 'Belinda', the girl in the piece. I telephoned Maggie Smith to say that I'd just read a play with a marvellous part in it for her and she revealed that she had already agreed to play it. So within a week we were meeting again and discussing the play, what we would wear, where we would be touring and where we should stay.

The director was Peter Wood and the first read-through of *The Public Eye* was at his flat in Little Venice where I met Richard Pearson who was playing Charles. After he'd listened to the three of us reading the play, Peter Wood said, 'Yes, well that was all very hieratic,' gave us all a meal and sent us home. Outside the house I asked Mags what hieratic meant. 'Search me,' she said. So I asked Richard if he knew. 'I think it's something to do with priests,' he answered. I began to wonder what was expected of us. As it turned out, Peter was so engrossed with *Private Ear* that rehearsals for *Public Eye* were kept to a minimum. Once the geography had been settled we were left very much to ourselves. There was a tour of four weeks with a dodgy moment in Oxford when Binkie attended a performance.

He suggested that the second half needed pruning. Peter Wood made several cuts in the play and we were instructed to revise our performances. We were against any cuts. I felt that it might seem overlong at the moment but once the dialogue was second nature it would flow that much more quickly, and Richard agreed that it was just a question of picking up cues. I maintained we should refuse to implement the cuts. Mags said, 'No, let's do them *badly*.' I thought that was genius and that's

97

exactly what we did at the matinée. The management didn't like it. By the evening the excised portions were all back in.

We opened in London on the 10th of May 1962 at the Globe Theatre and were a resounding success, but I little dreamed then that I would still be there over a year later. The more I played with Richard Pearson and Maggie Smith in *Public Ear* the better it became, with vocal patterns established so that we accelerated to climaxes, built properly to the laugh lines, and picked up each other's cues crisply. We even suggested overlapping so effectively that one critical visitor backstage complained that we went on talking during the laughs, so that he missed a lot of the dialogue. 'Well, the play is published now,' Maggie told him, 'so you can go and buy a copy. You'll find you've missed nothing.' She was right of course; the conversation during laughs was extemporary, put in to sustain realism, and to avoid the artificiality of articulate people suddenly falling silent during audience laughter.

Maggie introduced me to her boyfriend, the writer Beverly Cross, whose adaptation of the French comedy, *Boeing Boeing*, was running at the theatre next door, and the three of us often met for supper after the shows. One of our favourite haunts was Lyons' Grill and Cheese in Coventry Street. Every time we went there we met fellow-actors who would come across from their tables to chat. It was like old home week. Once we passed John Gielgud on the stairs and he said he thought our show was 'very droll'.

I didn't realize it to begin with, but with lunch and tea and the late meal after the performance I was beginning to put on weight alarmingly. Only when I could no longer struggle into the costume did I go to the doctor where I was told, 'This is the shadow of a man's hand that turns into a cloud.'

Thereafter I started to cut down to one meal a day. One bunfight I didn't miss, however, was held backstage at the theatre when my Gran came to a matinee and Maggie gave a lavish tea for her in the dressing room after the performance. I'd often spoken about Gran's graphic accounts of her neighbours but Maggie wasn't convinced that I hadn't embellished the stories, especially one concerning an elderly bald lady who bewigged herself for visitors and frequently peed the bed. Gran came in smartly on cue when I prompted her. 'Tell Maggie about Mrs Houth.'

'Oh, her!' she said as if she were discussing an errant child.

98

'She lives next door you see, says she's bedridden but I think she's just lazy. She bangs on the wall and I have to go in and see what she wants, run errands for her and do a bit of shopping, you know.'

'Tell her about the knickers,' I urged her.

'Oh yes,' said Gran. 'She bangs on the wall one day and I go in to see her and she says she's had an accident if you please and would I get her some new knickers with the money on the mantleshelf. All she had was one and eleven, but I put the rest to it and went over to the drapers and got her a nice pair of interlock bloomers. When I come back she was still laying there – terrible smell there was. I said she ought to get up and wash herself. "You're a dirty cow laying here and letting everyone else do the dirty work", and she gets out of her bed all lady-like and she says, "That's all right, Mrs Williams. Sit down a minute and I'll play the piano for you." "Moonlight and Roses" she played, not that there was any moonlight.' Gran laughed, 'And it didn't smell like roses either, I can tell you. Mind you, you couldn't hear much 'cos the piano was full of green boots. It was the damp, you see. She kept her shoes in there and of course they were covered in mildew.'

'What did I tell you?' I asked Mags triumphantly – 'the green boots, you see. They smelled worse than the knickers.'

'Oh it's kooky,' laughed Mags and she agreed I hadn't varnished the tale. Old Mrs Williams had impressed her.

'What a marvellous face your Gran's got,' she told me afterwards, 'a wrinkled old bun with a couple of currants stuck in it for eyes, like Rembrandt's housekeeper', and it wasn't a bad description.

The warm summer seemed never-ending. Maggie and Beverly had a cottage in Broxbourne and there we played games on the lawn with their chow, Tuffet, and went blackberrying in the surrounding fields. On one particularly bright morning Maggie, dressed in a pink dress with matching hatband round a straw boater, drove me down to Beckenham for a day with Richard Pearson and his family. It was an open car and, at every traffic light, motorists and lorry drivers looked twice at this elegant lady motorist. I felt very proud sitting beside her.

I don't think I had any idea then how fruitful and satisfying the days were. It comes back to what Robert Bolt described as 'the negation of the moment'. What he meant was that because men worried so much about the future and knew so much about the past they had lost the ability to enjoy the present.

My tranquillity was soon disturbed when my father's health began to decline. Ever since Charlie's enforced retirement he had been on a downward path. Having lost his beloved shop there was nothing to take its place in his affections. After a spell in the Brompton Hospital he returned home and began to pursue all sorts of eccentric activities, designing telescopic scaffolding and collapsible beds and ringing people in the early hours to ask for financial backing. He became increasingly strange and on more than one occasion he called on me in the dressing room at the theatre with unusual requests. 'Lend us a tenner, will you. I fancy some spaghetti in this Italian place over the road.' I knew Louisa cooked all his meals and I found this very odd. When I checked with her she admitted that he often went out for whole days and she didn't know what he was up to. 'One week he hired a taxi, went round to Grandma Williams and bundled her into it and told the driver to take 'em to Eastbourne. He was rambling and shouting and she got frightened. She jumped out at the Oval when they stopped at the lights. She was in a terrible state.'

His irrational behaviour worried us all. The crisis came in October when he got up in the middle of the night and drank a concoction which resulted in collapse: it was a cleaning fluid, carbon tetrachloride, which he'd mistakenly labelled 'Cough Syrup'. Louisa called an ambulance and he was taken to St Mary Abbots' Hospital where he died on the 15th of October 1962.

Any sadness I felt at his death was outweighed by the relief of knowing that Louisa would no longer be subject to his erratic and eccentric behaviour. Peter Eade was adamant that I must not attend the inquest. 'You're performing in the theatre every night and this could provoke the wrong kind of publicity. I will accompany your mother and see she's properly looked after, but you must not be seen. This way we'll keep it out of the papers.'

The inquest returned a verdict of 'Death by misadventure' and the funeral followed on the 23rd of October. It was only reported locally and even then simply as a 'Mr Charles Williams of Kensington' with no mention of me. Louisa seemed resigned to living alone. I bought her a Jack Russell terrier to keep her company in the flat, and didn't have much

100

time to mourn because Maggie decided to leave the play at the Globe and do *Mary Mary* next door at the Queen's.

Her part was taken over by another actress so I was busy rehearsing the Shaffer plays all over again. By the new year, 1963, Judith Stott was playing Doreen and Belinda in *Private Ear* and *Public Eye* and the business was as brisk as ever. I had not had a holiday for a long time and was beginning to get restive, so I asked the management when I could leave. They said they wanted more time to find an actor to assume the role, but all being well I could go away at the end of May.

At the first opportunity I told Maggie and Beverly over supper one night. By then we had switched the restaurant rendezvous to Biagi in Upper Berkeley Street. Beverly expressed interest in the Greek Islands and I seized upon that. 'Yes, I'd love to go there, that would be fine! When can you go?' I badgered him until I got an answer. He thought he would be able to come with me on the 1st of June. Everything seemed to be falling into place, but suddenly there was a stumbling block. For a month or so I had been aware that Robert Bolt was going to send me a copy of his new play. He'd written saying the character for which he wanted me 'was alternately despicable and terrifying; he must disturb and you do disturb'. I realized this was some kind of a challenge.

Just as I was finishing at the Globe, a copy of *Gentle Jack* was delivered to me at the stage door. After reading it I found myself torn between conflicting emotions. I felt enormously flattered that a playwright of Bolt's distinction had singled me out for a part but I was also deterred by the play. It seemed to me more concerned with philosophy than drama. I couldn't envisage an audience readily understanding its message. In the end I took the coward's way out. I departed with Beverly to Venice, writing from there to Robert Bolt saying I would rather he found someone else for the role.

We boarded the yacht SS *Romantica* on the 2nd of June for the cruise round the Greek Islands, calling at Athens, Istanbul, and Dubrovnik. I spent most of the time sipping the eau de vie on deck but Beverly ploughed ashore and trudged over Lemnos, Delos, Skiathos and even got me to the Parthenon. Bev was the best kind of travelling companion, amusing, informative and flexible about an itinerary. If you didn't feel energetic he'd go off and explore on his own and give you a fascinating account when he returned.

101

We stayed at the Danielli in Venice, with Bev insisting on the old wing with the Titian ceiling and the minstrels' gallery. The heat was exhausting and one day I left off my shirt. I got the most appalling rash as a result, and I've never risked undressing on any holiday since. Sitting outside Florians' in St Mark's Square I told Beverly, 'Don't look now, but there's a man in a blue shirt three tables away on the left. He keeps smiling at me but I don't know him.' Bev immediately lowered his airmail edition of *The Times* and looked. 'Take off your sunglasses,' he said, 'it's Clifford Evans'. It was indeed Clifford, and when he had finished his coffee he walked over to our table, and we sat chatting. He said all visitors to Italy fell into one of three categories – Roman, Florentine and Venetian. 'I've just come from Rome; it's one long traffic jam – but here you can relax and forget about the traffic fumes. Henry James was quite right, you know, about St Mark's Square. It *is* the Drawing Room of Europe'.

My ploy for opting out of the play did not work. There were various communications from Robert Bolt when I came back to London and on the 14th of July I went down to his home in the country to discuss the project with him and the director Noel Willman. They both made it clear that they thought I was the only actor for the part. If you tell a performer he is brilliant often enough, he will start to believe it. So I read *Gentle Jack* again, but my doubts persisted.

For me the crux of the problem now ceased to be the philosophical nature of the work and became instead the 'divine' element in the character of Jack the wood god. It seemed paradoxical to me that a figure endowed with such power should resort to appeals for compliance. I was particularly apprehensive about one entreaty in the form of direct address to the audience. The play used the convention of realism within the proscenium and then broke it by having Jack talk to spectators outside it. This sort of licence can be taken in the theatre; the chorus, the 'aside', and the interior monologue are all examples of it, but Jack was supposed to be divine. I thought he should speak with the tongues of angels, within the stage frame, not appeal to the audience with curious bits of Middle English and quotes from Wordsworth. It didn't smack to me of the god-like. It seemed to diminish the character and make vulnerable what should appear invulnerable.

Noel Willman argued persuasively for the play and Robert

102

pointed to the truth of originals creating their own conventions, and I succumbed, but with the proviso that I should be contracted for only three months and not for the run of the play. I had a premonition that this would be a lonely role.

In August I recorded Gogol's *Diary of a Madman* for that most brilliant of all animation film-makers, Richard Williams. I don't think I've ever met such a taskmaster in the recording studios as Richard. He would order retake after retake to acquire the precise quality he desired and my vocal ability was stretched to the limit. Richard and I had worked together previously when I did the voices for his film *Love Me Love Me* and I thought he had created a little masterpiece with that: its conclusion was a choral chant, 'When it comes to love, no one really has it Good' – and the solemnity of the crescendo made wonderful comedy.

The lowering nature of the Gogol dialogue must have aroused the dormant depression in me because on the 22nd of August I wrote, 'The madness screaming up inside me. So many awful thoughts – this terrible sense of doom hanging over me. I wonder if anyone will ever know about the emptiness of my life. I wonder if anyone will ever stand in a room that I have lived in and touch the things that were once a part of my life and wonder about me? How could they ever be told? How to explain that I only experienced vicariously, never at first hand, that the sharing of a life is what makes a life and that I cannot share because I dare not risk the vulnerability involved. Now I am thinking all the while of death in some shape or another. Every day is something to be got through. All the recipes of the past are no longer valid. I've spent all my life in the mind. I have entered into nothing.'

The wretchedness seemed to have been dispelled with my decision to move, because two days later I viewed an apartment in Farley Court, overlooking Madame Tussaud's. I set in train arrangements to buy the lease and on the 26th of August my diary recorded quite a different mood. 'I feel so buoyant and elated I could fly. Just want to get into my new flat so quickly. I know it's going to feel good being on the ninth and top floor.'

Peter Rogers and Gerald Thomas started shooting *Carry On Jack* in September 1963. My part was a milksop sort of Captain Bligh who was seasick every time his ship sailed. The first day was spent at Frensham Ponds with Bernard Cribbins, Charles Hawtrey, and Juliet Mills. Delightful weather with delightful people. The cameraman said, 'The sun always shines for Gerald, doesn't it!' and everyone agreed that location filming went uncannily well for him.

The picture was something of a reunion for me because the midshipman was played by Juliet Mills, whom I'd met doing *Twice Round the Daffodils*, and the bosun was Donald Houston, with whom I played long before that in the Festival of Wales production in 1951. Cecil Parker played the admiral, and this was a very adroit bit of casting, rather like Wilfred Hyde White's role in *Carry On Nurse*; both of them actors who were absolutely right for the parts, but not the people you expected to see.

With Juliet I talked about our mutual chum Andrew Ray, and I told her of our visits to the Old Bailey. As actors, Andrew and I were both fascinated by the art of cross-examination and together we sat through numerous trials for murder, mayhem, assault and battery. In one case of incest that we saw the father denied everything, saying that the daughters had 'done it with boys at school' whereupon counsel for the prosecution said, 'But the court has been told by the surgeon that their condition was caused by regular intercourse with a fully grown male penis.' Nevertheless the accused protested his innocence and claimed that the girls had misbehaved with schoolboy chums. The defence, to support the story, called a doctor to the witness box and asked him, 'At what age is the male penis fully developed?'

'Why, at puberty, of course,' came the reply.

'What is the age of puberty?'

'About 14.'

'But have you ever seen a younger child with a fully grown member?'

'Sometimes, there can be exceptions.'

'Even at the age of twelve?'

'Oh yes, I've seen some whoppers – I mean – I've seen some big – some unusual . . .'

There was an embarrassed pause before the Judge told him, 'Yes, doctor, in your own words – some whoppers.'

I told Juliet that Andrew and I thought it could have been a scene from a *Carry On*. She asked, 'What was the verdict?'

'That staggered us,' I told her. 'The jury acquitted him! But when we mentioned our surprise to the policeman on the door coming out he told us the man was re-arrested immediately afterwards and charged with assault.'

In the middle of October I moved into the new flat, continued filming, and started rehearsing *Gentle Jack* with a cast headed by Edith Evans, Sian Phillips and Michael Bryant. One day Dame Edith asked me, 'Don't you find these lines difficult? I do. Perhaps I should retire.'

I told her about the forgetful complainant with the doctor: 'Nowadays I just can't seem to remember anything.' 'When did this start?' 'When did what start?'

The play opened at the Theatre Royal Brighton on the 7th of November for just over two weeks and since Dame Edith and I were staying at the same hotel, we used to share a taxi back to from the theatre. On the Monday she said, 'None of the actors come along to my dressing room for a chat.'

'You're something of a myth, they view you with awe.'

'No, I am very ordinary really.'

'They don't think so.'

'But I am. I sit at home on my little stool with my apron on and I baste the joint with my old wooden spoon. Oh yes, I am very ordinary, roast beef and Yorkshire pudding.'

On the Wednesday she seemed out of countenance and confided, 'Binkie Beaumont came round to the dressing room after the rehearsal and said Hardy Amies had designed very regal costumes – I should look equally regal in them. Do you think that is justified?'

'I think any criticism of your deportment is tantamount to impertinence,' I replied.

'You're a very pleasant young man', she murmured, patting my knee affectionately. 'There is no reason why the right girl shouldn't come along.'

The production had a lukewarm reception in Brighton and on several occasions my original reactions to the script were vindicated when visitors backstage expressed bewilderment. There were several rewrites which rather threw me because having got one set of lines in my head I found it difficult to supplant them with new dialogue. The result was a tentative performance. Stanley Baxter came down with Moira and depressed me by saying that my performance was inhibited. However, I returned to the hotel to find a letter from Ned Sherrin which contained such a glowing tribute that my morale went up again.

105

On the 28th of November 1963 *Gentle Jack* had its opening night at the Queen's Theatre in London. I thought my performance was laboured and nervous. The audience was bemused and mystified. At the end the stalls applauded but there were murmurs of dissent from the gallery and one rude cry. Dame Edith misinterpreted this, saying 'Well, that was one bravo'. I told her, 'No, it wasn't bravo, it was "go home".' Apart from the *Daily Mail* and *The Times*, the rest of the notices the next day were spiteful and rude. Maggie and Beverly came on the 6th of December and said much the same about the play as I had originally: there was not enough conflict, and not enough for me to do. I told them how lonely I felt in the role.

A few days later Richard Williams came to see it and he too told me it was boring and undramatic. He said that with this kind of writing the direction needed to be exciting and that this was too formal. On the 10th of December I wrote in my diary: 'All the adverse criticism of last night has stayed in my head; people just don't know how sensitive one is about a play one is in. When anyone talks to an actor after a show, they should remember: love me, love my dog. If they don't see that, then they don't see anything. When the play is off the actor can take all sorts of knocking, but after a performance all the "I'm going to be frank" and "You wouldn't want me to lie to you" stuff is totally unwelcome.'

The dressing room became a dreaded place for me once the curtain was down. Invariably the visitors backstage were either carping or unforthcoming about the play and I felt torn between conflicting loyalties. Sometimes in order to avoid any atmosphere, I left the theatre so quickly I was gone before anyone had time to get backstage. This stressful situation was brought to a head by that disinterested arbiter, the box office. Our business dwindled and Tennent's withdrew the play at the end of January 1964. At the end of it all, I could only feel relief.

In February I started work at Pinewood again in *Carry On Spying*. It was on this film that I met Barbara Windsor and I was immediately taken with her. The rueful irony of her humour suited me exactly and we became firm friends on the set. I waxed eloquent about a holiday I was planning in Maderia: 'When it's winter here, it's summer there, palm trees under an azure sky.' Barbara was so impressed she rang the travel agent and booked the trip for herself.

106

'You made it sound so attractive' she said. 'Hope it doesn't turn out like a wet weekend in Wigan.'

'It's a beautiful island,' I assured her. 'Elizabeth of Austria found it a haven.'

'Who?'

'The Empress of Austria'.

'Where was her husband?'

'Women don't take their husbands to Maderia.'

'I'm taking mine,' she said firmly. 'We've only just got married.'

So it was decided that Barbara and Ronnie Knight would spend their honeymoon in Funchal. I was taking my mother and my sister Pat. (Since her divorce in Australia, Pat had returned to London and had been sharing the flat in Brunswick Gardens with Louisa.)

On the 28th of March 1964 all five of us met at Heathrow and sat talking in the restaurant of the departure lounge. Barbara began to express misgivings. 'I bet we end up in the khazi,' she predicted darkly, as she signed autographs for fans who were milling around the table. I began a harangue against pessimism, which was endorsed by Ronnie: 'Yes, you've got to look on the bright side, Babs.' We were so engrossed we failed to hear the flight call. At the eleventh hour an irate airline official bundled us all into a car which took us to the waiting aeroplane, and we were shown to our seats under disapproving gazes from the waiting passengers.

Then the nightmare began. On arrival at Lisbon we waited two hours for the flight to Porto Santo which took another two hours. Again we had a long wait before a lighter came and took us out to a ship anchored in the bay. We boarded this in a heaving swell, and the vessel got under way, lurching through the water like some monstrous drunkard. The passengers became groggy and many were violently sick. Ronnie was looking green and appeared stupefied on learning that there was no doctor aboard; he lay uncomprehending in Barbara's arms predicting an early demise. Louisa and Pat were prostrate.

I made my solitary way to the dining salon and found all the tables empty, so I went to the kitchen and loudly demanded dinner. 'None of the passengers require food,' a white-coated steward informed me. 'Well this passenger does,' I replied spiritedly. 'My ticket stipulates a cooked meal on board, and

107

I'm going to stay here till I get it.' Reluctantly they laid a place for me and served some watery soup, followed by an omelette and then some rather tough chops. As I chewed doggedly through the mess, while the ship swayed precariously, I became aware of faces staring at me through the deck windows. Several passengers, including Barbara and Pat, were looking on in amazement at my gourmandising – they couldn't understand how anyone could eat under those conditions.

We arrived at the Funchal docks in semi-darkness and shuffled to the shore standing with the other passengers in a muddle of misery while the confusion of baggage-sorting took place in falling rain and stygian gloom. When we found the cases we called for taxis and got to the hotel at about 3 am. It was a decaying colonial pile with bare, friendless rooms, and hard, prison-like beds, and not a bath to be seen. After remonstrating furiously with a sleepy manager roused from his bed our travel booking was shown to us: no bathrooms had been specified. I sat in dejection on the verandah as the dawn appeared, wondering whether it was worth going to bed. Barbara came along and justified her scepticism. 'I told you we'd end up in the khazi!'

I mournfully agreed. 'It's not up to much.'

'It's a dump,' she said. 'It might have suited your Empress friend but I think it's horrible, that filthy boat with everyone sea-sick and now this rotten hotel in the middle of a rain forest.'

The water dripped noisily on to the roof above us.

'And the beds are too short. My Ronnie can't stretch out.'

'Don't worry,' I comforted her, 'later we shall laugh when we look back on it.'

'In these beds we'll be lucky to have any back to look back on.'

Then there was a crash from Louisa's room and we found she'd fallen trying to reach the high wardrobe rail. Pat, rushing to help, tripped over the hem of her dress and as Barbara and I were sorting out the mess, a disconsolate Ronnie arrived asking, 'Anyone got something for a terrible headache?'

We all said that things could only get better. We were wrong. They got steadily worse. Day after day the rain confined us to the hotel and members of the staff assured us they'd never known such weather, that it was all most unusual. The girls departed in taxis to the hairdressers, and I sat with

Ronnie playing cards and commiserating about his ill-starred honeymoon. We went regularly to the airline office in Funchal asking to be got out, but they tirelessly iterated that the weather prohibited any sailings to Porto Santo and therefore the flights were grounded.

If two is company and three's a crowd, then five is a disaster, and we began to get increasingly short-tempered as a party. When we split up it was fine. I used to sally forth with Ronnie, visiting sad little bars with names like 'Naughty Pigeon' and 'The Flamenco', where morose British tourists sat clutching their drinks with no sign of either naughtiness or birds, let alone dancers, and we swapped stories about the myths of foreign travel. Ronnie and I had a lot in common: we both liked sentimental songs – not pop music – and neither of us could add up very well. Every time currency had to be exchanged Pat or Barbara had to explain the intricacies, but we only listened with half an ear as we always left money matters to them.

On the 8th of April rescue was announced at the airline office. 'We can take you to Lisbon tomorrow.' We rushed off happily to pack our bags for departure on the following day. It was another voyage to Porto Santo and after more interminable waiting we got a plane to the mainland, and by 1 o'clock on the 10th we were all ensconced in the Ambassadors Hotel in Lisbon.

The rooms were clean and spacious, the sun was shining brightly and things had taken a distinct turn for the better. We were lunching in the hotel's rooftop restaurant congratulating ourselves on the change of scene when a familiar voice at my elbow asked, 'Will you be requiring room service?' We found ourselves joined by Lance Percival, my old chum from revue days. He was performing in cabaret on one of the cruise ships and had a few days' leisure in the capital, so he offered to show us the sights. Now we were a party of six.

Lance took us to the Coach Museum and to Manuel's sixteenth-century Cathedral and in the evening he provided free tickets for a night spot. This was the sort of clip-joint serving inferior champagne and featuring elaborate striptease acts. One of these depicted a nude lady posturing before an arclight while a vocal commentary told us she represented Eve greeting the dawn. She looked more like a Rubens' voluptuary than the product of Adam's rib. When a light faded the voice said she was preparing for sleep. 'Looks as though she's in a trance,' I whispered to Ronnie.

He said, 'It's her boobs, they've made her top heavy,' and we started to giggle.

An elderly blimp from a nearby table told us to be quiet. 'You are spoiling our enjoyment of a fine artiste!' he said. 'People like you make me feel ashamed to be English.'

Ronnie went across and inquired with deadly politeness, 'Are you complaining about our behaviour? Perhaps you'd like to come outside?' There was an instant volte-face ending with the man sending drinks to our table and protesting that he meant no offence. A mollified Ronnie returned to our table saying honour had been satisfied.

Ronnie never looked aggressive but when he thought he was being put upon he could certainly make his presence felt. I was grateful for his intervention the following day as well. At the airport when we departed some self-important official tried to disperse our party in different places on the plane. Ronnie put paid to that, firmly shepherding us to five adjoining seats, saying that my elderly mother needed constant attention and an immediate brandy. Louisa has been his fan ever since.

On my return to London, Peter Eade told me of an intriguing offer. 'The BBC want you for Napoleon in the Anouilh play *French Cricket*.' I was pleasantly surprised. I didn't see myself as conventional casting for the French emperor. When I met the director I asked him what had made him think of me. He replied, 'All the other actors I wanted were unavailable and the producer said when in doubt get a comic.' He may not have been flattering but he was certainly forthright. When he told me that the wily Chief of Police, Fouché, was to be played by Robert Helpmann I needed no further encouragement; this was a play I wanted to do.

Rehearsals were held in a drill hall in Broomhill Road, Wandsworth. Louis XVIII was played by David Horne, an elderly and distinguished character actor, whose everyday clothes had a dated period flavour: this was the time of drainpipe trousers, but David Horne's were wider than Oxford bags and actually covered his shoes. Once or twice he almost tripped when catching his toe in the hem, and Robert Helpmann warned, 'Watch your skirts, Lena!' The idea of David Horne even remotely resembling Lena Horne set me laughing straightaway and I sat giggling with Robert during all my stage

110

waits. Not only did he tell amusing stories but he was also an appreciative listener. So often with funny men you're aware that they're waiting for you to finish before they come back with a competing sally, but Robert delighted in hearing an anecdote: he'd drink it in and return to it, often repeating a phrase that took his fancy.

I told him about Grandma Williams's account of her husband being bitten while unloading cargo at the East India Docks. 'This horrible great black spider come right out at him! Bit him in the neck it did – great big lump come up the size of a football and they took him to the lying-in hospital – lying in, I said, he looks more like he needs laying out – then they told me how this horrible black thing came right out at him. Oh, I nearly died.' Months later I received a postcard from Robert Helpmann in Florence of Hercules and Diomedes with 'A great big black thing come right out at me' written on the back.

Because I was playing Napoleon, it was decided I should wear padding round the abdomen and during the recording all this cotton wool became displaced, so that I ended up with no stomach but a huge posterior. The director discounted it ('Don't worry, no one noticed') but Robert Helpmann said it wasn't every day you saw a Bonaparte with a behind like a balloon.

June 1964 was a month of socialising and my diary recalls endless luncheon parties and engagements. I saw a lot of Gordon and Rona in their new house at Hampstead. Stanley and Moira had moved to Highgate, and with Andrew Ray I continued to visit the Old Bailey, then going on to his flat where we talked into the early hours. We were both admirers of Samuel Johnson and he quoted with approval the doctor's maxim, 'Any man abed before midnight is a scoundrel', and I countered with Kenneth Tynan's 'Actors are like owls – they blink in the daylight.'

Another friend, Basil Henson, who had been the Marshal in the Anouilh play, was responsible for introducing me to the ballet. He took me to Covent Garden to see Nureyev and Fonteyn dance Margeurite and Armand in a ballet based on Dumas' *La Dame Aux Camélias*, with music by Lizst. In the interval, as I pushed through the crowd at the bar to get drinks, I suddenly felt myself being goosed. I decided to ignore it. Then it happened again. I turned to administer a haughty rebuke but the words froze on my lips as I found myself face to face with Judy Garland. She smiled dazzlingly and asked, 'How's your asp?' Not sure whether I had heard aright, I hesitated and she continued, 'I've got your recording of the asp sketch from *Pieces of Eight*. I've played it so often the grooves are practically smooth!'

When I found myself again, I could only ask this sylphlike creature in bolero and ski slacks: 'How do you look so young? Is there a secret elixir under the bed?'

She laughed and said, 'Dieting is useless. I just go without for a few days.'

The delectable Miss Garland joined us for the rest of the evening and sent my social standing soaring.

The following evening I went to Wyndham's to see Joe Orton's first West End play *Entertaining Mr Sloane* which I found absorbing; Gallic in its construction and Wildean in its wit. It is significant that Michael Codron was presenting it. He was quick to see the potential in Harold Pinter when he presented *The Birthday Party* for the first time at the Lyric, Hammersmith, and Joe Orton was another singular new talent. When I told Michael how impressed I was by the writing he told me that Joe Orton liked my work, too. He thought I ought to meet him. I readily assented. 'I warn you,' Michael added, 'we'll have to have the Friend as well, they're practically inseparable' – and that was the first I heard of Kenneth Halliwell. When we did meet I was surprised at Joe's patience, because Halliwell constantly interrupted his conversation, correcting Joe about times and places ('No, you've got it wrong – that was Thursday when we went to Holloway Road') and Joe would meekly acquiesce. Halliwell continually halted Joe's narrative in this irritating way.

I warmed to Orton immediately. His mixture of naivety and sophistication was a constant delight. He seemed genuinely surprised to find that people set so much store by formality of any kind. 'Why do I have to wear a suit?' he asked in bewilderment when someone invited him to dinner. He wandered about London dressed in sweat shirt, denims, army boots and a dustman's jacket: he thought they were perfectly serviceable. He talked amusingly about a report he had read in the newspapers about a policeman called Challoner who allegedly planted bricks on some students demonstrating against the visit of Queen Frederica and talked of the man's obsession with physical fitness, instancing his camping out under canvas

112

in a London park and undergoing all sorts of physical privation. Joe thought such behaviour bordered on fanaticism and said it was already forming the basis of a character he envisaged in a play. This was the first inkling I had of Inspector Truscott in the play he was to call *Loot*.

Joe was darkly handsome and confident. Halliwell seemed a weak, defensive characer and his toupé always looked obvious even when it wasn't vaguely askew. Whereas Joe spoke easily, Halliwell's speech was pedantic and sibilant. I was shocked by the spartan nature of their apartment – two beds, with the sheets and blankets neatly stacked and folded on a bare mattress, two chairs (Halliwell on one, me on the other, Joe sat on a stool), and a painted desk. There were no curtains, only venetian blinds, and no decorations apart from an enormous wall collage which was entirely composed of illustrations from colour supplements and magazines. It had everything from classical male nudes to modern film stars. Halliwell offered me a ham sandwich, and eyed me closely as I took a bite. 'It's rather good, isn't it?' he said. 'We got this bread from a special shop round the corner.' I stopped chewing and pretended to savour the contents. I wondered if it wasn't some private joke of theirs, but then I saw that Joe was nodding perfectly straight-faced. I'd seen them prepare the sandwiches. I'd seen the packet of sliced bread from a well-known bakery and the ham in a bag with the brand name clearly marked. The bread was white, spongy and tasteless; the ham moist and salty. Joe was clearly enjoying his and said, 'Yes, it makes a delicious snack, doesn't it?' I realized they were both serious so I mouthed some pleasantry about the food, but secretly I thought it deserved no compliments.

On a later occasion when they served some boiled haddock the same elaborate ritual occurred, 'Doesn't this taste really delectable?' one was asked in all earnestness, and the ordinary was awarded an accolade. Any objective comment would have been superfluous: they were wrapped up in their own world where they created their own values.

On the same evening they played a tape-recording of a sketch they had written. Joe told me, 'It's about this man with a magnetic member. He's been at Harwell, you see, where the radiation causes metal to be attracted towards it and he's got this job as butler to a duchess who secretes these pins in various orifices and sends for him to get them out.' I listened to

113

the performance in which Joe played the butler and Halliwell the duchess. I asked afterwards, 'This *is* for your own amusement, isn't it?' and was amazed when they told me they thought it would make a good revue sketch. 'You'd never get anyone to stage it,' I told them, and we had a long discussion about censorship. I was the one who was proved wrong, because this sketch was indeed staged. It was produced some time later in the London revue *Oh, Calcutta*. The intervening years had seen a revolution of social mores.

Chapter Six

In July 1964 I was filming *Carry On Cleo* back at Pinewood Studios. I was playing Julius Caesar in this burlesque of ancient Rome; Sid James as Mark Antony addressed me as Julie and Joan Sims as Calpurnia was a comically complaining matriarch forever bullying and bashing me with whatever object came to hand.

Kenneth Connor played a stalwart centurion who was bodyguard-cum-dresser and there was a sequence in which he used curling irons to wave my hair. There was a lot of word-play about iron from Cockney rhyming slang – iron hoof – poof – and during the fight sequence where he and Jim Dale shielded me from attack, I continually goosed them with a short-sword. Since I always did it when the cameras were rolling and they didn't want to spoil the shot, they had to suffer it all without complaint, but once the take was finished, they rounded on me angrily and I was chased all over the set, till I could hide behind the safe skirts of Joan Sims.

They got their own back in the crowd scene. When I had to address the mob in a mock Friends-Romans-Countrymen speech on the steps of the Forum, I was supposed to be pelted with rotten eggs and fruit. The stuff came hurtling at me from all directions – tomatoes smacking me in the mouth before I could deliver a sentence. Gerald allowed it all in the long shot, but when it came to the close-up , he relented, telling them, 'Take it easy this time, aim for his body, not the face, I want to hear the dialogue,' and I earned a respite.

While we were making *Carry On Cleo* the earlier *Carry On Spying* was released and several newspapers carried favourable reviews. This was interesting because initially these films were given scant attention, and then only disparagingly, but now I was surprised to see good notices in some unexpected places. *The Spectator* for the 17th of August 1964 carried a piece by the film critic, Ian Cameron: 'The *Carry On* series may lack subtlety but at least it avoids a weedy refinement that passed for it in Ealing Comedies. *Carry On Spying* which should only be seen with a large audience, is probably the funniest and crudest to-date. The inspiration is obviously the

115

Bond films, although one can hardly call it either parody or satire. It is burlesque and at its best thoroughly outrageous . . . let's hope for more burlesque from Rogers and Thomas, and more good old English camp from all concerned. Give lines about Carnival Queens or Barbara Windsor doing her bit to Kenneth Williams and they're played for much more than they're worth. And that's how it should be.'

On the 9th of August the *Observer* headed a column 'In Praise Of Carry On' with a picture of me in the middle. I began to wonder why the climate of opinion had changed so much in the last few years. As far as the business was concerned, they'd been enormously successful – *Carry On Nurse* was the top box-office film of 1959 – but critically they'd been mostly damned with faint praise. Now they were suddenly becoming fashionable. They had enjoyed commercial success from the outset, but good notices only came later. Stick around long enough and even the critics will accept you.

If I wasn't exactly feeling prosperous at this time I was certainly behaving like it. I arranged a holiday for Louisa and Pat on a cruise to the Greek Islands – my enthusiasm had infected them. I also concurred with my accountant when he suggested I invest £963 in a single premium assurance policy to mature at £1500 in ten years which he assured me would be a buffer against poverty in the years ahead. I nodded sagaciously, but we were both wrong. Simple interest at 4 per cent didn't even keep pace with inflation, but it certainly taught me how insurance companies made so much money.

I hired a motor to bring my mother and my Aunt Edith down to the studios where Gerald gave permission for them to watch the filming. This was quite a concession because Peter Rogers didn't encourage visitors on the set. Aunt Edith was my godmother and always had a very special place in my affections; it was she who persuaded her husband to give an interest-free loan to my father which ensured that he had a business in Marchmont Street – and of all my mother's sisters she was the closest. Another of my guests brought down from London was George Borwick whom I had met when he had been one of the backers in Michael Codron's *Pieces of Eight*; he'd proved a stalwart during the dark days of my father's death. He was a fan of the *Carry Ons* and watched shot after shot with keen interest. Often the layman finds it boring to watch the repetition of establishing scene, dual sequence and

116

close-up of the same dialogue, but George enjoyed it all. He particularly enjoyed meeting Charles Hawtrey, whom he had admired in the Will Hay films as well as in such classics as *Passport to Pimlico*. Charles was always courteous to guests on the set – not all actors show such consideration – going out of his way to make them feel at home.

By early September I had finished filming *Cleo* and I was approached by Norman Newell of HMV to do a recording of some Noël Coward songs. I said I was chary of attempting 'Mad Dogs' because I feared it would sound like an impersonation of the Master. Norman said, 'If I telephone him and tell him of your reservations and he okays it, will that make you happy?' I said yes, and subsequently he informed me that Noël had approved me for the project. I started rehearsals with Cyril Ornadel's orchestra. The Coward lyrics are not easy to sing. They require the author's clarity of diction and an awful lot of abdominal breathing. Taken at speed, lines like 'In the Malay States/there are hats like plates/which the Britishers won't wear' are particularly challenging, because you must avoid elision. It's rather like some of Liszt's piano compositions; they're too difficult for the average instrumentalist, you need a technical virtuoso.

Coward's lines obey the rules of metre, and they're immaculately constructed. His 'Nina' is a masterpiece. As a story it's got a beginning, a middle and an end, plus a superbly satisfying tag-line. The satirical comment of Latin-American dancing is mordantly accurate and the musical technique enhances every funny point he makes. There's not a bit of padding anywhere; the wit is wonderfully economical and the rhythms brilliantly contrived.

I just about managed to get through 'Mad Dogs' without mishap, and then went on to tackle 'Mrs Worthington'. I became a little over-confident here and in the concluding stanza I actually used an ad lib – I'm still amazed at my temerity. After 'On my knees, Mrs Worthington/Please Mrs Worthington/Don't put your daughter on the stage', I added, 'or your son' – and then reprised the last line. Norman Newell didn't object, and to my surprise neither did Noël. So it stayed on the recording which included Joyce Grenfell singing one of the most poignant renderings of 'The Party's Over Now'. The Coward songs contain as much effervescent humour as they do wry melancholy and I was more than pleased in later years

117

when I found that Philip Larkin had included him in the *Oxford Book of Twentieth-Century English Verse.*

In October 1964 Michael Codron sent me Joe Orton's latest play, which was then called *Funeral Games*, in which I was to play Inspector Truscott. I went to see Joe and Kenneth Halliwell at Noel Road in Islington and we had a long discussion about the various characters in the play. The suggestion of Duncan Macrae as the father was greeted lukewarmly by Joe but I urged that his was the kind of style that could make a highly individual Mr McLeavy. Michael Codron had got Ian McShane for the son and Geraldine McEwan for the Nurse. ('It's all getting very Scottish', Michael had written to me, 'D'you fancy playing Truscott in a kilt?'). It was on this occasion that Joe told me about Terence Rattigan's admiration for *Mr Sloane* and about their subsequent meeting. They had got on very well and Rattigan had asked Joe to go to Hong Kong with him, leaving Halliwell behind. I said that seemed unreasonable and Joe answered that many people didn't understand how inseparable he and Halliwell were. Halliwell remained silent.

I changed the subject and said I didn't like the title of his play. *Funeral Games* didn't sound very inviting on a poster. K.H. suddenly said, 'I've always thought it should be called *Loot*', and I seized upon that. 'It's a brilliant idea, and it epitomizes what the play's all about!'

After that I told them both about an extraordinary coincidence which had occurred that week. 'I was in Piccadilly Circus and an open car stopped, the driver called my name, and I found myself face to face with a chap I'd done basic training with in the Army. He gave me a lift and told me he'd gone into the Paratroops, then after demob he got a job with a brewery and now he shares a flat with this Irishman in the same block of flats I moved into. I am meeting them tonight for a drink.' Joe said he'd love to meet an ex-paratrooper, so I suggested he and K.H. join me and we all went to Endsleigh Court where I introduced them to Stan Walker and Terry Duff. Halliwell contributed little to the conversation apart from, as usual, correcting some of Joe's anecdotes which were mostly about sexual promiscuity.

When they'd gone I asked Stan what he'd thought of Joe. 'He doesn't give anyone else a chance, does he?' he said. 'All he

118

does is talk about himself.' I thought this was much too sweeping; while Joe delighted in describing his encounters, he told you a lot about other people on the way. I especially enjoyed hearing about Joe's eccentric neighbours. He'd told us about a married couple inviting him and Halliwell to spend a weekend with them 'at our little place in Holland'. He said they got their passports and packed their bags and the couple drove them for miles and miles till they realized they were a long way from Harwich. In fact they were appalled to find they were nowhere near the Netherlands at all – they ended up in Holland, East Anglia, in a holiday chalet. 'The path to the front door was all crazy paving with the stones actually painted in different colours, and before you could cross the portal we were asked by the lady to close our eyes and only open them when she called out. She said she wanted us to get the full effect of her hall. When she cried "Now" we looked and saw this formica-panelled lobby with china birds stuck all over the place, and she said her husband had removed every trace of timber from the house and substituted deep plastic.'

Orton had a keen eye for the incongruous and the actor's gift of a retentive memory and he could give just the right accent and colour to a quote that appealed to him. He recounted the Holland woman talking about her hospitalisation: ' "Unfortunately I was placed in a communal ward, but I have no complaints of the National Health because I received top class penicillin." '

I was anxious to introduce Joe to a number of my friends but it wasn't always successful. After an afternoon spent with Gordon Jackson, I remember sensing a lack of enthusiasm, and I pressed Gordon for an opinion. 'I see what you mean about him, he's very funny,' he admitted, 'but his eyes are so cold.' With Louisa, however, Joe was a great success. He described a torrid coupling in a Leicester doorway. 'It wasn't a very big porch and most of the time my behind was exposed to the elements.' 'Oh Joe!' said Louisa, 'You are a fool. You could've caught double pneumonia'.

By January 1965 I was rehearsing *Loot* and thinking what a very good company had been assembled. Geraldine McEwan was coolly insolent as the Nurse, Duncan Macrae played a startling McLeavy, Ian McShane made a wayward son alarmingly acceptable and David Batley as his friend was mournfully droll. I began to think that everyone else was good and that I

119

was bad. Peter Wood was directing and he insisted on so many rewrites that the script began to bulge with amendments. In the second week I asked how much more dialogue was to be altered and he said there would be no more. I wrote in my diary of my doubts about this and learned painfully in the coming weeks just how much my misgivings were justified.

On the 28th of January the cast arrived to find a metronome ticking by the footlights. We eyed it apprehensively, wondering what it was for, when Peter Wood appeared; apparently it was in order to 'keep a sense of rhythm for the actors'. I could hardly believe my ears. Geraldine looked bemused, and Duncan laughed in disbelief. 'Ah! you're joking of course!' When this was denied he said, 'The actor has to have his own natural sense of timing – he doesn't need this clockwork tick-tock to teach him!' I put in my twopenny-worth, 'This machine is ridiculous.' The metronome was removed.

At the director's instigation two front-cloth scenes had been added: the Inspector and his assistant Meadows appeared in front of the house wheeling a pram in which there was a wound-up horned gramophone playing a record of Clara Butt singing 'Abide With Me'. I felt this sequence stuck out like a sore thumb. At the dress rehearsal in the Cambridge Arts Theatre on the 31st of January I asked Peter Wood to cut it, saying that I found it embarrassing. After some acrimonious argument he reluctantly agreed that the scene should go, but at 9.30 the next morning he telephoned me at the hotel and said firmly, 'The scene is going back', and refused to budge.

On the opening night, 1st February, at Cambridge, the audience watched this curious prologue with Truscott and Meadows wheeling on the gramophone and 'laying the plot' as it were, and then the front-cloth flew away and the set was revealed and the play proper began. What with first-night nerves and the obvious distaste shown by the spectators for much of the dialogue, the performance was ragged. I didn't help much by wearing a chrome-yellow make-up which Peter Eade said made me look like a pint-sized Charlie Chan.

He had motored up from London and said he felt that it failed in the second act, not the third. I said I thought the perambulator sequences should go and the rewrites, too. I was convinced we should return to the author's original conception.

By the next day, after a conference with Michael Codron,

120

Joe and the director, the front-cloth scenes were cut. In the evening the play went a little better but there was only reluctant applause at the finish and we hardly managed a third curtain. On Wednesday a drastic rewrite was rehearsed and the entire piece was put into two acts, the first finishing with the entrance of Mr McLeavy after the funeral accident. In my diary I wrote, 'It went a bit better and the final applause was not as tepid as before – it justified three curtain calls without a feeling of embarrassment.'

On the following night Michael Codron came backstage and said we'd come from a disastrous Monday to a potentially good show on Thursday. On Friday, author and management returned to London and we continued with the altered script feeling a little more confident, but on Saturday the evening performance was booed, and Geraldine and I left the theatre feeling utterly dispirited. She said that performing that week had been quite unreal for her. It was almost as though it had never happened. When we entered the hotel a square dance was in progress all round the tables in the dining room. 'Oh dear,' I moaned, 'we've come from one nightmare to another.' Supper was eschewed and we fled to our bedrooms.

The cast returned to London on Sunday. Duncan Macrae was in a buoyant mood on the train telling us how, for £1000, he'd laid a stone terrace outside his Millport home. 'I feel the expense is justified, one might as well go the whole hog, it's the same with my work – in for a penny in for a pound,' he said, getting expansive, with the back of his right hand covering his face, his mouth and chin, his eyes staring relentlessly above, and his left arm outstretched with the fingers spread wide. 'The body should speak as well as the mouth, limbs can be eloquent, do you not think?' Geraldine shrank further into her furs and huddled in the corner of the railway carriage, silent and despondent. Duncan was undeterred, 'I think the Russians demonstrate it very well – the complete physical immersion. Och! I've always been a devotee, I'm naturally balletic.' He kicked a leg in the air and waggled his foot. 'I was up there in the gods watching the Moscow Arts when they came over here in the '20s. Did you see them?' Geraldine said she wasn't born then. After a pause, Duncan enquired wonderingly, 'Oh were you not?' by which time Geraldine had curled up on the seat opposite and gone to sleep.

Our next date was at Brighton where the Monday

121

performance got four curtains and I began to feel our luck had changed. Gordon Jackson came down to see it and was loyally enthusiastic afterwards. We returned to the hotel for supper. Near us in the dining room we heard two women loudly holding forth about the play. 'It is quite disgusting – all about pregnancies,' the first one told their male companion, and the second one said, 'I left at the interval: I thought it was awful.' I had my back to them but Gordon could see them and he mimed their descriptions across the table to me, making dreadful faces. I had trouble stifling my laughter.

On Tuesday Michael Codron and Peter Wood arrived bearing yet more rewrites. When I said I thought they were all patches for a leaking hulk Peter reproved me saying that my destructive comments were spreading discontent through the company and sapping everyone's confidence. We rehearsed the new stuff and put some of it in the evening performance with the result that the play became sporadic and tentative. At Thursday's rehearsal I pointed out how much harm the rewrites were causing and Peter reminded me that this was what the management wanted and lectured me all about 'the evil of negative thinking'. After another shaky performance that night Sir Laurence Olivier came round and took me in his arms, saying sympathetically, 'Oh Kenny, you haven't got a *play* here, that's your trouble.'

We continued in this fashion – half original text and half new – to the end of the Brighton week, and made a herculean effort on the 14th at the Oxford New Theatre to put in all the new moves and dialogue – rehearsing until late at night on Sunday and again on Monday, so that with the performance of the 15th February, we got all the different versions staged. But my diary entry was cheerless: 'Died in much the same way as the opening night in Cambridge – we're back to square one.'

On Tuesday I complained again at rehearsals that the rewrites were all a mistake and that our only chance was to go back to the original script. Peter said no. I telephoned Michael asking him to come down and see the mess we were in, but he refused saying he had to obey the director. The performance that night was again dreadful. Hysteria mounted and by the end of the play I was barely controlling myself. There were several bouts of ill-repressed giggling. It was the nervous laughter that comes from desperation. Geraldine caught it and

122

at one point she went offstage shouting 'I can't go on with this stuff any more!'

Wednesday was calmer and I left Oxford that night because I had to be in London for the radio show with Kenneth Horne on the following day. What had begun as *Beyond Our Ken* with Eric Merriman had changed. The script was now put together by Marty Feldman and Barry Took and the show was entitled *Round the Horne*. Some new characters had been added. There was a send-up of a folk singer – called Rambling Sid Rumpo. Hugh Paddick and I played 'Jule and Sand', a pair of camp interior decorators, with lines like 'Oh yes, Mister Horne we'll brighten up your patio, ducky! Shove a couple of creepers up your trellis!'; and talking about our yachting experiences – 'Oh Mister Horne, there was this terrible storm blew up and this great wave washed us overboard; we clung to the edge of the boat for dear life!' When Kenneth Horne asked, 'Did you manage to drag yourself up?' I answered, 'No, we wore casuals.' Another character was the fortune-teller Madame Osiris – 'I will tell you all, dear, cross my palm with silver – yes, your lucky sandwich filling is salmon and shrimp, your lucky stone is gall, and uranus is in its last stages.' Betty Marsden continued with her indignant charladies and Russian spies. Bill Pertwee performed his patriotic characters and songs and Kenneth Horne presided confidently over the proceedings like a ringmaster putting us all through our paces. It was to prove one of the BBC's most popular revue formats.

The Paris Studio attracted huge and eager audiences and I returned to Oxford feeling as though I'd had a holiday. The respite was short-lived, for when it came to the evening performance the reception could only be described as politely indifferent. My diary entry reads: 'Playing this stuff is like trying to catch bath-water; it keeps slipping through your fingers . . . Geraldine felt so ill and shaky that a doctor was called to the theatre and on our return to the hotel, David Batley suddenly started crying uncontrollably and ran out of the room. What an awful effect this show is having on us all!'

Monday the 22nd of February was not my happiest birthday. I awoke conscious of a cold, my eyes heavy-lidded and my temples throbbing with a headache. I decided to do something to take my mind off my ailments and began cleaning the windows. I spilled the pail of dirty water in the bedroom and it soaked the carpet. I bent down to clear up the mess with a

123

towel and saw two beetles by the telephone plug. I recoiled with horror upsetting the receiver which fell to the ground breaking the mouthpiece. I rushed for the DDT spray but the nozzle was blocked and it all shot back in my face. After that I gave up, wheeled the divan over the wet patch and went back to bed.

Loot had now moved to Golders Green but, at the evening performance on the 22nd, we 'lost' the audience in the second half. There was an inquest afterwards in a nearby restaurant with the producer, the director and the author. Joe looked defeated, utterly beaten into the ground, but Peter Wood insisted that we had to have more rewrites. On Tuesday the cold moved down to my throat and every time I swallowed it was agony. I went to the chemist for linctus and played that night with my voice grating and my chest as tight as a drum. Wednesday was spent rehearsing more amendments resulting in an evening performance full of stops and starts. Everyone was hesitant because the new material and the old dialogue didn't synchronise. On Thursday I felt so ill that I went to the doctor and croaked out my woes to him. He telephoned the management cancelling my appearance at the matinée saying I should save what was left of my voice for the evening performance. I got through that all right and by Friday I was feeling better. The audience was receptive and the play received spirited applause. Perhaps word-of-mouth caused the box office to pick up, because by Saturday the mood had changed enormously and the last performance at Golders Green was amazing; a packed house clapped and cheered at the final curtain. Everyone went home with morale boosted and perhaps, if our next date had been appropriate, the mood might have been sustained. But on Monday the 1st of March we opened not to a metropolitan audience ready to be in the vanguard of new ideas, but to freezing conditions at the Bournemouth Pavilion.

We couldn't have fared worse in Reykjavik. With a gale-force wind blowing loudly in the bleak auditorium, voices were drowned and performances reduced to ludicrous dumb show. This sort of seaside concert-party date might have suited a pierrot show in the summer but for an Orton comedy in winter it was disastrous. With snow-storms flurrying round the resort our audiences dwindled nightly. The cast was still rehearsing more inserts sent from London but everyone was

124

greatly demoralised and any hope of the play's ultimate success was rapidly receding. Saturday provided the only decent house in the whole of the week and I departed from Bournemouth the same night anxious to erase the experience and put miles between me and the misery.

At Manchester Opera House, the following week, *Loot* aroused the hostility of the local Watch Committee and since the endless rewrites had meant that no complete script had been submitted to the Lord Chamberlain we did not have his protective seal of approval. The local arbiters of taste were now our censors. They decided I was not allowed to say 'I have come to turn off your stop-cock.' I protested that the line was perfectly permissible for a man allegedly representing the Water Board, but they were adamant. And they cut one of Ian McShane's lines as well. During one of my speeches about his friend Dennis I asked, 'Where does he engender these unwanted children – there are no open spaces, the streets are well lit, the police patrol regularly. It should be next to impossible to commit the smallest act of indecency, let alone beget a child. Where does he do it?' Ian, playing Hal, replied, 'On crowded dance floors during the rhumba.' The Watch Committee thought this cast an unwarrantable slur on the local terpsichorean haunts and demanded that it be excised from the play. For good measure, they had several burly policemen standing in the wings observing. We were assured that if one offensive word was uttered, the actor would be swiftly removed. Some of the things happening offstage in *Loot* were almost as incongruous as what was happening onstage.

In Manchester, the audiences seemed evenly divided, with parts of the house applauding and laughing while others sat silent and disapproving. On Saturday I was surprised by a visit backstage from Clifford Evans. He made no secret of his dislike for the piece and told me that whatever I did, I should get out of it before London. Many visitors backstage said that Orton's dialogue was shocking but Clifford went further. He thought it was impermissible. I mentioned it to Duncan Macrae after the show and he said, 'I've heard the same thing from people in the dressing room. Och, they're all carpers, moaning minnies with no stomach for anything new in the theatre. It was the same when I did my fireman sketch in Scotland: a very distinguished critic, Mamie Crichton, came backstage, and said it was scandalous what I was doing with the hose-nozzle between my legs – I said to her, "Och Mamie, the precedent for phallic comedy goes right back to Aristophanes." There wasn't a peep out of her after that.' Duncan pronounced it 'Aristo-far-knees' which made the story even funnier.

Our last week was played in the vast theatre at Wimbledon, the wind and rain lashing down on the 15th of March for our first night there. The audience received it coldly and afterwards Michael Codron addressed the cast. He told us that there were no further dates, that we were in the last week, and that the only available London theatre, the Phoenix, would rather be dark than have us. He said that if everyone was agreeable it might be possible to re-engage us when and if a suitable theatre did turn up. We dispersed wondering what was going to happen next.

The rest of the week found us all in a state of limbo. The usual differences of opinion were voiced by visitors backstage. George Borwick said he found it entertaining but that it needed a different set, and naturalism, not stylisation – 'it should be played for realism'. Richard Pearson on the same night told me, 'It is an extraordinary play. Every time you laugh you feel ashamed afterwards.'

On Friday Andrew Ray and his wife, Susan, came, with my mother and sister, Pat. They were chatting in the dressing room discussing the play quite favourably when in walked a man with whom I was barely on nodding terms. Before I had time to put a name to the face he began, 'I'm sorry but I must tell you: I think this play is disgusting. I have never known such uncomfortable moments in the theatre. I don't know why you ever agreed to appear in such a perverted – '

I interrupted him. 'If you haven't anything constructive to say, you shouldn't come backstage at all.'

There was a pause. 'But I came to see you. After all, we're acquainted.'

'Then we must get quickly unacquainted,' I said, 'Goodnight,' and ushered him to the door.

The others were clearly embarrassed. 'You were rather rude, Kenneth,' said Pat raising her eyebrows.

'I've had adverse comment till it's coming out of my ears', I replied. 'Even if what he said is justified I don't think he's earned the right to say it.'

By Saturday the end was in sight. Michael Codron made a last effort to save the play saying he could get the Lyric,

Hammersmith, if the cast would agree on some weeks out, but they didn't. One day, I knew, Orton would be accepted in the same canon as a Congreve or a Sheridan, but that night, sadly, I wrote in my diary: '*Loot* died tonight after 56 performances of about three different editions.' I hadn't the prescience then to record that, once staged with full trust in the Orton text, and not in the technicalities of production, it would enjoy such a successful revival within a matter of years.

Chapter Seven

March 1965 was summerlike at its close and it was warm enough on the 28th to sit in Stanley Baxter's garden at Highgate. After listening patiently to all my moaning about the travails of *Loot*, he said, 'You should do another revue.' I pointed out that there was always the problem finding the right material.

'You wait until you've assembled the right material.'

'But I don't like long runs.'

'You stipulate that in your contract. Your agent arranges a release clause, that's what agents are for. It's called negotiation. Then you take the whole show to America. You'd be a great success in America.'

'I don't want to go to America. They asked me to go with the Shaffer play but I said no, and Alex Cohen wanted to do the revue in the States but I said no to that as well.'

'Don't you want to see Broadway?'

'I feel like Johnson, I suppose: it may be worth seeing but not worth going to see.'

That started the conversation on quite a different tack. We were both devotees of the great 'Cham' and we fell to discussing his unequivocal and forthright manner. Stanley relished the story of the clergyman who asked the Doctor if Dodds's sermons weren't addressed to the passions. Johnson told him: 'They were nothing, sir, be they addressed to what they may.' I said I had been re-reading Johnson's life of Richard Savage. 'The sadness of his illegitimacy, the pathetic appeals to his mother, his lack of success in writing and the trial for murder; there are all the ingredients for a marvellous play,' I said. 'And Johnson's description of his envisaged exile is delightful: "He could not bear to debar himself from the happiness which was to be found in the calm of a cottage, or lose the opportunity of listening without intermission to the melody of the nightingale which he believed was to be heard from every bramble." I don't think modern people's dream of retirement would be very different.'

Stanley was interested to hear about Savage and next day I sent him a copy of *Lives of the Poets*. Strolling back from the bookshop I felt vaguely envious of all my friends who had houses with gardens. Only a day or two earlier I'd been visiting Gordon and Rona at Hampstead; since their removal from Chelsea they were now the proud parents of two young children, Roddy and Graham, and I was playing with them on the lawn, and thinking how pleasant it was to enjoy the grassy space that wasn't open to the public. My only recourse to sylvan surroundings lay in Regent's Park – a stone's throw from my flat – but even a brief stroll through the gates involved recognition, requests for autographs, the moron's nudge and the cretin's wink.

The days drifted by and I did no work. Peter Eade sent me scripts which I thought unsuitable and I turned down so many suggestions that he became quite edgy with me. Lunching with him on 22nd April he asked, 'Have you any clear idea of what you would like to do?'

'No, the last two plays flopped, and my poor old career is in tatters. The offers I do get are for asinine parts.'

'Yes, well, you see they all connect you with high camp.'

'Yes, I do see.'

'And if you're not careful, you'll find over the years that you've actually become the label they put on you.'

I felt all my accomplishments dripping away from me. I might as well have been sitting there naked. I continued chatting about job prospects but I was inwardly thinking of Eliot's line, 'I keep my countenance: I remain self-possessed.'

My jaunts to the Law Courts with Andrew had ceased because he, too, was suffering from the effects of unemployment and a depression had brought him to the Middlesex Hospital. I visited him there and he told me, 'They're giving me psychiatric treatment. They came round the ward today offering everyone a trip to Watney's Brewery.'

'I should have thought the wine vaults were more in your line.'

'Well, they don't have any vineyards round here.'

'No, the inner cities have less and less to offer, even Miss Gerrard is giving up, she's leaving the area and returning to her native haunts in Caledonia.'

'Who's Miss Gerrard?'

'She does my feet.'

'Oh, the chiropodist?'

'Yes, I've got this convoluted toe-nail and she says it's the result of calcium deficiency so I've got to see the dietician. I think I'll tell him about the palpitations. I always seem to get them after eating.'

'You're a hypochondriac, Kenneth, that's your trouble.'

'Hypochondriac? What are you talking about! It's not imagined. I know when something's wrong with me.'

'There's nothing wrong with you: it's all in the mind!'

'Since you're in the psychiatric ward, that makes two of us.'

We both laughed and I predicted, 'You won't be here long, you're far too rational.'

The following Sunday I met Stanley and we drove to Maidenhead where we hired a motor launch at Boulters Lock and spent an hour on the river. He told me he was going to take over from Brian Rix in *Chase Me Comrade* at the Whitehall and then tour Australia with it.

'What, and leave that lovely house, just as you've got it all looking so nice?'

'The house is no substitute for a career. I enjoy the theatre, I like the challenge of a different audience every night and the reciprocal thing it entails. Can't bear being away from it for long.'

I said that after my last two experiences in the theatre it couldn't be long enough as far as I was concerned. I suggested we have tea at Skindles. 'I've never been there,' he said. 'It's famous!' I told him. 'You remember Phil Gilbert who was in *Share My Lettuce* – he took his Canadian aunt there and she had an appalling enteric attack after devouring a toasted teacake. The waiters were superb, they erected screens round her table, did the ablutions, found her another dress and within the hour she was taking her ease on the terrace.'

Stanley expressed his admiration for such resourcefulness but when he scanned the menu at Skindles he expostulated: 'Twelve and six for tea?'

I pointed out it was a set tea. 'You get scones and cakes as well as the tea.'

'At this price I should want the pot. Come on, let's find somewhere else.'

I had to agree with him. We left hastily and found an hotel opposite where an ample tea was served for half a crown and we returned to London feeling we'd scored a minor victory.

Later that week it looked as if the darkness on the work front had lifted. Peter Eade told me that Peter Glenville (who had

130

directed *Hotel Paradiso*) was making it into a film and he'd arrange an inteview for me. 'He wants to see you to check on whether you look youthful enough to play Maxime on the screen.'

Wearing a young-looking outfit I walked across the park on the appointed day but a sudden downpour soaked my finery and I arrived very damp at a house in the Brompton Road where a secretary bade me wait in a reception room. I tried to dry myself standing by an open window, but it wasn't long before I was ushered upstairs and a smiling Peter Glenville rose from the other side of a desk to shake my hand.

'I had expected to meet a middle-aged man!' he said. But I felt more like a damp derelict as I hitched up my sodden trousers and sat down opposite him.

'Of course it will all have to be cast differently. Most of the people in the stage production are too old now, they don't all wear as well as you.'

I dimpled at such flattery, and then he said, 'I hate asking actors to do this but would you mind terribly if we did a screen test?'

I was still smiling and replied unthinkingly, 'Certainly not, a screen test, yes of course.'

'That's good. Here is a script of the scene we'd like you to learn. It is marked. Go along to Bermans straight away and they will fix you up with a costume.'

He gave me a swift handshake and as I departed another actor was being shown in by the secretary. He looked much younger than me and I began to feel uneasy. At Bermans an assistant looked surprised when I said I wanted a suit for 'Maxime'.

'You as well!' he asked, and added, 'I've already fitted three other blokes for the part.'

'Sounds as if there'll be quite a queue', I said dismayed. Rembering the humiliation of the tests for the *Seekers* at Pinewood, I felt a sudden revulsion. 'No, don't bother about a suit for me,' I said, and left Bermans, going straight to my agent's office and telling Laurena, Peter's secretary, what had occurred. Laurena was Scots and uncompromising. 'Yes, well, you should never have agreed to test in the first place; it's your own fault.'

In an attempt to dispel my gloom I went up to the Baxters at Highgate and helped to construct their rockery, and did so much digging I ended up with three nasty blisters. Afterwards I remarked on how extraordinary it was that my close friends were all Scots – 'You and the Jacksons', I told Moira and she replied, 'Of course. It's the Celtic influence, you see.'

I said, 'The Celts are all right within the framework of English discipline – it doesn't work if they stay in their own country.'

She agreed. 'No, and the climate isn't so good either.'

'That's right. Stanley always says the air gets balmier as you travel south from Scotland.'

London was shimmering with warmth and I wanted more and more to get out of the city. At the end of May I visited Maggie and Beverly in their new abode, The White House at Beaumont in Hertfordshire. I sat with them drinking champagne on the lawn and feeling very sybaritic. Since Maggie was with the National at the Old Vic she couldn't go away but I asked Beverly if he was game for a holiday.

'I'd be interested in Crete,' he said. 'I'd like to look at the Minoan sites at Knossos and Phaestos and Mahlia.'

None of that took my fancy. 'I want to go to Turkey,' I countered. 'That glimpse we had of Istanbul, when the ship called there that day, was fascinating.'

'Do half and half', Maggie suggested. 'Spend some time in both places.' So we got out maps and started to plan a route. Before I left, Beverly had worked out a rough itinerary – London to Athens, boat to Istanbul, then Heraklion, then boat to Naples and home from there. The plan was to leave on the 10th of June returning about the 3rd of July.

We bought tickets and on the appointed date I flew with Beverly from Heathrow at 7.15 pm for Frankfurt where we had dinner in the airport. I asked him what the E stood for on our flight number to Athens. 'It can't be Ecuador, can it? They wouldn't do Greek routes, would they?'

'Shouldn't think so.'

'And Estonia's ceased to be independent. I wonder what it means.'

'Probably Ethiopia.'

'Oh heavens. That will mean a very restricted menu, I should think.'

Beverly turned out to be right and we boarded the Ethiopian Air Lines plane at 10 pm. Once we were in the air I asked the black stewardess slowly and carefully, 'Could we have

132

champagne please?' She smiled, 'Sure, honey, its on ice.' 'You don't sound Abyssinian to me,' I said and she told me, 'We're Ethiopian airlines but we are trained by TWA.' I was certainly impressed by her efficiency because within minutes she produced the Moët & Chandon superbly chilled.

'I think this is going to turn out rather well,' I told Bev, and we toasted so many absent friends we were soon calling for another bottle. The friendly stewardess kept the bubbly flowing all the way to Athens and the party mood lasted after we'd landed.

A taxi took us to the Grande Bretagne. We briefly inspected the rooms and then went out into Constitution Square at 2 am for more drinks in the balmy air. The combination of champagne and ouzo was heady to say the least, and the following day my skull felt as if it was atrophied.

Beverly was anxious to see where Clytemnestra and Aegisthus did their abominable deed so we drove via Corinth to the Palace of Agamemnon. But I was so full of lethargy I didn't take much in, and a viciously hot wind didn't improve my humour. I fell asleep in the car on the return to Athens.

After a bath and a change of clothing we wandered up to the Plaka area in the evening and dined at a rooftop taverna in the shadow of the Parthenon: sardines followed by moussaka washed down with retsina. That restored my feeling of well-being and we returned to the hotel to find a message from an American film-casting director who was also staying at the Grande Bretagne, suggesting we join her for drinks in the American Bar.

'How did you know I was here?' I asked her when we met.

'This is a very small place and these things get around,' she replied. I realised someone in the hotel must have recognised me and felt rather flattered. Then she said, 'We're making a screenplay out of Peter Shaffer's *Public Eye*. You were very good in the stage version but of course we want a Name for the film.' I began to feel not so flattered. 'We're thinking of either Peter Sellers or Laurence Olivier.' I murmured something about the cleverness of both these actors before making a headache my excuse for departing.

On the 12th of June we boarded the M.V. *Marmara* for Istanbul, and sailed through the Aegean with a trio playing 'Ramona' as we took tea in the saloon. We got to Izmir next day and, by 8.30 am, were strolling through the sun-baked

133

streets to the bazaar. Bev said, 'We must go to Inciralto, it's the Southend of Izmir.' I eagerly assented since he'd named one of my favourite resorts.

When we arrived we had a bit of trouble getting a bathing hut but an obliging Turk took us to an office where we had to deposit money and watches and valuables, then he escorted us to the allotted cubicle. The beach was packed with friendly people and after a swim we found a taverna by the waterside where we ate grilled mullet, Turkish meat-balls with salad and a bottle of wine. Bev scrutinized the bill and said, 'This lot has come to a pound each. We congratulated ourselves on such thrifty enjoyment, and then bundled into a taxi with four other people to return to the boat for about fourpence each. I decided Turkey was not only friendly, it was very reasonable.

We watched a school of porpoises cavorting in the sea of Marmara before disembarking in the Galata Quay in Istanbul. Porters pushed and shoved each other to be first up the gang-plank: it was like a bear-garden. The tumult was in total contrast to the sight of the city from the water: the minarets and domed mosques capped by St Sophia twinkled in the sun, all peace and dignity.

A taxi conveyed us through the city to the suburb of Yesilyurt and the Cinar Hotel. After unpacking I walked to the shops to get shampoo and returned to join Beverly on the hotel terrace where a young man in the uniform of British Eagle Airlines approached us. After some introductory compliments about my work he invited us to join him and the rest of the crew for drinks. 'We're room 225, say seven o'clock.'

Pleased by the recognition I graciously agreed and afterwards I asked Beverly what we ought to wear to the party. He thought we should be formally attired in suits. Later on, therefore, we sailed down the corridor in sartorial splendour and knocked on their door. Our host opened it to reveal the depressing spectacle of pilots lounging about in vests and shorts and stewardesses in bathrobes downing duty-free gin as if it was going out of style. Our lounge suits looked incongruous and we stood awkwardly as these indolent figures cried out introductions and invited us to get tooth-mugs from the bathroom and help ourselves.

This wasn't quite the cocktail gathering I had envisaged. I remember Peter Nichols telling me about the Harrods' work-force with whom he'd once found temporary employment at

Christmas. As soon as the employees were in the staff rest-room jackets and shoes were discarded, they put their feet up and talked a different language: 'You wouldn't recognize those sprawling layabouts as the immaculate and courteous assistants who serve you in the store.' It was the same with these airline people: usually we only see them in blue jackets and gold braid, but for their leisure they obviously dispense with their finery as quickly as possible. The illusion of uniformed elegance was shattered. We had a quick drink with them before going down to dinner and an early night.

Next day we caught the electric train from Yesilyurt to Serkici and walked through the bustling streets of Istanbul to St Sophia where we gazed upon this architectural miracle that had withstood military onslaughts and earthquakes and still stands, much as Justinian knew it, to this day.

Beverly described how on that fateful day in 1453 Mehmet's victorious troops slaughtered the people of Constantinople till the blood ran in rivers down the streets from the heights of Petra to the Golden Horn. The great cathedral was still thronged as the Turks overran the city; the service of mattins was being sung and the worshippers were praying to be delivered when the doors were battered down and the troops poured in. To stand in its vast silence today and think of the carnage that ensued when the congregation was almost torn to death as the captors fought over women and children, is to be reminded of one of the most shameful episodes in Christian history. Why no powerful princes helped Constantine, as he fought so heroically in the last days of the beleaguered city, probably has its origins deep in the original schism of the Western and Eastern halves of the Roman Empire.

St Sophia is the palpable example of what happens when a universality is broken. It is one of the saddest monuments in the western world, haunted for me with the same melancholy that pervades the Inigo Jones Banqueting House in Whitehall where another martyr, King Charles I, prepared for death. There are some buildings that are paradoxical. They appear mute, but when you think of what their walls have witnessed you realise they can still speak to you eloquently over the years.

Every day Beverly chose another area to investigate and we visited places like Justinian's Palace or the Suleiman Mosque

135

in the mornings and a resort in the afternoons. One of these was Heybeli in the Princess Islands, which we reached by boat from the Karokoy bridge. You could stroll round the beaches and find a sandy deserted cove, and as a taverna was never far away I could sip a glass of tea while Bev swam and did snorkel diving. But our favourite place was a little town called Menekse on the shore of the sea of Marmara, where we found a restaurant with tables outside under vine leaves and a proprietor who spoke English and went to no end of trouble seeing to our wants. He even arranged for us to hire a fisherman's boat for four shillings, in which we took turns to row round the bays.

All in all the Turkish holiday was very successful, though Beverly never grasped the pronunciation of Tesekkür which is Turkish for 'thank you'. It always came out as 'Tay she cocoa', but our smiling hosts never seemed to mind.

After Istanbul we flew to Crete, staying at a tatty hotel in Heraklion and visiting the Minoan sites. Knossos is particularly fascinating because part of the archaeological reconstruction of the great Palace shows the enormous columns coloured with the original scarlet dye and you are startled to realise that Greek architecture was all embellished in this gaudy fashion. When you gaze at the bleached-white stone pillars of antiquity you tend to think that's how they always looked, but of course they didn't, they were decorated with exotic colours which have been eroded by time. An agent in Heraklion with the glorious name of Ulysses Adamis arranged all our trips: Mahlia, Phaestos, and Sitea, and we were driven in a black Mercedes by a chauffeur called Stavros who was filling in between his studies at university by taking tourists round the island. Ulysses told us that when we stayed overnight in Sitea in Eastern Crete we could visit Topolu monastery and stay the night with the monks.

When we arrived I was amazed to see a Greek Orthodox priest on the battlements with a feather duster. Any cleaning seemed pointless to me because a hot wind blew everything back in his face. Another monk took us round the building, describing the mosaics, showing us the chapel and finally the cells in which we were to sleep. 'Only straw pallet beds are provided, but you are very welcome.'

Beverly suddenly said, 'No, we can't stay, we have to get back to Heraklion,' and practically flew out of the room.

136

Outside in the corridor I asked him why he'd turned down the accommodation. 'I saw the lice in his beard,' he said, 'and it turned me right off.' For the rest of the journey I felt as if I were itching in a thousand places.

At Fedhele Beverly went swimming and a young Greek boy gazed enviously at his flippers and snorkelling equipment. Our driver, Stavros, told Bev, 'He admires your swimming gear and wishes he could afford to buy such things,' whereupon Beverly presented the child with all the stuff. The boy's face was transfused with joy as he stammered his thanks and rushed off to his father's house nearby. 'That's put an end to your scuba-diving,' I told Beverly, but he said he could always buy some more and that anyway it was worth seeing the look of delight on that young face. Just as we were packing up the picnic things and loading everything back into the car, the boy reappeared with his father, both of them carrying armfuls of cucumbers and lettuces which they presented to us. Stavros explained that this was their crop and they were giving us all they could afford. It was very touching and it would have been graceless to refuse, so we drove back to Heraklion with enough greenstuff to supply the entire hotel.

We sailed from Crete on the SS *Bernina*, which was full of British snobs, and after three days we disembarked at Naples. It was like walking into a sauna. The wet heat was so oppressive that I had a perpetual headache. After dragging ourselves round some museums and the Galleria Umberto we decided to call it a day and get a plane back to London. It was 20° cooler at home and we felt relieved to be back.

Nevertheless those days away had established a set of new rhythms and I felt buoyant enough to start work for Gerald and Peter at Pinewood on another film. This time it was *Carry On Cowboy*. I was to play a corrupt judge and I thought I'd use the Hal Roach voice. I demonstrated it for the director and producer and though they weren't over-enthusiastic about the diction they thought it would be all right.

On the 13th of July 1965 I was tackling the first shots on location in a barn at Chobham. I used greying sidepieces and a moustache to make me look older. By the end of the first week one side of my face had become very painful and I realized that my American voice, which was spoken out of one side of the mouth, had taken my jaw out of alignment. I was stuck with it – in more ways than one – because whatever characterisation

137

you choose for the first day of filming you have to keep till the end. The doctor gave me some tablets and advised resting it as much as possible but it was the newspaper man at Baker Street Underground who gave me the best advice: 'Shut your mouth, tie a scarf tightly round your head and chin and go to bed.' It certainly did the trick and proved to be excellent advice from a most improbable source.

In *Carry On Cowboy*, Joan Sims played a Mae West-like saloon-owner, looking as if she'd been poured into a skin-tight gown, and Angela Douglas was the courageous gunslinger who saved the hero of the story, Jim Dale. He had to keep popping out of sewage manholes to shoot the villians. It was an engaging story line with a proper moral ending and to see an entirely British cast successfully emulating a 'western' was very satisfactory indeed. There was great attention to detail with all the riding done in the American style with special trainers brought in for the purpose. They had quite a job with me because on the one occasion I had to ride it was on my stomach. The gangsters sent me into the town trussed over the saddle.

There was a mock gambling scene in the saloon and I was at the gaming table with Peter Butterworth, the pair of us looking intense and menacing as we announced our cards, 'Mrs Bun the Baker' etc. from Happy Families. There was the reiterated cry, 'One for the pot' as we upped the ante, and at the end of the game a chamber-pot was brought from under the table. Every time this incongruous object appeared, we started giggling and spoiled quite a few takes.

I said, 'Sorry, Gerald, but you can't help laughing.'

He remarked drily, 'I'd rather hear it from the audience than from the cast.'

Towards the end of the picture when we had a day off, I met Joan and Angela in town and we all had lunch at the Grill and Cheese in Coventry Street which was still famed for its cheapness – soup, steak and salad and coffee, all for seven and sixpence.

When I asked the waiter if he would split the bill three ways, Joan expressed astonishment.

'Surely, Kenny, you're not going to ask the ladies to pay?'

'If you were ladies, you wouldn't be in *Carry Ons*.'

Angela joined in the protest. 'Surely you're not that mean!'

'Mean!' I echoed, counting out my contribution. 'I've got a burglar alarm on my dustbin.'

They both had to dig into their handbags and when we emerged on the pavement Joan began to harangue me. 'You're the last of the big spenders, you are!'

I quickly boarded a 53 bus which happened to be handy and laughingly bade them farewell as it sped away. Unfortunately the bus got held up at the traffic lights and Joan and Angela seized the opportunity and jumped on the platform pointing out to all the passengers, 'Here, it's that bloke from the *Carry Ons*! Fancy seeing him on a bus. They must pay him peanuts.' My embarrassment was their triumph and of course I wished I'd never divided the bill in the first place.

After the holiday in Turkey and Greece I saw a lot of Beverly because he'd found a play by Roger Longrigg called *The Platinum Cat* which he wanted to direct and which he thought provided a good role for me. The part was Bernard and the plot dealt with a man's obsession with his work causing marital problems. I thought it read amusingly enough but would need expert casting. Bev was confident we could achieve this and I became keen to do it.

My unfortunate experiences with the last two plays had left me uncertain about acting in the theatre and I was enormously heartened by the prospect of being directed by a chum and decided the best answer to hydrophobia was to jump in the deep end. So in September I started work on the play and was delighted to find that Bev had got Richard Williams to design the posters for it. During the four weeks of rehearsals I decided to diet because I wanted to effect a lean and youthful appearance for the stage. I managed to shed about 21 pounds. When I was being fitted for the trousers, the tailor said, 'It's very good to have a 28-inch waist when you're 39 years old,' and I was pleased with the compliment.

We opened in Brighton and had a fair reception; though faults were appearing I thought they could be ironed out as we became more familiar with the script. There were the usual inquests after the show with management and cast, extra rehearsals etc. and then the rewrites appeared, and I started seeing all the omens of doom that had surrounded the Orton production.

From Brighton we went to Oxford where the reviews were discouraging and then to Birmingham where they were even worse: J. C. Trewin, the critic, pronounced me 'inaudible'. We

139

opened in London at Wyndhams on the 16th of November 1965. The notices were universally bad and comments from friends ranged from sympathy to surprised dismay. Michael Codron expressed shock at my appearance. 'Why have you got so thin?' Gerald Thomas said, 'You look quite haggard – about as thin as the play.' Stan Walker asked, 'Why did you want to do a load of rubbish like this?' When Maggie Smith came backstage on the 30th, she said, 'The play is no good and you've got an impossible task! It must be exhausting for you; you're acting for everyone in the cast.' But she added a lovely postscript, 'I heard a group talking in the bar during the interval and they were interpreting the play for a French girl but she told them she understood all that you were doing because your face and body said it so well.' Peter Eade, too, was comforting. 'There is nothing for you to be ashamed of. I know the audiences are small but the management has agreed to cut the matinées in two weeks' time.'

When I went to the hairdresser's, however, the assistant bluntly said, 'I hear your show at Wyndhams is a flop,' and suddenly I realised that this was the plain unvarnished truth. The knowledge made me more depressed. I went off my food completely. A nervous stomach caused digestive problems, and by early December I caught a nasty bout of 'flu, alternately going hot and cold. When I was performing on the 6th of December I felt so faint I could hardly focus. I mistimed a piece of business on stage and cut my face just below the eye. I finished the performance bleeding and instead of walking home I got a taxi to the flat.

Next day I felt so ill I stayed in bed and telephoned the doctor who examined me. 'You are in no condition to go on performing,' he said, and instructed me to stay in bed, while he talked to the company. Some days later the management sent another doctor to examine me and after his report they announced they were withdrawing the play the following day.

I went to the London Clinic for X-rays and a blood analysis because both doctors suspected a shadow on the lung as well as anaemia. My spirits sank to zero and I was pervaded by listlessness. In the midst of this my friends were towers of strength. George Borwick came in to see me and counselled, 'You must get away from this murky climate and get into some sunshine and start eating properly again. Once you get the all-clear from the doctors about these tests, let me know and I

140

will ring my friend Joan Walker at Cook's. I should think somewhere like Beirut in the Lebanon would be suitable.'

Stanley Baxter was in Australia but I knew that he was leaving shortly to return to England. Moira gave me his telephone number and I talked to him. His reaction was swift. 'I can fly from Sydney to London via Beirut and meet you there. As soon as you know the dates, let me know. Don't worry about anything.'

Once the medical verdict was known and it turned out to be nothing serious, the doctor agreed with the holiday idea, and George Borwick pulled all the stops out for me, fixing a flight to Lebanon and a suitable hotel. I departed from Heathrow on the 17th of December at 8 am arriving in Beirut that evening at 6.30 pm. My room in the Hotel Phoenicia overlooked the bay and, apart from noisy air-conditioning, it suited me admirably.

For the first few days I spent the time leisurely strolling along the Corniche or sitting reading *Catch 22* on the hotel terrace. When I did sally forth into the town I found everything reminiscent of back streets in Istanbul: the same thronging crowds, street traders, music and smells. In the Place des Canons a youth pestered me for several blocks. 'I take you to the Turkish Bath with massage, you know sir, all that you like.' He looked disbelieving when I said I'd rather have a cup of tea and some aspirins.

Joan Walker of Cook's had told me to contact their man in Beirut, Mr Haddad, and I called on him to complain about the prices. 'Even the simplest meal at the Phoenicia hotel costs a fortune. Steak and half a bottle of Beaujolais is £4.10. I'm not going to last long on my travellers' cheques here.'

'But you're only supposed to sleep there, Mr Williams,' he told me. 'I will give you a list of suitable restaurants where you can eat very reasonably. Never eat in the hotel.'

After that I didn't. I took his advice and dined at a restaurant called Angelo's where a 3-course meal and a glass of wine came to thirty shillings.

On Christmas Day it was raining heavily when I set out in a cab to the airport and waited for Stanley's arrival. I saw him before he came out of the customs hall and he was miming horrific happenings through the glass partition. When we met he told me, 'That lovely Jaeger sweater Moira gave me! It's been lost. I know it was in my case when I packed in Australia, and now it's vanished. Of course the stuff is literally turned

141

over the customs people. You turn your head for a second and the next minute something's disappeared. I particularly liked that Jaeger sweater – it was perfect for the chilly evenings, you know. Don't think much of this dump. Is the weather always as bad as this!'

'Not all the time,' I told him as we struggled with the luggage to the taxi rank. 'Yesterday it was sunny and the temperature was up to nearly 70°.'

'Hmm, it's much warmer where I've come from,' he replied as we got into the car. 'Now how much is it at the Phoenicia?'

'About £18 to £20 a night.'

'I'm not paying that,' he retorted swiftly. Then he asked the driver, 'What is a reasonable hotel here?' and was told 'The Alcazar', so he stayed there for a quarter of the price.

After unpacking we went for lunch and I poured out all my woes to him. I told him about the disastrous tour, the flop in London and then my subsequent illness and loss of confidence. 'It's a temporary lapse,' he assured me. 'You may feel now that you'll never act again, that you've got no talent, that there's a jinx on you. But you simply have to live through the time when everything hurts. It's the same as I told you after your spell in hospital – the pain goes away eventually.'

Then he launched into a long account of his Australian tour and waxed lyrical about the country, especially Sydney. 'Now that's the place to retire to – vast sandy bays, and a warm sea, perfect for swimming. With the drophead coupé and the beach-house it could be idyllic and the climate is glorious all the year round. Mark my words, New South Wales is the place of the future.'

By the time I left him at the Alcazar I was convinced that the New World wasn't America but definitely Down Under.

The fact of Stanley's arrival in Beirut sent my spirits soaring – nothing is so valuable as old acquaintance and his lively companionship was exactly the sort of stimulus I needed. The next day he announced his intention of replacing the lost sweater and we wandered round the bazaar looking for something suitable. His eye lighted on a black woollen pullover and he asked the price. There ensued the endless haggling which seemed a way of life in the Levant and after a while Stanley shook his head and smiled regretfully. 'Let's walk away,' he muttered to me, 'they always call you back with a better offer.' And sure enough, we hadn't taken more than a few steps

142

before the vendor was calling out a compromise. In the end, the purchase was agreed at the English equivalent of 12/6d, and Stanley carried off his prize in triumph.

'It's a bargain,' he told me delightedly and after confessing to a feeling of jetlag it was agreed that we would meet for dinner in the foyer of the Phoenicia at 7 pm. 'I'll wear the black sweater,' he told me. 'It'll look very smart with a white shirt.'

You were conveyed to the reception area of the Phoenicia from the street by escalator into a magnificent marble hall where clusters of chairs and tables nestled under exotic plants and ornate fountains. I waited here keeping a weather eye out for Stanley's arrival. When he appeared he had the black sweater over his shoulders with the sleeves knotted round his neck and I asked him why he wasn't wearing it properly.

'I've been done,' he announced glumly. 'It's full of holes, I'll show you when we get outside. I'm not revealing it in all this grandeur.'

Out in the street he unfolded the garment and it was obvious he hadn't exaggerated. 'But it looked fine when you bought it,' I exclaimed.

'Yes, I mentioned that to my friends at the Alcazar. They said there is some brilliant sleight-of-hand involved in these markets – the article you select is deftly substituted when it's packaged so you come away with something which is similar but not what you've examined in the first place.'

I murmured sympathetically but he grinned and shrugged. 'Oh, what the hell, at least it keeps the shoulders warm, let's have a drink.'

We found a bar near the sea front and had just ensconced ourselves when an American sitting nearby suddenly yelled, '*Fast Lady*!' and Stanley turned enquiringly. The cry was repeated, '*Fast Lady*, am I right?' Stanley nodded. 'You were great in that picture, I saw it twice.' He was referring to a film in which Stanley played a very determined racing cyclist.

The American rose and came over to where we were sitting and insisted on buying more drinks, then recognised me and cried out, '*Carry On Sergeant* – oh, this is great! Two stars in one night! Oh you've got to meet my friends! They'll never believe me, they'll think I made it up.' Whereupon he rushed off and reappeared with more Americans who chorused *Fast Lady* as they gazed at Stanley rapturously and insisted on buying us more drinks and telling us all about their favourite

British films and the places they loved in England and their address in the United States. We never got to dinner at all. We were still there at closing time with the barmaid protesting that they'd lose their licence if we didn't go. It wasn't easy extricating ourselves and endeavouring to stand up straight but we staggered out somehow, clutching each other's shoulders unsteadily as we sang songs from Alice Faye movies ('No Love No Nothing') and laughed uproariously all the way back to the hotel.

Sore heads the next day taught us more sobering habits and thereafter we took it easily in Beirut. We used to walk along the Corniche to Long Beach and sit in the sun sipping non-alcoholic beverages, chatting to English expatriates, most of whom were from Bahrain, and confining our drinking to the odd glass of wine with the evening meal. The days passed pleasantly enough till it was time to get the plane back to London. This was a VC 10 and the BOAC crew were very kind to us both and we were taken to the airy cockpit and shown the magnificent view from this brilliantly designed aircraft.

By the time we were home it was 1966 and the fearful events of the past year were thankfully receding.

Chapter Eight

The beginning of 1966 saw me arranging another move for my mother. Louisa had never really enjoyed living in Kensington and though my sister Pat had shared the apartment with her to assuage the loneliness after my father's death, it hadn't worked out happily. After a long discussion between the three of us it was agreed that Pat would stay on at Brunswick Gardens because she needed to be near ICL – a firm she'd joined since her return from Australia – and that Louisa would move to Osnaburgh Street. She chose a flat there because it was back in an area she liked and it was near to her sister, Edith, at Baker Street, the two of whom met regularly.

I began another film at Pinewood on the 9th of January, this time *Carry On Screaming*, so I was busy going back and forth to the studios and rushing round in my spare time organising removals, decorations, carpets, curtains and all the paraphernalia of setting up a new home. By the 21st of January I saw Louisa safely settled in the flat and she expressed satisfaction with the second-floor location: 'I like being able to look out of the window on to the trees.' Louisa had always lived in the King's Cross area or Bloomsbury and now she was adjacent to all her old haunts.

Carry On Screaming at Pinewood meant a delightful reunion with lots of old chums, and I was especially pleased when the lighting cameraman Alan Hume told me it was good to have me back on the set. Gerald, too, gave me a warm-hearted welcome and I told him and Peter Rogers that in the nine years since we had started together no working relationship had ever been better. We had a newcomer to the team in Harry H. Corbett and when he told me he was suffering from a painful bunion I took off my shoe to show my own malformation. 'Cover it up,' cried Peter Butterworth. 'This is a film set not a surgical ward.'

Carry On Screaming was a spoof horror movie in which I played a scientist who'd created a Frankenstein monster with the aid of his sister. She was a Charles Addams-like voluptuary played with seductive guile by my erstwhile companion in revue, Fenella Fielding. I had a sinister appearance with a pallid make-up, sunken eyes and a facial twitch. The pair of us looked suitably ghoulish. In one scene we had to sit in a gig jogging along the road with the camera in the horse-shafts and Gerald instructed me to get 'very close to Fenella: it's a two-shot with just the faces in frame.' As I pushed in tightly, Fenella turned with devastating seriousness and asked, 'Why is your bum so hard? Do you leave it out at nights?' She had an uncanny knack for the devastating riposte and I've often quoted that remark as an example of her surrealist wit.

On the 7th of February I had a particularly tricky scene to play. The monster I had created had to turn on its master. I had to back away from the creature and fall into a boiling vat of noxious fluid. In fact, this was an enormous tank full of hot water with hidden pipes providing the necessary bubbles and steam machines creating the finishing effect. Gerald told me before the shot, 'When you fall in, go under the water. It will be all right if you take a deep breath first. Stay under the surface while we pan over the top, because you're supposed to drown in the vat. Don't worry about resurfacing because I'll have the stunt men standing by to pull you out.'

As soon as he called 'Action' the monster advanced according to plan. I babbled out horror-stricken pleas for mercy and retreated, tripped and fell into the cauldron. I was so busy acting I forgot all about taking a deep breath before submerging. I went beneath the bubbling water, sank to the bottom and stayed there. They got the shot all right and then Gerald told the stunt men to jump in and get me out. I must have become momentarily unconscious, for I was hardly aware of the rescue until I was safely deposited in a chair on the set and wrapped in towels. Only then did I discover that I had no trousers.

I asked, bewildered, 'What happened?'

It was explained that one diver had pulled my legs and the other had pulled my arms. 'When they got you to the surface your trousers and pants had come off – you lost the lot!'

'It's extraordinary; I don't remember anything after falling in. It was all over in a flash!'

'It was more than a flash when they pulled you out,' laughed Gerald.

'But the cameras weren't turning then, surely – you cut, didn't you?'

'Of course I cut! Don't want to frighten the audience to death.'

146

At lunchtime I went to the bar feeling I deserved a drink. I said, 'Mine's a large one,' and forestalled Peter Butterworth's joke by adding, 'And I'm not boasting, I'm ordering.'

On the 9th of February I went to Studio One in Oxford Street for the trade show of *Carry On Cowboy*. The finished picture turned out to be my favourite of the series. Sid James astride a horse looked as if he'd been a cowboy all his life; his expertise with six-shooters and his laconic delivery made him perfect for the role. I have never seen him better. Sid always found praise slightly embarrassing and I knew he distrusted the superlatives actors often use, but when I saw him afterwards I grasped his hand warmly and said, 'You made that part, Sid,' and I meant it. He held me at arm's length and looked searchingly before he said quietly, 'Thanks, Kenny. I appreciate that.' I told Peter Rogers, 'It's the best one of the lot. At last the *Carry Ons* have found the juveniles. Jim Dale and Angela are this year's screen couple, and all the character actors are marvellous, including me.'

I telephoned Gerald who was on the set at Pinewood and congratulated him and then I went to lunch and celebrated with Peter Eade. He was quieter in his enthusiasm but he agreed that it was a successful picture. 'That meeting with Hal Roach wasn't wasted. With his voice and those whiskers it provided the basis for your first character role in a film.' I drank to that and told him I felt more buoyant than I had for years.

The radio series of *Round The Horne* started in March and I began increasingly to enjoy the solo spots like Rambling Sid, where I was able to hold the audience on my own and know that the success of the performance depended on no one else. I began to wonder about my acting ambitions. Was I mistaken in wanting a success in the legitimate theatre? Apart from school plays, hadn't I begun as a stand-up comic in troop shows? Shouldn't I perhaps be seeking a way back to that original path? The last three flops had left me determined never to be vulnerable to that sort of hurt again. Peter Eade kept insisting that I read the plays which managements sent me, but I invariably found excuses for rejecting them. Everything about the idea of casting and direction frightened me. Finding the kind of like-minded people such as our marvellous

147

threesome in *Public Eye* seemed a once-in-a-blue-moon affair. The average production seemed to be hit-and-miss as far as true co-operation was concerned and I began to think the term director should have commas round it, so many of them were bogus.

Yet in spite of the failures I must have been quite fashionable because Binkie Beaumont wrote, 'All I want is a splendid part for you in a play. I never stop reading scripts but little seems to present itself. I am now reaching the stage of reading all the Shaw, Galsworthy and Pinero plays . . .' A letter from Peter Bridge suggested Somerset Maugham. He'd discovered that the original title of *Home and Beauty* was *Too Many Husbands*. 'You have inferred to me and to Peter Eade that you want to do something different so why in heaven's name can't you see the enormous possibilities in this play? The part of Freddie is a classic originated by Ronald Squire.' Michael Codron envisaged a revival, too, and took me to see a production of the play *The Gay Lord Quex*. But nothing fired my imagination.

The radio series came to a temporary halt in June and I received a postcard from Joe Orton at Marina Residence, 21 Rue de Meuchamps, Tangier: 'Wonderful weather etc. I've taken an apartment for one month though I plan to stay for three months until July. Love Joe. K sends love too. P.S. Marina Residence sounds quite Edna-ish but it isn't really.' (This was a reference to 'Edna Wellthorpe' the pseudonym under which he wrote outrageous letters to various newspapers and individuals.)

The missive intrigued me and on the 11th of June I flew out to Morocco for a holiday. In those days Tangier tended to be full of English people. Government fiscal restrictions at that time meant we could only take fifty pounds abroad but one of the reasons Tangier was so popular was that there were expatriates there who gave you dirhams which you repaid in pounds when they visited Britain. I found an apartment midway between the beach and the Boulevard Pasteur, and a kindly man called Baudouin showed me how to use the Calor gas stove, though I had little intention of cooking. It was only a stroll away from the Café de Paris where I often sat at a pavement table with Joe and Kenneth Halliwell watching the world go by. For them that was generally in the evenings. In the mornings they frequented the Windmill which was a beach

148

café on the front. The owner was frequently cross with them because they spent practically nothing. They brought along their own sandwiches and fruit and they would sit on his terrace throwing their orange peel and banana skins over the garden wall and then ask for a glass of water when they'd finished. During the day they seldom touched alcohol, unlike most of the clientèle in the Windmill who seemed to be half drunk from early morning onwards.

Joe and Kenneth's apartment at the Rue de Meuchamps was as threadbare and frugal as Noel Road and I told them they might just as well have stayed in London. But, as Joe said, the climate was better. He enjoyed the langorous heat of Morocco, the sunbathing and the swimming. 'We went for a dip to the diplomatic beach. An Englishman called Hubert invited Ken and me to join him for a picnic. He had this hamper and a huge Rolls-Royce, the wine in special coolers and everything. He wouldn't change, like us, on the beach. He lowered the blinds in his car and disrobed in private. Then he came out wearing his white towel robe with purple lapels – very grave and majestic. These Moroccans walking by pointed at him and laughed, "Vous êtes une femme!' but Hubert boomed out "Pas une femme! Un Roman!" It was quite a moment I can tell you.' Joe had risen to declaim the lines and the tiny performance created a perfect picture of the remembered incident.

A message from Peter Eade reached me in Tangiers and brought me back to London to do something which I had never before attempted. I had been asked to appear on the Eamonn Andrews show and Peter was anxious that I should accept. I had always refused to appear on television chat shows because I thought working ad lib was dangerous. I have never possessed the ability to marshal argument, my conversation meanders and flits and I thought it would be unsuitable for a chat show. Peter argued about it till I gave in and on the 26th of June I went down to Teddington Studios full of fear and apprehension. My diary records, 'Stomach going over and over – Oh the thousand natural shocks that flesh is heir to.'

Looking back on my reactions I'm surprised to read about my trepidation. Appearing on a chat show today is like falling off a log as far as I'm concerned and after accepting such an engagement I usually forget about it till the appointed hour. But, then, I lost a night's sleep, worried about my appearance and constantly asked myself, 'Will I know what to say?'

149

When I got to the studio, before going on, I talked to Dora Bryan who calmed my fears. She is a stalwart on such occasions and told me not to worry about it, just be myself. When Shirley Bassey appeared with her manager, Kenneth Hume, there ensued such irate disagreements about the scoring of musical arrangements that I soon forgot my nervousness. I went on thinking it was a good thing I didn't have to sing, and everything went very well. Eamon was the sort of host who did his homework. The façade of easy-going charm hid a computer-like mind stored with information. Even if I strayed off the subject he brought it deftly back in order to restore the tag line and he ensured that all the right anecdotes were related in their proper order.

Peter was delighted with my performance. 'I told you you could talk well in public if you wanted to – you were fluent and you were funny.' His verdict was obviously endorsed by other people because he was telephoned by lots of producers the following day and suddenly there were several offers of work in entirely new spheres for me. The one which interested Peter most came from Tom Sloane at Television Centre. He was organising a project called International Cabaret for BBC2 and wanted a host for the series. Peter thought this was the right vehicle for me. 'You've told me how much you enjoy working a house on your own' (the Rambling Sid bits on the radio show had been so successful they wanted me to do a record of them) 'now here is your chance to handle an audience in cabaret. It's the perfect ambience for a stand-up comedian. It will be fine as long as you don't gabble.' This last proviso was a favourite of his. Speaking too quickly was something I was often accused of by agents and producers alike. I had been reluctant about the Eamonn Andrews show for this reason, and Peter had proved me wrong, so I decided he might well be right, too, about this new departure. Certainly I wanted to steer clear of the theatre and solo performing seemed a challenging alternative. So I said yes, and signed a contract for eight episodes.

Probably one of the things that swayed me was Tom Sloane's suggestion that I should work on the scripts with John Law. 'I think he'd be the ideal editor for this because we want your kind of conversation – narrative rather than jokes – and it needs to be put into shape so that you do just enough to whet the audience's appetite between each act.' John Law had been one of the writers in the revue *Pieces of Eight* and we knew each other well so there was no ice to be broken. He was an amiable, fuzzy-haired Scot with a dry sense of humour, lots of patience and tremendous optimism. I worked with him in a tiny office at the Television Centre where we fashioned the material for the series. The first show was performed on the 5th of July 1966 and the nervous tension throughout made me self-conscious. I talked through quite a few laughs. Do this often enough and they stop coming. At the end I felt that I had failed miserably. Georgia Brown was top of the bill that night and she said, 'You can't judge yourself – there's the audience at the tables round the stage and there's another audience in the auditorium watching them – you need to see a rerun on the screen.' I was unconvinced.

Tom Sloane came round with the Controller of Channel Two, David Attenborough. When Tom smiled and congratulated me, I said, 'You're being kind – I think I was bad in the show.' 'You are wrong,' he told me. 'You concentrate so much on what you're doing you can't take in the reaction of the entire house. It's the total effect on screen, that's what we're interested in. You'll find when you see it that it works very well. I think you'll be pleased.'

Three days later I was shown a play-back and my fears were quelled. I looked composed throughout and the laughter was there whatever I had imagined. I did the second show on the 12th of July and this time it was live. I was more confident and acquitted myself well. Gordon Jackson telephoned afterwards to congratulate me. I was tremendously heartened by this and went off to Hampstead for supper with him and Rona. Gordon said, 'It will become the sort of show where they're waiting for the acts to finish and for you to come on.'

At the end of July I was very touched when Maggie Smith asked me to take part in a documentary programme about her work, as part of a BBC TV series, *Acting in the Sixties*. The producer was Hal Burton and he told me, 'There'll be a long interview with Maggie first and then I would like to bring you into it talking about your early days with her. I think it would be enlightening if you could jointly discuss how you achieved such spontaneity together in the Shaffer plays.'

As soon as I turned up at the Television Centre on the day of the shooting I realized Maggie was nervy and highly strung. She had just completed an interview which she described as 'a

151

1½ hour inquisition' and greeted me like the lone Englishman in the middle of Red Square. The programme people watch on the television screen is very often a distillation of what the camera recorded. The final edited version which is shown may be only a segment of a whole mass of dialogue and naturally a producer selects what he thinks are the best sections; but the serious probing interview is exhausting for thinking actors because it subjects them to psychoanalytical questions, expects seriousness and yet requires very entertaining replies.

When we came to do our bits together I stressed the need for creating the illusion of immediacy in acting and I talked about the controlled hysteria which is the basis for so much of Maggie's comedy. I thought it made sense but that it was conversationally woolly and repetitive. When I was asked afterwards if I would agree to its being printed in book form for BBC Publications, I demurred ('Oh no, it will be full of oohs and aahs'), but they assured me that it read very well. And surprisingly it did.

This was an interlude – the only harking back to straight acting in the year – for the rest of the time was spent in gruelling sessions with John Law cobbling together lines for the solo spots in *International Cabaret*. Some of the days were barren and we would sit despondently bereft of ideas and committing little or nothing to paper. At other times we really got the bit between our teeth and the writing flowed. Occasionally a conversational gambit provided the stimulus or a recounted event spurred us to action. Talking about troop entertainers in Singapore, I told John Law about a lady accordionist who'd squeezed the instrument across her bosom, catching the material of her dress in its concertina folds and her pique when the comic in the show remarked, 'You must have pleated tits, Maudie.' That, coupled with a true story about a girl who turned up every year for auditions with Tennents and never accepted a job, led us into a sequence for *International Cabaret* where the character of Maudie Fittleworth was born. It occurred in one of the rambling monologues that were typical of my style in the show, and went like this:

> I went round to meet the famous scriptwriter, Boris Stakvitch. The door was opened by this extraordinary creature who looked like a floor mop. Figure

like a beanpole with a ginger wig on top. There were no ankles; the legs simply continued on into a scruffy pair of plimsolls. She looked like a do-it-yourself famine. I thought, surely this bedraggled wraith is not employed by Boris Stakvitch, author of so many Hollywood epics? Perhaps I'd come to the wrong house? She stood there quizzing me under severely plucked eyebrows, volunteering no information. I feigned delight and smiled disarmingly.

'And who are you?'

'I am the cellist-cum-char.'

'Cellist-cum-char,' I echoed. 'I didn't know cellists did charring.'

'Oh yes, that's why they engage me. I do the low dusting and the odd Celtic lament by the bedside.'

'Are you doing it by the bedside of Boris Stakvitch, the famous writer?'

'That's right. He likes a lament to lull him off.'

'Don't we all, if it comes to that. Do you live in?'

'I couldn't very well live out and do the Celtic Lament by the bedside. I'm not al fresco.'

'You're not Al Jolson either, if appearances are anything to go by.'

'You'd be surprised!' she cried. 'I can go right down to baritone. I can do Ol' Man River'. Whereupon she began bawling, 'You and me, we sweat and strain . . .'

I quickly interrupted 'Yes thank you, riveting, but please don't mention sweat and strain. I've got this thing about BO.'

'We've all got it,' she asserted. 'How else would our little doggies tell us apart? I've studied these things. I know about canine characteristics. I also do poodle clipping.'

'Well, you are the busy bee, aren't you. What with your cello and your charring and your poodle parlour.'

'Why shouldn't a woman be versatile?' she asked aggressively. 'For years you've had your Jack of all Trades — now you've got your Jill.'

'Of all trades?'

'Yes, there's not a trade I can't turn my hand to — I even do French polishing on the side.'

153

'Oh I had a girl for that. She did all the parquet flooring, made the carpets slide everywhere, nearly ruined my coccyx. I don't want any more of that thank you, but I am partial to the cello and I do fancy the odd Celtic lament by the bedside. You must pop round to my place sometime, I've got terrible myopia.'

'You mean insomnia.'

'No I mean myopia. I can't read the music.'

'What's that got to do with it?'

'Well, obviously if I could read the music I'd play the Celtic lament for myself, you stupid great Nelly!'

'Don't call me Nelly, call me Ermyntrude. Ermyntrude Smythson actually, but I also go under Gummer for accountancy."

'You're into that as well, are you?'

'Of course, many of my clients ask me to handle their tax returns, and don't forget I come under deductible expenses.'

I thought privately that with her figure there wasn't much to deduct but aloud I said, 'Well, it's certainly a change from cellist-cum-char.'

'Not really,' she replied winking hugely. 'I'm still on the fiddle!'

Her laughter continued as I ascended the stairs to the first floor where I found Boris Stakvitch reclining on a chaise longue with sheets of paper scattered on the floor around him.

'What a curious cleaning woman you have,' I exclaimed and he peered over his horn-rims saying, 'My cleaning is done by a man.'

'But that woman who opened the door . . . ?'

'That was Maudie Fittleworth. I've been interviewing her for a part.'

'You could have fooled me. She is a brilliant actress.'

'I agree, but I can't get her for the role.'

'Why not?'

'She only does auditions.'

On the 12th of August, Bill Cotton, who was then Head of the variety side of Light Entertainment at BBC TV came into the office where I was working with John Law and commented on how well the weekly shows were going. He felt it would be lunatic to stop the series just when it was starting to gel, and asked me not to leave after the eighth show but to go on with it to the end of the year.

This enthusiasm, after only six episodes had been transmitted, was a gratifying surprise, but when I discussed it with Peter Eade he pointed out that future dates were complicated. 'You've got the film coming up in September – *Don't Lose Your Head* – with Gerald and Peter, you know. Their films always have a tight schedule and I don't think they would agree to release you early from the studios so that you could get back to London in time to do the Cabaret show.'

Of course I felt that my first loyalty was to the film committment, and I left it to Peter to sort out. When I saw Bill Cotton again I told him about the complications but he waved it all airily aside. 'Don't worry about the film, concentrate on the television series, that's what keeps you in the public gaze, and that's what makes you a name; it is the medium of the future.' In the end there was no clash because Peter and Gerald agreed to let me go early on the *International Cabaret* days, and so I was able to do the film as well as the TV series.

Before starting at Pinewood I embarked on another new venture. I made a record for Decca entitled 'Kenneth Williams in Season'. This came about because of meeting Ned Sherrin years before when he'd shared an apartment full of actors, including my old chum Peter Nichols, on Chelsea Embankment. Since that period he had introduced the satirical *That Was The Week That Was* to BBC TV and was involved in a host of other activities. In collaboration with Caryl Brahms he had prepared some amusing lyrics for a Yuletide record including a satirical number called 'Drop your Portcullis for Christmas'. The three of us had several sessions together talking over various ideas for other songs, including a '60s version of 'Good King Wenceslas' and a soprano being rudely interrupted by me while she tried singing the ballad, 'I Saw Three Ships'. We got together with composer Eddie Braden and on the 5th of September went to Decca studios in Lansdowne Road for the recording session.

It all went surprisingly smoothly, everyone was pleased with the results and we finished up in a nearby pub having celebratory drinks afterwards. I told Eddie Braden, 'I thought it

155

was all going to be much more difficult than that – after all I'm not a professional singer – I know nothing about music.' 'Maybe', he replied, 'but you've got a very good ear,' which pleased me greatly.

I started filming *Don't Lose Your Head* at Pinewood on the 12th of September. It was a send-up of *The Scarlet Pimpernel* and the opening sequences were mainly shot in a huge open-air set of a square round the guillotine, and during the second week I was with Sid James – who was playing the English rake-turned-rescuer – when a call-boy arrived saying there was an important telephone call for me, they'd rung three times, could I go back to the studios to take it? I hurried off. It was Tony Hancock on the line. He had taken the Festival Hall and urgently wanted to know if I would do the snide character in the Test Pilot sketch from *Hancock's Half-Hour* with him on stage there. I was astonished at the request. He had never disguised his abhorrence for this particular voice in his radio show, dismissing it as 'cardboard comedy not based on truth'. Now here he was asking me to perform what he had previously castigated. I blethered a bit to cover the initial shock and said I'd have to call my agent to see if the dates fitted and then let him know. In fact I telephoned Peter Eade to acquaint him with the facts and asked him to get in touch with Tony for me and say I wasn't available.

When I returned to the set Sid James asked me, 'What was so urgent that you had to rush to the phone, Kenny?'

I told him and he was amazed. 'You're joking, aren't you?'

'No, he says he's taken the Festival Hall and wants to do some of the old radio scripts.'

'But you're not going to do it are you!'

'No, I'm not.'

'You'd be mad to work with him again, the man is a megalomaniac.' Sid wasn't given to hyperbole and at the time I agreed with him. Looking back on it now I think that the apparent selfish behaviour was only the outward sign of an inner turmoil. Hancock wanted to cut himself off from the conventional concepts in search of a totally new approach to his work. His praise for the documentary-like reality of Jacques Tati's *Monsieur Hulot's Holiday* was significant. Tony was vainly seeking comedy in life itself, whereas the

156

Beyond Our Ken was first broadcast in 1958. The team, clockwise from top,
Betty Marsden, Douglas Smith, Eric Merriman, K.W., Kenneth Horne,
Hugh Paddick and Bill Pertwee.

First and second left, K.W. & Maggie Smith, in *Share My Lettuce*, which opened in London at the Lyric Hammersmith in 1957.

With George Borwick in Morocco.

Carry on Teacher, the third in the series, 1959.

With Maggie Smith sightseeing near Stratford-on-Avon, 1962.

With Charles Hawtrey in *Carry on Jack*, 1963.

L–R: Aunt Edith, Charles Hawtrey, K.W., and Louisa on the set of *Carry on Cleo*, Pinewood Studios, 1964.

On location with Sid James in *Carry on Cowboy*, 1965.

Carry On: Follow that Camel: L–R: Peter Butterworth, K.W., Jim Dale and
Phil Silvers. (Reproduced by courtesy of The Rank Organisation plc.)

With Hattie Jacques in *Carry on Doctor*, 1967. (Reproduced by courtesy of The Rank Organisation plc.)

Joe Orton, K.W., and Kenneth Halliwell on the terrace of the Windmill beach café, Tangier, 1965.

Ingrid Bergman as Lady Cicely Waynflete in *Captain Brassbound's Conversion*
Cambridge Theatre, 1970.

With Louisa wearing her WRVS long-service medal on her 80th birthday.

Sharing a joke with Stanley Baxter at a voice-over session for Richard Williams, 1980.

performer requires the alchemy of the story-teller who knows that we need art lest we perish from the truth.

The filming stretched on to the end of October and thereafter it was a relief to have only one set of lines to learn every week for the television series. My social life remained much the same. I saw Stanley and Moira, Gordon and Rona and Andrew and Susan pretty regularly. Andrew now had a baby son, Mark, and I was asked to be the godfather. An old chum, Henry Davies, with whom I'd worked in the Welsh Pageant at Cardiff back in 1951, had agreed to be a sponsor at the christening and I'd roped in Nora Stapleton as well. She was a friend from *The Buccaneer* days and we'd never lost touch. At the christening the baby cried in his mother's arms but when I took him to the font he was quiet, and the vicar said, 'They're always better with a man.' I nodded gravely.

I had wanted Louisa to be there but her WVS work kept her away, and I always encouraged her to busy herself since she'd taken to living alone. She was enjoying her new flat. I saw her at least once a week and heard all about her voluntary work, her Old Time Dance club and the regular jaunts with her sister Edith. It had been a very wise move for her to leave Kensington and there had been an enormous improvement in her general health and appearance.

Of the several letters pasted in my 1966 diary two are of note. One is from Joe Orton, dated 16th October, saying that the new production of *Loot* was 'an unqualified success' and was going to the Criterion Theatre in November. 'I hope this won't affect our friendship,' he wrote. I suppose he thought I might resent not being asked to play the role he had written for me but of course I didn't. That was all in the past, and I was delighted to hear of his new success. Terence Rattigan's judgement of the play – 'a superb comedy of manners' – had been vindicated. At the end of his letter he said, 'I haven't rung you because Kenneth says you're working on the film and learning lines on Sundays,' which is a measure of the consideration I always received from him and Halliwell.

The other letter is from Marty Feldman and Barry Took, writers of *Round The Horne*. They had sent me an outline for a TV series which I had declined because, with *International Cabaret* every week, I felt I had enough on my plate. Their reply was delightfully amicable, 'We enjoy R.T.H. too much to disturb the pleasant relationship we have with you. It is a case

157

of chacun à son goût: that's yer actual French! Yours till the stars lose their glory, Marty and Barry – spinsters of this parish.'

I was still working on scripts for *International Cabaret* in November as well as performing it and I was involved in another record project, again for Decca. This time it was for an LP of original songs by Myles Rudge and Ted Dicks. The orchestral arrangements by Barry Booth were ingeniously colourful but not easy to sing because they ornamented rather than stated the tune and I found it difficult to sustain the melody line. In the 'Mesopotamian Tango' I wanted to sound like a sort of Victorian strangulated tenor but my voice kept cracking up on the high notes and eventually I had to use a different vocal characterisation. 'Minnie Dyer' was a straight-forward West Country ballad, and a charming satire about computers, 'Above All Else', lent itself to a Cowardesque delivery. There was a Cockney number, 'Three Cheers for Charlie', sending up Labour MPs elevated to the peerage, that required all the gusto of a Harry Champion. But the one I liked best, 'The Sound of Children', was done with lavish sentimentality and organ accompaniment. On the record sleeve Myles Rudge wrote, ' "Mesopotamian Tango" may revive poignant memories for some and it's interesting to note that Mr Williams had the entire studio floor covered with sand before recording it.'

Well, I don't think I was quite as authentic as that; if the floor was covered in anything it must have been perspiration because the temperature in the studio, plus my own exertions, made it very hot indeed. When finally put together, the LP owed much to the producer, David Platz, and all of us were pleased with the record. Excerpts were played on various radio programmes long afterwards and it was good to find that the humour hadn't dated one iota. The studio sessions were spread over a period from the 7th to the 16th of December and apart from television that completed my work for the year.

I spent the evening of the 31st with Gordon and Rona at Hampstead and we toasted the New Year in champagne together. I wrote in my diary, 'My first year spent entirely out of the theatre and I haven't even missed it: I have kept busy with the radio, the two films and 21 episodes of the television series. I have successfully achieved stand-up comedy and the satisfaction of getting laughs on my own – no new friends . . . still the old and probably the best ones.'

158

Chapter Nine

In 1967 the run of *International Cabaret* was extended and I did ten more programmes which lasted from January to March. Again John Law and I prepared a lot of new material and we worked pretty speedily with the penultimate script completed by the second week of January. We tried to accomplish as much as we could before John went off to Rome to work on a new Peter Sellers' film.

About this time I had a call from Leslie T. Jackson who produced the TV panel game *Call My Bluff*. He told me that Frank Muir was unwell and asked if I would take over the captaincy of his team on the show until he was able to return. Frank had often popped into the little office where John and I laboured over our scripts and more than once he'd helped us out with ideas as well as encouragement, so I had no hesitation in saying yes. I was very touched when Frank telephoned from hospital to thank me for taking over at such short notice. I did the first programme on the 15th of January and it all began beautifully. I had two chums on my team: Dickie Wattis and Dilys Laye with whom I'd worked at Pinewood and they both entered splendidly into the spirit of the thing.

The game went well but my team lost and then things went wrong for me. There was a hospitality room where one of the guests, a woman, asked me, 'What does it feel like to be a loser?' I said something like, 'It doesn't matter, it's only a game,' and she announced firmly, 'Nobody likes losing.'

'Rubbish,' I replied. 'I am a very good loser and I showed it in my performance on the box.'

She said, 'There is no such thing as a good loser.'

I said crossly, 'Oh, do think for a minute before you make such wanton assertions! What about Jan Smuts – he lost the war but behaved most graciously afterwards.'

'No,' she told me, 'he won.'

'The Boer War?' I asked.

'Yes,' she affirmed, 'He won!'

Finding myself faced with such invincible ignorance I retreated with a polite excuse about having to go to the lavatory. The entire episode left me very depressed. It wasn't until the next day that I realised I should have quoted Wellington to

159

her – 'If you believe that you'll believe anything'. But alas, that was *l'esprit d'escalier*.

The second *Call My Bluff* went well and provided another reunion with Juliet Mills who was on my team and whose company I always enjoyed. For the last one, on the 12th of February, I got Joe Orton onto the panel and he was very successful. All his bluffs worked brilliantly. I said to him afterwards that he'd made his definitions sound utterly convincing, fooling everybody. 'Well,' he reminded me, 'I did start off as an actor.'

Gordon Jackson, too, was on my team and all his ploys also worked splendidly. My team won and I was quite exultant in the hospitality room afterwards, and when we were joined by Kenneth Halliwell, I invited them all to dinner. I told them about the woman asking what it felt like to be a loser, and Joe wanted to know what I'd said.

'Oh nothing witty, I'm afraid, I just said I had to go.'

Halliwell said, 'You should have said to her "*You'll* have to go".'

Looking back on it I think he was right.

John Law returned from Rome and we continued working on the cabaret scripts. He used to come to the performances with a portable tape machine so that we could have an aural record of how the material had been received, see what had got laughs and what had died the death. He was a joy to have around backstage. At one show he was standing in the wings while I was on stage in the middle of one of my spots and I suddenly said, 'Oh dear, I've forgotten my lines, what should I say, John?' He stared at me with incredulous bewilderment. I called out, 'Could you bring the script on, ducky?' and he came on to the stage proferring me the page. Then I said, 'It's all right, I was larking about. I know it really but I just thought the audience would like to see a genius!' They laughed and clapped and John bowed and then he took the rolled-up script and bashed me smartly over the head before exiting into the wings. When I came off I told him, 'That was quite a blow you caught me, and it disarranged my hair, you know.'

He said crossly, 'I was furious, I really thought you had dried. I didn't know it was a gag.'

'I'm always talking about you so I thought it would be nice for them to see you.'

160

'I didn't want to be seen like that?'

'Why not?'

'I wasn't prepared?'

'What sort of preparation do you want?'

'I should have been made up.'

In all the years I'd known him that was the reply I least expected.

'Surely you're not vain,' I laughed, but when he replied, 'You can be very insensitive,' I saw that the joke had misfired.

There was a curious echo the next day. I had lunch with Andrew Ray and we went to the Old Bailey afterwards. We tried three courts and they were all trial preambles or summings-up – no cross-examinations which was all that interested us both. So we left in a disgruntled mood. Outside it had been raining and as we waited to cross the road at the lights a man swung his folded umbrella so that it hit me. I rounded on him.

'Watch where you're swinging your umbrella!'

'I'm sorry.'

'I don't want your filthy muck on me.'

'Sorry.'

'You stupid great poof.'

As I walked away I saw that Andrew was scarlet and I asked him why.

'It was embarrassing the way you went on about it. The bloke had apologised. I thought you were very insensitive.'

'I was furious.'

'There was no need to be so rude. If someone called you an old poof what would you think?'

'The thinking is done in retrospect,' I said excusing the contretemps but feeling I'd been chastised twice over.

Nemesis was imminent because shortly afterwards I was brought low with an appalling bout of influenza; again I was alternately hot and cold and every bone and joint ached. I managed the *Round the Horne* broadcast and the *International Cabaret* episodes and saw John Musgrove, the ENT surgeon, on the 6th of March. 'You've got an infected left antrum, chum,' he said. 'I'll give you these drops and an antibiotic to be taken every four hours; you'll have to get up in the night and take it. I'm afraid you're going to feel a lot worse before you get better.'

I went to see Joe Orton and Kenneth Halliwell to tell them

161

of my woes but instead they told me some of theirs. They had just returned from Tripoli. 'It was disastrous,' said Joe. 'A nightmare,' said Ken. 'The natives were all right but the English and the Americans were awful.' Joe said, 'The hotels were all miles away from the town. Not that we could get into any of them, they were all full. We were forced to spend the night on a terrible cruise ship paying an exorbitant rate for a tiny cabin, over ten pounds! Ugh it was disgusting. We got the same plane back as we came out on.' 'With the same crew,' K.H. put in. 'We told the stewardess how ghastly it all was and she looked surprised and said, "Oh, didn't you know?" Apparently everyone except us was aware that Tripoli was a hell-hole. It is disgraceful, travel brochures should warn one about these tourist traps!'

Before I left Joe gave me a copy of *Loot* which he inscribed, 'To Kenneth, the original Truscott, with love from Joe', and that gave me a great deal of pleasure. He also showed me two letters he'd written under pseudonyms to *Plays and Players* magazine. The first pseudonym was a new one to me, 'Donald H. Hartley', and the letter began: 'I take great exception to the Green Room piece in *P & P*. Mr David Benedictus in my opinion shows a lamentable want of tact in suggesting Joe Orton's *Loot* was not the best play of 1966' and ended: 'Really if every pip-squeak circus pony were to give awards for the Horse of the Year, goodness knows where we should be!'

The other was from our old friend Edna Wellthorpe, the persona he'd invented to typify the respectability of the Home Counties. 'I agree that no one should seriously nominate as the play of the year a piece of indecent tomfoolery like *Loot*. Drama should be uplifting. The plays of Joe Orton have a most unpleasant effect on me. I was plunged into the dumps for weeks after seeing *Entertaining Mr Sloane*. I saw *Loot* with my young niece, we both fled in horror and amazement well before the end. I could see no humour in it. Yet, it is widely advertised as a rib-tickler . . .'

The magazine published both letters, believing them to be genuine. Joe's choice phraseology was evident throughout and reflected the authentic sound of the characters in his plays.

The *International Cabaret* series finished in March 1967 and Bill Cotton said he wanted to bring it back from September to December for another fifteen episodes. *Round The Horne* was also enjoying a great success every week, running from January until the end of June.

In April I had costume fittings for the uniform of a commandant in the Foreign Legion and the location shooting for the film *Follow That Camel* started on the 1st of May at Camber Sands, Rye. This was the first time we had had an American actor in the team; Phil Silvers, who played the Sergeant. He told us he was having trouble with his contact lenses. 'I lost one in the soup at the Dorchester. Another time I was on all fours searching under the bed, growling with frustration, when the maid came in and asked if I was doing a dog impression.' His third mishap was losing one at Camber Sands. Jim Dale, Peter Butterworth and I all scrabbled to help him but we failed to retrieve it.

The beach at Rye was used to simulate the Sahara and the cameraman had to be careful to miss any sort of recognisable English shoreline. Gerald was again lucky with the weather, the sun obligingly peeping out at the right intervals. We were accommodated in a nearby hotel and on the first night I had dinner there with Jim Dale, Gerald and Phil Silvers. 'I've got second wind', Phil said. 'That marching up and down on the sea-front all day exhausted me. I hit the sack when I got back after the shooting. I nearly didn't come to the dining-room tonight but I thought, I'm not going to let this thing beat me! You'll have to read the menu for me – I lost my contact lenses on the beach, remember. Last time someone had to read for me was when I did a Paul Robeson impression and I couldn't see the cue card.' He began to sing 'Ol' Man River' and all the other diners in the room turned and stared in surprise. After a few bars he stopped and suddenly asked Gerald, 'Am I boring you?' I made a face, and Gerald kicked me under the table and said, 'No, not at all.' Phil continued, 'Cos the thing I can't stand is a bore!' Gerald kicked me again and said he couldn't stand bores either.

'Yeah, a bore is a thief! You know that?' continued Phil. 'He's a thief because he steals your time.'

Jim Dale, scarcely suppressing laughter, said that was very true. 'You bet your sweet life, it's true,' said Phil. 'Time is money.' Gerald said, 'Money is time.' I chorused 'A stitch in time saves nine'. And Gerald said, 'You must excuse me,' and left the table. I followed him into the gents where he was doubled up over a wash-basin laughing. 'It's terrible for me,' he said. 'I'm in front of him and I can see you and Jim pulling faces but *he* can't. Oh it's awful trying to contain oneself. You and Jim must stop it, I can't digest my food properly.' When we returned to the dining room, admirers had recognised the actor of Sergeant Bilko fame and several of them came over to the table with requests for autographs. Jim Dale recounted a tale from his pop star days when a young belle had bared her bosom at the stage door, offering him a biro to sign his name there. 'And you had to do the breast stroke?' quipped Phil, guffawing all over again.

On the 8th of May I couldn't do any filming because I had to be in London for the recording of *Round The Horne*. Peter Eade came to watch it and took me to lunch afterwards. He told me that EMI definitely wanted to make an LP of the Rambling Sid Rumpo songs with an invited audience. We both agreed that the radio serial was getting better every week with listening figures rising as well.

A car took me back to Rye where Jim Dale told me that filming had finished early because there wasn't much they could shoot without me. We dined in the hotel with Jim and his wife Trisha, Gerald Thomas and our lighting cameraman Alan Hume. Phil Silvers joined us and immediately launched into a long saga about Frank Sinatra.

'I was with him in one of the USO shows touring Italy and when we got to Rome he said we could drop in on the Pope. I said, "Don't be silly, Frank, you can't just drop in on the Pope. These things take some organising". He said, "Shucks to that" and he could pull some strings with the Embassy, and sure enough the next day we were standing in the Sistine Chapel and this Cardinal ushered us in and said, "The Holy Father will see you now." In comes the Pope. "Well my son," he says to Frank, "I know you are a very fine tenor,' and Frank says, "No Father, I'm not a tenor, I'm a baritone: everyone gets it wrong," and the Pope says, "I am sorry my son, I thought you were a tenor," then he turns to me and says, "But you, Mr Silvers, I know that you are a comedian", and I gave him a rundown on my early days in burlesque. It got a few laughs. He was cute. Then he asks me if there is anything he can do for me, and I showed him this rosary I've got in a tobacco tin and I said if he would bless it personally I could take it back to give to Bing Crosby and tell him that no one had touched it but the Pope. He said, "My son, I will do better than that." He turns to

164

this acolyte and speaks in Italian and the next thing is he brings back six rosaries all in cellophane packets and stamped with the Vatican seal and he said, "Take these with my blessing to Mister Crosby and his family, my son," and I'm stammering, "Gee thanks Your Holiness, 'cos I know Bing'll be over the moon when I tell him you have blessed them personally." Then we back away and leave, but when we're on the steps outside Frank hits me right in the solar plexus and it really winded me. I said, "What d'you hit me for?" And he said, "You bum! I get you an audience with the Pope and you plug Crosby!"'

The next day we had a cloudless sky and sunshine after midday, and were able to shoot more desert scenes till about 6 pm. Phil Silvers had to have a fly button resewn by a ward robe assistant. As she knelt down he said, 'If you find anything down there, let me know'. It made everyone collapse with laughter. His involuntary sallies were often more amusing than his long stories.

By the 22nd of May the Camber Sands location work was over and the company was back at Pinewood where everything was much more convenient. Soon we were doing the parade-ground sequences. I was playing the sadistic commandant who forced the legionnaires to march with full pack under a pitiless sun and there was a moment when the recruits enjoyed my discomfiture as Jim Dale dropped his rifle on my foot and had me hopping with pain and anger. Before the scene I had said to Jim, 'We'd better rehearse this because slapstick can go wrong and people can get hurt,' but he pooh-poohed the idea. 'Don't worry, Kenneth, I'll see that the rifle falls on the ground all right.' In the event it didn't. It fell on my foot and the metal butt cut the boot leather. When I jumped with pain I wasn't acting. 'It's agony, Gerald,' I told the director and after noisy recriminations to Jim Dale I went crying to the nurse who soaked a wad of cotton wool in witch-hazel and applied it to the bruise. Needless to say I affected a limp for the rest of the day. But after Jim had plied me with drinks at the bar when shooting was over, I departed for home with a sprightly if unsteady gait.

On the 25th of June I was invited to appear on the Eamonn Andrews *Sunday Night People* television show for the second time. I was on first, then Roger Moore and then Phil Silvers. I played a very old trick on Phil and it worked. I said, 'Doctors

165

will tell you that the outward sign of impotence in a man is his inabiliteer. Phil asked, "His what?" and I said loudly, "His inability to hear.' It got an enormous laugh, but I apologised to Phil afterwards. Phil told his Sinatra and the Pope story.

Peter Eade came down to Teddington to watch the recording of the show and he drove me back to his flat in Duke Street where we watched it on television. Obviously they'd run out of time because the Vatican story had disappeared. Peter thought it was a pity because Phil had timed the tag-line beautifully. I said I wished Phil had mentioned writing the lyric for the song 'Nancy With The Laughing Face'. Very few people knew he was the author and it would have been good on the show.

In the television column in the *Observer* the following Sunday, George Melly wrote about the Eamonn Andrews show: 'Williams was definitely the star of the evening and rather penetrating about his father's disapproval of his choice of profession. "He didn't want the poetry," he said, his little round nostrils turning triangular with assumed distaste, "and the gin and tonics". All very diverting, and I might as well admit I look forward to the programme's return in the autumn.' What I actually said about Charlie was that he wanted a son who enjoyed football and beer, not poetry and gin and tonic, but I'm not carping about such a cordial mention.

On the 3rd of July I did the Rambling Sid recording at EMI studios in Abbey Road before an audience of about two hundred people. It went like a bomb. The laughter was so intrusive that it broke up the rhythm of some of the songs. I said to one of the organisers after, 'I have never known such an uninhibited audience – all that laughing was extraordinary. At times it sounded almost hysterical. I didn't think it was as funny as all that.' He revealed that they'd given them a party first, with wine and cheese – 'It puts them in a good mood.' Obviously he wasn't concerned about *my* mood because there was no hospitality for me afterwards, and I felt very put-down.

Peter Eade was with me. 'I can see your chagrin,' he said, and I laughed, 'You shouldn't be looking.' We went off to a restaurant to have supper by ourselves. In many ways our lives were comparable, both of us had bachelor pads in central London, preferring the town to the country, and both of us lived for our work. Whenever I quoted Shaw's line, 'If you want to be single-minded be single,' he nodded with approval.

166

His thoughtfulness was remarkable. After hearing me talk about the glories of St Sophia he specially got me a copy of Steven Runciman's *The Fall of Constantinople*; seeing my tatty suitcase in the studios he presented me with a fine new one; and when I'd complained about the bore of having to roll up dressing-gown sleeves to wash off the make-up he sent me a linen kimono which I have to this day.

I was back with John Law in the office at Television Centre working on scripts for *International Cabaret* on the 5th of July and in the evening Louisa came along to my flat to discuss her planned holiday cruise in the *Reina del Mar* with my sister Pat and to show me the brochures etc. Joe Orton and Kenneth Halliwell called and we all chatted merrily. Later we were joined by my ex-army chum Stan Walker: he knew Lousia well and had arranged all the transport and the catering at my father's funeral. Conversation veered round to that because Stan had driven my Aunt Alice home afterwards and his van (a converted ambulance) had broken down. 'We all had to get out and push,' laughed Louisa. 'Alice was furious saying she shouldn't be pushing a van in her best black dress.' I said, 'Aunt Alice always had trouble at funerals; it was the same with Eliza Cod's cortège when the publican rushed out of the Plumber's Arms with the Gates of Heaven Ajar.' 'Oh yes,' said Louisa, 'she didn't like that. Well, she'd bought the same wreath and she said only the family should give the Gates of Heaven Ajar – when it was put on the hearse she tried to push it off.'

Joe asked who Eliza Cod was and Louisa explained, 'She was my step-mother. Eliza Cod was her name before she married my father, Henry Morgan, but we always called her Tin Lizzie. Tin was slang for money and she used to hoard hers.'

I said 'Yes, she was so mean she wouldn't buy butter, she used to get the eightpenny roll at the Maypole Dairy which was half margarine.'

'Her generation was always skimping,' said Louisa. 'Lizzie Williams, Charlie's mother, she always gave her family condensed milk in their tea and everything. They never had cows' milk, always a tin of condensed on the table.'

'Eliza Cod never got on with Charlie,' I put in, and Louisa said, 'You know why. She was round our house that night during the war – we were in the basement sitting round the fire

167

and Charlie went out to get some coal from the cellar and there was this grating overhead where people stood to look in the shop window. These soldiers were standing on it peeing down into the area. Charlie looked up and shouted at 'em to stop it and they took no notice. 'Course they'd been drinking and he came back into the room furious, and said "I've been peed on! Peed on in my own house!" and Gran started laughing – she thought he was joking. He shouted at her and said it wasn't funny but of course that made her worse. Then he said she needn't bother to come round to do the shop any more. She used to scrub out the saloon and he gave her a few shillings for it but after that I did all the scrubbing myself.'

Stan said it must have been a lot of work running the shop and Louisa said, 'Oh I enjoyed it. I used to do the till in the gents' salon and chat to all the men waiting to have their hair cut.' I reminded her of Peter Nichols sitting there telling her about the new Ekco television set. 'Oh yes,' said Louisa, 'he said it was a 17-inch console and I said 17 inches should console anyone!' Everyone laughed at this sally and when Louisa had gone home Joe Orton said how much he'd enjoyed seeing her. 'She likes a joke, doesn't she? Very different from my mother. I could never talk like that with her.'

Joe had just returned from another holiday in Tangier. 'We stayed at the Favier flat and it was a great success except when that daft old French gardener below played the hose on the bougainvillea round the balcony. We were lying there sunbathing and the water went all over us.' He also confided that he'd begun writing a diary which would contain details of all the sexual encounters in his life. When he and Halliwell had departed, Stan again expressed disapproval – 'He's so boring – always talking about himself' – but I pointed out that it was a fascinating self to talk about.

The heat of July 1967 was not conducive to scriptwriting. John Law and I sat in a daily torpor of perspiring tiredness, the comedy ideas eluding us. Often we'd pack in about 3 pm. One day I went up to Noel Road to see Joe and Kenneth Halliwell and they were full of the new Bill passed in the House of Lords legalising homosexuality.

'While we're going forward, Morocco is going backwards,' said Ken. 'While we were in Tangier that Captain in the Gendarmerie came to the flat and said that there were to be no more visits from boys. He said they must be of a proper age.'

'I doubt if the police here would call upon you so courteously,' I said.

Joe said, 'Yes, but let's face it, it's supposed to be easy over there.'

'It will never be easy anywhere, society will always regard it as abnormal.'

'It isn't abnormal as far as I'm concerned,' said Joe, 'it's normal.'

Then we fell to discussing relationships. 'Sharing of any kind means an invasion of privacy,' I said. Joe talked about his horror of involvement: 'I need to be utterly free.' I quoted Camus' line, 'All freedom is a threat to someone,' whereupon K.H. declared, 'Love is involvement and you can't live without love.' 'There are many definitions of love,' said Joe, 'it depends on your point of view. You can love your work and be entirely committed to the pursuit of perfection.' Sexual promiscuity, he said, now provided him with material for his writing: 'I need to be a fly on the wall.' But Kenneth Halliwell disagreed: 'It's all right letting off steam on a holiday but a home life should have the stability of a loyal relationship.' 'You sound like a heterosexual,' Joe countered, but Halliwell stuck to his guns and said that promiscuity led to wasted aims: 'You can only live properly if it's for a person or for God.'

There was obviously some unresolved friction between them. Joe told Kenneth that he would walk with me to the bus-stop and we left the house. There was no bus in sight so I said I would walk down Pentonville Hill. Joe offered to accompany me. 'But what about Ken?' I asked. 'He'll be on his own.'

'That's all right,' said Joe. 'We've been getting on each other's nerves lately. It's not a big flat and it gets a bit claustrophobic at times.' He talked about the possibility of taking a place in the country. He thought Brighton might provide a convenient base for Kenneth, leaving the London flat just for Joe. 'I could go down and see him at weekends.' Then he stopped walking and told me, 'I'll never leave him, you know. We've been through too much together for that.' He spoke about adversity forging the tightest bond and he came with me all the way to King's Cross where we said goodbye.

In a few weeks the weather was cooler and John Law and I worked profitably on the scripts. My diary entry for the 7th August says, 'Finished script 26 and feel now the pressure is

169

off. Re-read script 1 to see how it played and found it was terrible so the pressure is on again. Will have to do more work on it.' Some of the faults in the script were to do with working against the clock and some were to do with writing as opposed to playing. What looks funny on paper doesn't always work in performance. The thought of so much revision plunged me into gloom. John said the editing could be delayed, the series didn't begin till September and we were only up to the first week in August. So we didn't meet for regular sessions at the Television Centre after that.

On the 9th of August I had a telephone call from my old friend John Hussey. He was now with the RSC and Peter Brook, but he hadn't rung about that. He came straight to the point. 'Joe Orton and Kenneth Halliwell are dead. Apparently Ken murdered Joe and then killed himself.' I was stunned. I had seen them only a few days ago and it didn't seem possible. Requests immediately started coming in from the television news people to appear on the screen discussing Joe and Kenneth posthumously. I said no, thinking that such tributes to the dead were done with indecent haste.

Peter Butterworth and Janet Brown took me out to dinner that night and said it was wrong to brood over it. 'Joe's work will endure, don't worry,' said Peter. 'They'll be laughing years after this aberration is forgotten.' I said that Halliwell must have thought that something was threatening his life with Joe, that some sort of split was imminent and that rather than face such a divorce he'd killed him. It was so extraordinary to think of a languid, passive creature like Kenneth Halliwell using such violence to destroy his love. Peter Butterworth quoted Wilde, 'Each man kills the thing he loves,' and Janet Brown said it didn't sound like love to her. Suddenly, it didn't to me either.

I had to get all the script revisions on the TV series finished in August because the film *Carry On Doctor* began in September and so did a new series of *International Cabaret*. I had to time everything by recording the dialogue and ensuring it didn't go over the allotted span. I met the director, Stuart Morris, to tell him that I'd checked them all.

'It's really a gamble, Kenneth,' he told me. 'You know that with the right house your stuff can get longer and longer. The laughter put on five minutes in some of the episodes in the last series. Ideally I should be able to do the timing during the show, watch the other acts and say to you on the night: stretch it out or pull it right in.' I said it sounded more like a corset than a compère.

On the 1st of September I met Yvonne Caffin, the designer, at Bermans. She was selecting the clothes for the film *Carry On Doctor* and we went through all the stock rooms, Yvonne limping with her broken leg in a plaster cast scattering items right and left. 'Quite unsuitable, no good at all, dreadful selection. Come on, let's go to Burton's,' she said. 'We've got to find the right sort of suit for a hospital consultant and we need the track suits for your exercises in the room. We have to have two lots in case anything goes wrong when the door bursts open and you ricochet across the room.'

I was apprehensive immediately. 'Exercises? Ricochet?'

'That's right,' said Yvonne, 'Haven't you read the script?'

'Oh yes, yes of course,' I returned, but secretly determined to read it again. My cursory scanning was always for dialogue. I invariably missed the movement descriptions; same with a play, I never bothered with stage directions.

We couldn't get everything on that day and on the 6th of September I was having fittings again for more clothes. This time Gerald Thomas turned up to give his approval. Over lunch Gerald said, 'I was particularly pleased with your performance in *Follow That Camel* because you sustained the character throughout.'

'With that German accent it wasn't easy,' I replied.

'Don't worry, in this next one you're back to standard English, you can do your posh voice playing this very grand consultant.'

He told me that Frankie Howerd would play the man who imagines he's only got a short time to live when in fact he was perfectly healthy. Under this illusion he marries his faithful old secretary out of sentiment, only to find later that he was not going to die after all.

I said I thought it was very good casting and how ironic it was that I, who was always accused of hypochondria, should be playing an autocrat who dismissed such ailments as psychosomatic. 'Nothing wrong with you,' I had to say to a distressed Charles Hawtrey suffering a sympathetic pregnancy. 'You will attend all the prenatal keep-fit classes with the ladies every day till we knock this out of you!'

Before the first day of filming I had an opening night at Talk

171

of the Town in Leicester Square which was the new venue for *International Cabaret*. Instead of performing the show in a BBC TV studio it had been decided to shoot the series in this theatre as an Outside Broadcast every Sunday night. Playing my kind of comedy in a mock-up cabaret set in the TV studio, as we'd done hitherto, was one thing, but in the enormity of this new location things were very different. One walked on the stage to find a sea of faces in a huge auditorium, and felt, as an actor, that one wanted to play broadly – right to the back of the circle – but as the production was aimed at the intimacy of the television screen compromise was essential. The place had a theatrical atmosphere of plush velvet opulence but the contrast backstage was startling, with shabby staircases and flyblown dressing rooms.

The first programme on the 10th of September was fine – I really got the feel of the house by the second spot and the laughs were coming thick and fast, the supporting acts were very good and all seemed set fair, but alas, it was not to be. The last spot, featuring a couple slightly past their prime, evoked only polite applause and the programme plummeted to a very weak ending. They were a disappointing pair, and when Marty Feldman came backstage he said the show had been going fine 'till Burke and Hare came on', which certainly summed it up succinctly. Two days later the producers telephoned me and said they were 'scrubbing' that episode so it was never transmitted. The BBC had merely staged a very expensive dress rehearsal for the series.

I had little time to reflect on the vagaries of show business because on the 14th of September I started filming *Carry On Doctor* at Pinewood. The team was in fine fettle and it was delightful being back with all the old chums. The first day involved Barbara Windsor, Jim Dale and the adorable Hattie Jacques, playing Matron. When I saw her she was peering into the make-up mirror asking rhetorically how anyone could be funny at eight o'clock in the morning. Hattie was used to theatre hours, like me, and we never really adapted to rising at 6 am, journeying out to Buckinghamshire, and getting made-up and costumed by 8 am. It was worse for a woman because there was hair-dressing as well; everything had to look immaculate on the set. A lot of my scenes were with Hattie. She had to chase me round the bedroom and roll me on the bed in passionate embraces and we used to giggle a lot in the process.

I had to scramble out of her arms saying, 'No, no, matron, I was once a weak man.' As she grabbed me again, her reply was, 'Once a week's enough for any man.'

All my weekends were taken up with *International Cabaret* which was enjoying steadily rising viewing figures and I was getting mentioned by critics as a 'cult' figure. It struck me as a very funny term and I began to use it in performance. 'I'm a cult, you know. Oh yes, I'm one of the biggest cults you'll find around here.' I embroidered it incessantly, beginning with the accent of the governing classes and going off towards the end of the sentence, missing the aspirate as it finished as 'round 'ere'. Audiences always enjoyed the vocal gear change. The *Daily Telegraph* sent Patrick Skene Catling to interview me for an article on *International Cabaret* in their colour magazine. 'Peter Cook says you could be the funniest comic actor in the world if you tried a little harder and stretched yourself a little more,' he said. It sounded like a school report from a PT instructor. I said, 'Yes, well, all criticism is a form of vanity, isn't it?' and went off about Voltaire's injunctions to dig in your own bit of garden. I quoted Eliot, too: 'I am not Prince Hamlet nor was meant to be, am an attendant lord fit to swell a progress start a scene or two . . .'

When Patrick came to the flat with a photographer there were questions about my frugal furnishings and the bachelor existence. I said I thought André Gide was right about men being interested in absolutes and women in relationships, that I liked living alone, that I couldn't learn lines with someone else moving about and that love was an invasion of privacy. There were more photographic sessions in the street, in restaurants and at The Talk of the Town. In the end Patrick Skene Catling wrote about *International Cabaret*:

> Acts are imported from all over the world . . . singers, dancers and musicians. Some of them are not untalented, but no matter how bravely the poor dears strain their muscles or larynxes for the sake of their art, Williams invariably steals the show with his preposterous, long, meandering, almost entirely irrelevant introductions. This is probably the only television show that is watched most devotedly for its preliminary announcements.

173

So Gordon Jackson's prophecy of 12th September 1966 found its way into print on 15th December 1967.

By this time television had changed from black and white to colour. But not everyone went over the moon about it. George Melly in the *Observer* wrote,

> Most of the programmes on BBC2 are better for colour but only incidentally. Variety shows glitter more but it isn't the colour that makes Kenneth Williams' Molly Bloom-like introductions to the acts in *International Cabaret* so inventively outrageous – or helps that splendid comedian Dick Emery to overcome his rather poor material . . .

This was a pairing I particularly enjoyed because Dick Emery was a favourite of mine – and one of the most innovative female impersonators of his day. His lipstick-bedaubed coquette who told men, 'You are awful – but I like you', before hurling them through a shop window, was a comic original which never failed to amuse me. He went from a belle to a bruiser and was hilarious as both.

I think George Melly's point about the transition to colour is perfectly valid: seeing W.C. Fields in a television repeat recently, I found myself laughing without even registering that it was in black and white. Our response to humour is unchanging. The medium is not the message. What counts is the intrinsic nature of men's comments on life's endless dilemmas, whether it's Cratinus in Athens, Plautus in Rome, or Williams in London.

Chapter Ten

By the end of 1967 Andrew Ray was in India touring with Shaw's *Misalliance* and writing from Lahore: 'I've been doing things I wouldn't dream of doing in England: reading poetry in schools, speaking at universities . . . the change of environment has been very good for me. How are things at home? I hear that Wilson fought against the devaluation of the pound but it's happened. I don't know! The moment my back's turned everything starts falling to pieces . . .'

My replies to him weren't politically enlightening; they were mostly about show-business. In November I wrote to him: 'Dinner with Maggie Smith who translated an Italian newspaper article for me. She learned the language when she was doing the *Honeypot* in Venice. We've had snow and the roads are icy. Cast your mind back and remember our awful English winters. On *International Cabaret* last week I talked about being vetted by the BBC governors in the BBC boardroom: very grand with your deep Spanish leather and your Sheraton furniture and your framed photograph of Anona Winn. They said "Just sign here". I said, "But what's it for?" They said, "The usual procedure, just certifying that you've never been an atheist or a misogynist or a bigamist." I said "What if I have been a bigamist?" They said "In that case we lock all the doors and you have to tell us what it's like." That line got quite a laugh.

'I went with George Borwick to see Beverly Cross and he showed the film of our sojourn in the Greek Islands. It was a very good film but George kept leaning forward, getting in the way of the projector and all you saw was a great shadow of a head on the screen. We said, "Sit back, you're blotting out the picture." He said, "I'm trying to reach the ashtray, I'm not doing it on purpose." At the meal afterwards I noticed he took quite a few boiled potatoes and I said, "They'll put on weight, you should diet," and he said, "No, not until the winter winds die down," which I thought very amusing.'

With Andrew abroad I had to find others who might be interested in the Old Bailey. Ned Sherrin came along with me to a couple of sessions and in time he roped in Bert Shevelove, Keith Baxter and Gary Bond. During one case of

175

embezzlement Bert got very carried away, saying, 'This guy is innocent', so audibly that the clerk of the court looked up. We had to warn Bert that he must be quiet in the Public Gallery or we'd be thrown out.

Ned christened our group 'The O.B. Club' and I still have a note of his minutes of the first meeting. Bert Shevelove was listed as Treasurer (good with money), Ned Sherrin, as Secretary (literate) and me as President (knows about the juicy cases). The outing was described thus: 'The Club visited the Old Bailey to hear the case of Queen versus Calder and Boyars. Owing to a miscalculation by the President we heard only closing speeches of Counsel and no cross-examination. However the meeting proved extremely interesting and members not present do not know what they missed. The President (our most experienced member) was particularly impressed by the Clerk of the Court.' (This was because I'd said he'd chuck us out apropos of Bert Shevelove's outburst.)

Louisa went away to the coast for Christmas with her Old Time Dance Club and wrote of unseemly goings-on in the hotel: 'We twisted toilet rolls and hung them round the room for paper chains.' It sounded worse than the ladies' powder room at Port Said.

I longed to get away from wintry London myself but I was busy with radio, I did a special Christmas Eve edition of *International Cabaret* at The Talk of the Town with Sandy Shaw, and with John Law I wrote a spot for *Christmas Night with the Stars* organised by Stuart Morris – my first TV variety producer. I'd been loath to get involved in so much work and complained to John Law, 'I've got enough on my plate as it is,' but he said, 'What plate? Audiences eat out of your hand.' Stuart wrot afterwards, 'Your spot was the highlight of the show. You have a competence as a performer which gives adrenalin to any director.' So the compliments made it all worthwhile.

I had moaned about the freezing weather to Alyn Ainsworth who conducted the orchestra on the show and we both agreed it would be a delight to sit in the sunshine away from it all. On the spur of the moment I suggested we flew to Morocco for a few days. To my surprise he agreed. We departed for Tangier from Heathrow on the 31st of December and at midday we were sitting on the terrace of the Windmill beach café having

176

sandwiches and coffee under a cloudless blue sky, our English clothes uncomfortably hot in the warmth of North Africa. It was like a transformation scene. We only had a few days' free time but we used them to the full.

Alyn enjoyed exploring and we made several trips along the beach to Magoga and Malabata and one day we went by car to Chaoven in the Rif mountains. It was a jewel of a town and the first sight of the cluster of white houses nestling round the minarets of the mosque as you approach from the high road is most striking, like a glittering array of jewels in a valley between the ridge. The medina there was like a labyrinth and guides had a habit of disappearing once they got hold of a few dirhams. We had been warned not to pay till we'd completed the tour. The cobbled narrow streets were bustling with activity; in tiny back rooms you could see everything from tailors to bakers, silversmiths and corn chandlers. In the dark alleyways it was cool but when we emerged into the sunlight it was baking hot.

We progressed to the palace of Abdul Karim where they showed us the dungeons by candlelight. Afterwards we went to the Government Hotel and sat in the garden by the pool having coffee. With the mountains providing a natural backdrop, the vivid green foliage spattered with coloured blossom all around us was balm to our tired eyes.

We landed back at Heathrow on the 5th of January 1968 and I began learning lines straightaway for the television series. The performers on the first two episodes were Georgie Fame and Vera Lynn and both got deservedly rapturous receptions. The *Sunday Telegraph* television critic wrote on the 4th of February:

> *International Cabaret* is a very proper showcase for the occasional pop singer it engages. Kenneth Williams is so enmeshed in some high camp monologue (last week the saga of the apple turnover) that he has no time and probably less inclination to do anything more than name the performer and skip aside.

I did better than that. I praised Vera Lynn not only for her singing but for all she did to boost morale in the war for civilians and troops alike. I extolled the talent of Georgie Fame

177

saying his own piano accompaniment was almost as enchanting as his singing. Lack-a-day and rue – you can't win 'em all. Mind you, I would not describe either of these entertainers as 'pop singers' and on *International Cabaret* I exhibited no nimble footwork. I never skipped aside, the exits were heavy-footed. I was in too much pain to do anything other than move slowly – if not gingerly – because the old rectal problem had returned with a vengeance.

I was back in Mr Mulvaney's waiting room at Harley Street at the end of the month. He tried various treatments off and on till finally he had me back in the St John and St Elizabeth hospital where I occupied the same room I had had eight years before. I was wheeled into the operating theatre on the morning of the 20th of February. When I came round in the afternoon I was visited by the anaesthetist who said they'd found a fissure. I tried to sleep because I felt so drowsy but the telephone never stopped ringing with enquiries about my indisposition. It's astonishing how people justify nosiness under the guise of solicitude.

My favourite nurse, Sister Xavier, came in later on and told me, 'You had a terrible great fissure and the entire area was inflamed.' Then the surgeon assisting Mr Mulvaney appeared. 'Well, you've really been through the mill, I don't know how you've been performing every week in that condition. You deserve a drink. Do you fancy a whisky or a gin?' I told him I hadn't the energy to raise a glass to my lips and he said he certainly had and was going off to enjoy a very large scotch and soda.

Then the night sister appeared. She was the sort of person who maintained she was too busy to watch entertainment. She was so anxious to appear indifferent that half-closed eyelids made her bang into the furniture. My post-operative lethargy meant that I couldn't have cared less but the relaxation made me oddly lucid because when she said, 'You mustn't mind, but you see I never had time to watch your work', I replied, 'I don't mind, I've never watched yours either.' That killed the conversation stone dead. Impoliteness may be the result of indifference but its form can often provide a script – I used the incident later in a comedy spot which worked admirably.

The next day I had to endure all the agony of a barium X-ray. They inserted a tube into the rectum and injected a mass of white liquid. Then I had to lie on a camera which filmed its progress through the innards. An apprehensive nurse kept entreating me to 'hold it in for goodness sake or it ruins the apparatus' – and I dutifully obliged. The minute it was over I was rushed to a commode and the relief was merciful. Then I was liberally dosed with castor oil to ensure the evacuation of the remaining barium.

I wrote afterwards in my diary: 'It was ghastly and I hated every minute. Hospitals take all the dignity away from you. You're so much meat and bone to be lugged round on a trolley, cut open, sewn up, bandaged and dumped back into bed. Humiliation is unavoidable, I suppose, but I bitterly resent the shaved bum: it's like walking with a hedgehog between the cheeks.'

I was home again on my birthday, 22nd February, and sat alone in the flat while the rain lashed the windows, reflecting that I'd reached the age of 42 and was still learning lines every week just as I did when I started in rep twenty years before. I found myself remembering a verse beginning.

'Tissue of time held fast, are all things done or undone
Eternity makes no haste in Babylon or London.'

and it took me quite a time to trace its source. I located it eventually: it was by Francis Meynell. It's one of the most haunting poems I know, forever in my head like de la Mare's *The Listeners* – both of them deal with time in different ways and both conjure up a picture that is vivid yet mysterious. When I lost my copy of the Meynell poems I wrote to the author and received not only a kind reply but a substitute copy which I've treasured ever since. Sir Francis Meynell jolted my perceptions in more ways than one. I didn't connect a successful man of business with poetry writing. It was the same as the shock I felt on learning that the cricket commentator, John Arlott, was the writer of that superbly evocative poem about Brighton's Regency Ghosts. The modern mind falls into the trap of pigeon-holing people because of the demand for specialisation. I was quite startled when I learned that T.S. Eliot once worked for a bank, and that Roy Fuller was employed by a building society. Clio finds her fruit in strange orchards.

International Cabaret finished its run at the end of March but *Round The Horne* ran on till the end of May so I began the next film at Pinewood with Gerald agreeing to release me for the broadcasts on Monday mornings. I started filming *Carry On Up The Khyber* in April. I was playing an Indian Rajah called the Khazi of Kalabar and my first scenes were with Sid James and Julian Holloway, Charles Hawtrey, Roy Castle and Terry Scott. I complained about the tightness of the turban to Gerlad Thomas.

'It's giving me a terrible headache.'

'All top and bottom with you,' he replied.

'What do you mean?'

'If it isn't your behind, it's your head.'

The make-up man, Geoff Rodway, gave me a present. 'Here's something to put in your diary,' he said, handing me a photograph he'd taken of the poster for *Carry On Cowboy* which he'd seen outside a cinema in Sarajevo. The title was written SAMONAPRED KAUBOJU and Sid James got top billing as SIDHI DZEJMS with me second as EHET VILL-JAMS. It was a delightful souvenir. It's always been a mystery to me why *Carry On*s are so popular in communist countries. I thought our films would have been dismissed as examples of western decadence or something equally pejorative, but I have had fan letters from Jugoslavia and round robins from Cuba.

Soon we were shooting a scene in the Rajah's palace with me in gold robes and turban making love to the Governor's wife, played by Joan Sims. We were seated on a divan and I had a long speech about her comely attractiveness. In the middle of this I leant forward to embrace her and inadvertently broke wind. There was a loud report and Gerald Thomas cried out, 'Cut!' and stopped the cameras. Joan Sims rose with enormous hauteur and complained, 'Oh this is disgraceful. How can you make love to someone with this kind of thing going on!'

'We're all human,' I said defensively. 'Even Valentino used to blow off.'

'Yes,' retorted Gerald, 'but they were silent films.'

Everybody giggled and the lighting man, Ernie Smart, told me that the crew were laughing so much the camera was shaking.

On the 14th of May there was a hold up during the shooting when Gerald objected to my delivering a line with a *double entendre*.

'I told you at rehearsals I didn't want that.'

'I think it's funny.'

'Well I don't, and now you will have to do it all over again.'

'That's all right, I can take it.'

'I know you can take it. It's what you do with it that worries me.'

Things were getting fraught. By the 16th we were again on the love scenes, this time on the bed with Joan Sims and an elderly dresser from wardrobe took so long fixing my clothes I said impatiently, 'We're not filming in slow motion, you know,' and he quavered, 'My back hurts, I need a lie down.'

'Yes,' I said, 'preferably in the middle of the M1.'

I took the turban from him and tied it myself. He went off in high dudgeon to the producer, complaining that my remarks had reduced him to tears and within minutes Peter Rogers was on the set. 'I will not have you behaving like this – you can go over to him and apologise immediately.'

I went to the old man and put an arm round him. 'You mustn't take any notice of me. I say silly things when I'm in a temper, I don't really mean them, you must not upset yourself, my dear fellow.' Since he was shorter than me I could see over his shoulder and during the embrace I winked hugely at Joan Sims. When I got back to the bed to resume the scene she said, 'You really are wicked, d'you know that – you're a demonic little trouble-maker.'

'Into every life a little rain must fall,' I returned sagely.

'Oh yes,' she said, 'you're a dab hand at seeing someone else gets drenched!'

On 20th May I did *Round The Horne* at the Paris Studio in Lower Regent Street and the show got a rousing reception from the regular audience we'd built up over many Monday mornings. This was the penultimate episode in the series and afterwards Kenneth Horne took us all to a splendid lunch in the Loggia room of the Hyde Park Hotel and gave us each a specially designed fountain pen with 'Round The Horne 1968' engraved on the barrel. I couldn't stay long because I had to leave at 2.15 for Euston to catch a very important train. For the first time in its history the *Carry Ons* were sending us on location out of England: we were to film in Snowdonia, simulating the Khyber Pass in Wales.

We were based at the Royal Goat Hotel in Bedgellert, where I duly arrived and I had dinner on the first night with Gerald,

Joan, Charles Hawtrey and Peter Butterworth. I asked where Angela Douglas was and Joan said she was in bed with a stomach ache. 'You have to be careful what you eat when you're abroad,' I said.

'It's not that', said Joan. 'Someone lent her this massage vibrator and it's pummelled her abdomen.'

'That can be very nasty. I had the same trouble myself with a belly dancer in Istanbul – fifteen shillings a time with use of cruet.'

Joan interrupted, 'Don't start me off giggling before I've had my food – it ruins the digestion.'

The food happened to be very good – Welsh lamb – and Gerald suggested a glass of claret with it. I did not demur in spite of the dentist's warning that it is one of the worst teeth-stainers after coffee. I drank it because I hoped the iron content would help build me up for the rigours of mountain-climbing the following day.

Snowdonia proved far from rigorous. I was taken by jeep up to the mountain pass, made-up, costumed and then sat about looking lovely till 10.30 when, with Bernard Bresslaw as a bearded Hindustani, I charged down the slope screaming, 'I am the Khazi of Kalabar' – at the head of a band of warriors, to attack the British soldiers. My army was largely made up of Welsh extras – turbanned and garbed like hill-tribesmen of India, and very authentic they looked.

When Bernard and I had finished all our scenes in the picture, he drove me back to London and I was in time for the last episode of *Round The Horne* on the 27th of May. In the afternoon I went out to Pinewood Studios for the siege of the Residency. Bernard and I had to scream abuse at the Governor (Sid James) and smash the outer walls of his mansion till we came to the twin lines of Highlanders defending the British territory. We had to rally our men and charge the Scotsmen and then suddenly stop dead in our tracks when they lifted their kilts. For a horror-stricken moment we halted and then retreated in appalled discomfiture. It was a typical *Carry On* sequence.

The *Eamonn Andrews Show* asked me to make a return appearance on 2nd June and this time Joan Sims accompanied me. The other guests were Carol Channing and Matt Busby. Joan told the story about our love scene and the eructation. It got the biggest laugh on the show. Eamonn said something

182

about the kaftan she was wearing and Joan said, 'Yes, well I can't be bothered with all that dieting stuff, I just shove everything into this sack dress and let it all hang out.'

After the recording we went back to Joan's house at Hurlingham to watch it on television, and I told her, 'There's no question about it – we were the highlights of the show,' but she kept repeating, 'Oh dear! I look like an old boiler,' and ranted about her ample figure. She told me, 'The wardrobe people took me to that maternity shop to find a dress and the assistant found this black and white number and said they'd have to take a lot off the hem but I could have the excess material made into a sash. I said no thank-you, making a waistline will emphasise the figure. Let the dress just hang down, I don't want a sash. And she said, "No madam, I mean after you've *had* the baby".' I said to Joan that she should have told that on the show. She thought it might have given rise to all sorts of rumour and conjecture. 'You know what it's like on the box. The ad lib is blown up to embarrassing proportions, especially if it's a reference to pregnancy. My mother would have a fit. She always says you've only got to swallow a pickled onion and the neighbours start talking.'

In August I was working with Myles Rudge and Ted Dicks once again. Myles had written a satirical piece, *A Bannister Called Freda*, for BBC Radio, which was a send-up of all those eulogistic biographical tributes to Victorian worthies. Ted Dicks composed some appropriate songs and at the opening under a hissing sound you heard the quavering contralto of Joan Sims singing, as Dame Freda Bannister, 'I search for blossoms in life's garden,' and it sounded like an authentic 78 rpm record. I played the various men in the dame's life and John Moffat, as the narrator, had to question us both about our exploits. Needless to say some of the answers he got were outrageous. I could hardly keep a straight face in the studio when Joan sang the first song and the second one completely creased me. It was called 'Blow out the light, beloved', and to her everlasting credit she sang it totally straight-faced throughout. Only on the playback did she allow herself to laugh, and then, as is usual with Joanie, her mascara ran riot and we all gave fervent thanks that it was radio and not a television performance.

During the same month I worked on the David Frost show

sharing a spot with Ted Ray where we literally hit a comedy ball back and forth to one another, with a tremendous reception from the house. There was a strike of technicians at the time and we had to brave a picket line outside. 'Don't go in there!' and 'Don't be a scab, Kenny!' came the shouts, but I replied, 'I must go in, lads. I need the money,' which evoked a loud raspberry but was diverting enough for us to effect an entrance.

On the show I told the story about the actor who had to shoot the wrongdoer in the third act with a gun that failed to fire. After pulling the trigger vainly he flung away the revolver and gave the villian a hefty kick on the behind. It was essential to the plot that the bad man dies, so the actor held his posterior in anguish and struggled to the footlights crying, 'The boot was poisoned!' expiring as the curtain descended.

I talked to Ted Ray afterwards in the hospitality room. 'Adversity actually helps you with an English audience. Once a crisis is established and they see the pickets outside and the management manning the cameras, they respond even more warmly. It went very well, didn't it?'

'You could never fail, Ken,' said Ted, 'because you listen to people.' Coming from a performer of his stature I was greatly touched and complimented.

David Frost said that he wanted us both back again next week – the chemistry had worked beautifully – and so we did a second duet. Altogether I appeared four times with David Frost during that series, and when Peter Eade began muttering darkly about over-exposure on television, I asked him who it was who had persuaded me to do a TV chat show in the first place. After that he raised no objections.

The ability to ad lib in an entertaining fashion resulted in another engagement the following month when David Hatch was producing *Just A Minute* for BBC radio and asked me to join the team. This game has fiendish rules, designed by Ian Messiter, whereby the four members of the panel are required to speak for sixty seconds without hesitation, deviation or repetition. It's rather like putting leg-irons on a sprinter: one's chances of running the race, let alone winning it, are hampered from the beginning. If any competitor tries to abide by the rules, he's invariably doomed. Regular players resort to gimmicks. Clement Freud waits till someone has almost completed the time before challenging on some minor point, leaving the field free for him to speak for a few seconds and score an easy victory. Derek Nimmo will use such complicated vocal rhythms and attenuated cadences that any fault is difficult to delineate. Both of them indulge their idiosyncracies very comically. Freud will fantasize about armorial bearings depicting ceres, the fatted calf and a broiler chicken being goosed with a ball-point pen over an inscription 'Don't let the good life stop' reflecting gourmet interests. Derek will digress about anything from unfrocked priests to jelly babies and some of the more obscure islands in the Malay Peninsula – he's widely travelled. When I started with them in September 1968 I was tentative and nervous but I see from my diary that it was the encouragement of the chairman, Nicholas Parsons, that saved me. He gave me the best advice for this game: 'When you can't speak, keep challenging.' It certainly brings out the best in the inventive and fluent performers and occasionally it brings out the worst. If I'm given an unfair judgement I sulk or scream abuse at the chairman. 'You couldn't run a whelk-stall let alone a panel game.' 'You don't want a deck chair – you want a bath chair. You're an illiterate derelict!' An aggrieved Parsons once said, 'Really Kenneth, I couldn't talk like that,' and I said, 'Of course you couldn't – you haven't got my vocabulary.'

This raillery is fine when it's amusing and audiences enjoy it, but there can be uncomfortable moments in an ad lib show. People will make an unthinking remark and realize its import too late. In one programme Clement was given the subject 'Beauty' and he said that in the play Beauty and the Beast his wife had played Beauty. Nimmo immediately challenged. 'Deviation – have you seen his wife?' The audience fell about but Clement was not a little annoyed and there had to be a rapprochement with Derek saying, 'Come off it, Clay, it was a joke!' before good feeling was restored.

No misadventures occurred when David Hatch altered the casting for one episode and made me chairman. I'd shrunk from the offer initially saying I'd be no good as a figure of authority, but in the event I was businesslike, quick as a Coward, and as sagacious as a Solomon.

In October I went down to Pinewood for my first day on *Carry On Camping* thinking it was an appropriate title for the fifteenth in the series. The story revolved about an educational establishment that was a cross between a ladies' seminary and

185

Holloway jail. It was a girls' school called Chaste Place. I was the Headmaster and the Matron was played by Hattie Jacques. She had the name of the school written on her windcheater so that 'Chaste Place' was emblazoned across her bosom. Barbara Windsor played one of the rebellious pupils and her first scene was in a shower bath. She had to become aware of a peeping tom as she spied an eye staring thorugh a hole in the cubicle wall. She squeezed her toothpaste through the aperture and protested, 'Get away, you filthy snooper.' Since it was her first sequence in the picture, whatever voice she used for it was the one she had to maintain throughout, and she was secretly determined to play this schoolgirl as a wide-eyed, well-bred coquette and rid herself of the 'cockney sparrow' image she'd created in former roles. Her plans went awry when she came to shoot the scene. In rehearsal the hole had been empty but, when shooting, Barabara saw Sid James' eyeball appear in it, drew back instinctively and screamed, 'Get aht of it, you dirty snooper' in the lusty tones of a costermonger. Once the shot was taken everyone moved off to a new set and a very wet Barbara was left in the cubicle drying herself with a towel and moaning, 'Oh blimey, I meant to play it posh.'

Once out of the interiors most of our scenes were filmed in the orchard at Pinewood, and for once the weather was not on our side. It was cold and rainy and hardly conducive to sporting activities. Our PT lessons in the open air were dreaded by the girls. Barbara complained, 'My boobs are all goose pimples and my open-toed sandals are sinking into the mud while I'm trying to be buoyant in a bikini. Even the leaves are falling off the trees.'

Gerald solved the latter problem by having the prop men stick the leaves back on and spray all the branches with green paint. They sprayed the muddy ground green as well to simulate grass and played huge arc lights on the scene so that we appeared to be doing our arm-stretching in glorious sunshine. Morale wasn't exactly high during such bad weather and mine wasn't helped when Gerald remarked, 'I notice your jaw line is receding, it's probably due to tooth decay and gum recession. You'll have to wear a pad or something because it's very age-making on the screen.'

'Oh, that's very uplifting, that is. It's an old ploy of yours, isn't it? You told me in *Carry On Sergeant* that my hair was

186

receding. You said I'd be bald in a couple of years, but I've still got my hair, so your forecast was wrong!'

'If all my predictions were correct I'd never have to work, I could make a fortune on the Stock Exchange.'

'But I'd be unemployed.'

'You could always go back to drawing maps.'

'How can you revive the old ways?'

'As easily as you revive your old jokes.'

'Gerald, you shouldn't mention my defects.'

'Then don't mention mine.'

'Ah, in thy orisons be all my sins remember'd.'

'Yes, well, get back to the set, we're here to shoot a *Carry On*, not Shakespeare.'

I had forgotten that Gerald was the cutter on the film of *Hamlet*.

By the end of October the orchard was practically waterlogged and every squelching step one took on the green-painted mud almost pulled one's shoes off. During one scene when the overhead microphone boom was well away from us, Barbara Windsor said to me, 'It's disgraceful making us work in these conditions, freezing cold in PT clothes with sludge up to your ankles, pretending it's summer. Of course it's all right for Peter Rogers. He drives down here in his great Rolls-Royce, gets out in his cashmere coat and wellington boots, sits in the producer's chair calling "Carry on, girls," then departs to the bar for his glass of vintage champagne. We're treated like a load of rubbish but he falls with his arse in the marmalade every time.'

I had completely forgotten that, earlier in the morning, the sound men had fixed a radio microphone round my neck under my shirt and next day when we went to watch the rushes of the film, we were both appalled to hear the entire speech recorded. Barbara was beside herself with embarrassment. 'Oh blimey, they've heard everything I said.' There was a lot of giggling in the little cinema from the other members of the cast as well as the crew. Afterwards Barbara was indignant: 'Why didn't you *tell* me you'd got a microphone round your neck?'

As we left after the rushes she drew back fearfully as she saw Peter Rogers approach. 'Thank you for those few kind words,' he smiled, and passed before a blushing Barbara could attempt to reply. Later on she received an enormous consignment of Seville marmalade from Fortnum and Mason, and though the donor was anonymous, I think she knew where it came from.

In November we were still working in the fields at Pinewood, and I said to Gerald, 'Exterior locations under these awful conditions are not conducive to comedy. I don't like acting in the open air. I didn't enjoy all that stuff on the beaches at Camber Sands during *Carry On Camel*. You said yourself then that it was better to work inside.'

'Yes, I know I did. And we did *Doctor* after that which was inside.'

'Well there you are and a much better picture it was!'

'Well, you can't do everything inside.'

'I wish you could. The atmosphere on this is lousy 'cos we're all floundering in mud.'

'Yes, but it's knitting together very well in the editing.'

'Really!'

'Yes. It is looking very good indeed. I think it's going to be a success.'

His prediction in this case was completely accurate. The film was top box office. What had been miserable to produce turned out to be one of the funniest and most profitable in the series.

As soon as the film finished I was back again with John Law working on the script for a Christmas show, and an idea for a television special which was extraordinarily ambitious – a fifteen-minute programme with me doing eccentric conversation, talking direct to the camera. Bill Cotton was encouraging but warned us that it might not work. Not altering the shots could make for monotony. But he was prepared to give it a try.

We got two scripts prepared by the 12th of December and Bill Cotton came into our cubbyhole of an office and listened to me characterising some of the material. He said he thought we should do them as pilot shows in January the following year. In television terms a pilot show is shown initially to a planning committee which either approves its transmission or pronounces it unsuitable for broadcasting.

On the 15th of December I did a Christmas radio show from the Camden Theatre – the scene of many of the early Hancock shows. I reflected that since Tony's untimely death in Australia earlier that year (he had committed suicide), it would see him no more. I was working with my old chum from *Round The Horne*, Hugh Paddick, and we talked about the sadness of suicide. Hugh said, 'If only they'd wait a bit they'd invariably find things weren't so bad the next day.' I agreed. 'I find myself resenting it. I feel life is rather like a coach outing and if some passengers keep jumping off you start wondering whether the trip is worth making.'

The next day I began another television job narrating 'The Land of Green Ginger' for Jackanory. We had three days in which to record the five episodes and all the different character voices had to be clearly delineated. It certainly wasn't easy because one slip in the vocal delivery meant a hold-up and a very difficult editing job for the men in the cutting room. I made a mistake in my approach for this children's programme, because I spoke slowly and deliberately during the rehearsals, and the producer, Anna Home, told me, 'Never sound as if you're patronising the young. Take it at the same speed you'd normally use with all your own vocal gear changes and mannerisms. Children like that. Where the script requires a gallop, take the bit between your teeth – they'll follow you.'

I was directed by Jeremy Swan, a man with a lively sense of humour and infectious enthusiasm. When I was struggling to produce a regal voice for the queen and failing miserably, he suddenly said, 'Do your Edith Evans impression', and it fitted like an old key into a well-oiled lock.

By Christmas I was free of all work and spent the 25th with Stanley and Moira at their Highgate home. It was a happy day with Stanley at his most entertaining. We fell to talking about the unpredictable Duncan Macrae and Stanley mentioned how he had made an extraordinary entrance in *Cinderella* as one of the Ugly Sisters. The other Sister came on stage with a hat box, placing it on the floor, with the bottom open. Duncan came up on a hydraulic lift from beneath the stage, so that when the hat-box lid was removed, he appeared rising slowly out of it, in a tight black dress, saying his first line. This was, of course, drowned in laughter as the audience watched his weird arrival. The other Sister whispered 'Say the line again'. Duncan turned raising his eyebrows quizzically and bawled, 'I've just said it!' as if he were addressing the deaf.

'Oh, I can see it all,' I laughed. 'I remember his eccentric moments during the Orton play.'

Stanley said he was just as eccentric offstage. When Stanley visited Duncan and his wife at their holiday home in Millport he was gesticulating wildly on the quayside long before the boat tied up. With a black fedora and flowing cape Duncan was waving a knobkerry, striking outlandishly theatrical poses and calling greetings from afar. When Stanley came ashore Duncan said, 'Gladys and I came here last Thursday and just merged into the background.'

I spent the last day of the year with my agent Peter Eade and we talked about the motivation for acting. I said, 'In my case it was born of a desire for a façade: my romantic self required a shield against reality, plus the fact that I've never really liked what I was and welcomed the mask of another persona. Children love to pretend and Freud says that when the child dies in you, you're finished.'

Peter observed, 'Freud has been one of the great influences of this century and I don't know that it's always been a good thing. The belief in psychoanalysis as a cure for the mind's maladies doesn't always prove efficacious. The truth about ourselves doesn't always set us free, it sometimes frightens us into another kind of bondage'.

'Yes, Maugham's line in *The Constant Wife* reflects that – "What do we any of us have but our illusions, and what do we ask of others but that we be allowed to keep them." It's one of the secrets of celibacy, the preservation of the illusion.'

'Is that why you've chosen to live alone?'

'In a way. I certainly don't want any invasion of my privacy, but that's not the whole story. My first sexual arousals were with boys at school, all clumsy, furtive fumblings and really very innocent. Nothing happened in the army – barrack-room life put paid to intimacy – and after demob my second choice of career meant doing a lot of work in order to catch up, having started late in the profession. I was ambitious then. I thought, I want to have a public life even if it's at the expense of a private life. I succeeded in that but in the process the sexuality has been stunted. I've still got the same schoolboy yearnings I had at Bicester and since they don't fit in with Kenneth Williams today they're relegated to the dream world. They would mar my public image, and I want to earn the public's plaudits not its opprobrium. Besides, love takes many forms. With the right night and the right performance you can feel waves of affection from an auditorium. Desire isn't dammed, it gets channelled into creativity and that saves me from despair.'

'What about your faith? You've always expressed a belief in God.'

190

'Yes, I can't conceive of a world without Divinity but the doctrinal aspect of it depresses me. Once religion becomes institutionalised it ceases to attract me. That is the paradox. I need the message but I don't always care for the way it's delivered. I don't like worship in community. I'd rather be alone talking to God, then I can forget the bit about having to love my neighbour as myself.'

'Oh yes,' said Peter, 'that is difficult. The tenant above me behaves abominably – it sounds like a herd of elephants overhead when he's got company. Some injunctions are hard to obey. But you don't quarrel with the fundamental message of Christianity, do you?'

'No. The essence of the Nazarene faith lies in Auden's lines, "We must love each other or die" and it's the way we interpret love that decides our lives. St Francis says it's nothing to do with strong arms and beauty. He says real love is lying thigh to thigh and toe to toe with the leper.'

'That's pretty radical.'

'He was a convert, after all and they often are radical. The desire to do good in people is in direct ratio to their degree of personal misery.'

'Is that a quote?'

'Yes, I must have read it somewhere, taken it in: literature, music, painting, it's always through art that I've come to the truth. Never from experience of life. The learning has been vicarious.'

'You should get all those quotes down on paper – they'd make an interesting book.'

'Well I've got the diaries, that's a start I suppose.'

'Will they ever get published?'

'They'd need a very diplomatic editor: some sides of my character aren't presentable. What is it Emerson says? "We have as many personalities as we have friends".'

'You can comfort yourself with the knowledge that you've got some very loyal ones.'

Walking home afterwards as the New Year was dawning, I returned to the truth of Peter Eade's last remark and another Emerson quotation soon went into my diary: 'Our friends come to us unsought. The good God sends them to us.'

Chapter Eleven

In January 1969 Stanley Baxter was rehearsing Joe Orton's posthumous play *What The Butler Saw* and Gordon Jackson was playing Horatio to Nicol Williamson's Hamlet at The Round House. George Borwick was increasingly away in Pangbourne because his mother was indisposed and my social life became circumscribed. There were compensations, though for I caught up with a lot of reading. I was engrossed in Michael Holroyd's biography of Lytton Strachey and was weeping by the time I came to the death, which is depicted so poignantly: a man who never found that shared affection he so much desired, and yet who at the end was surrounded by love.

Then I started on John Motley's *Rise of the Dutch Republic* and I was struck by his historical picture of man's almost monotonous pursuit of evil: war is commonplace, cruelty rife, persecution arbitrary and savage. In my diary I noted, 'It is still going on today. In Vietnam, war, in Laos, war, in Nigeria, war. In China, the ideology of Maoists opposing Revisionists with all the resulting bitterness and strife. It's all waste. There is no *idea* worth dying for, because life itself, being God-given, is more important than any intellectual concept.' The last sentence in the Motley book must be one of the most beautiful ever written. He says of William the Silent: 'While he lived he was the guiding star of a whole brave nation, and when he died the little children cried in the streets.'

On the 19th of January I went to the Television Centre to do the pilot shows of my two solo programmes. The audience was not enthusiastic and I performed like an automaton. I was so determined not to gabble that I was over-careful about my diction and somehow lost the symmetry of the thing. At rehearsals the timing of each show had come out at fifteen minutes but at the performance audience laughter lengthened them to twenty. Bill Cotton appeared afterwards and paraphrased his earlier warning, 'I think that this length of show is really pushing your luck. People sitting looking at one set and one face for all that time.' He made it sound like a party political broadcast. Still, his end note was encouraging. 'If it doesn't get on the air it won't be because of me.' John Law was unshaken in his optimism. 'Don't worry, it will be a series. I'm buying my new car now.' But when I viewed a play-back later on with Peter Eade, I was not at all sanguine about its prospects. The endless grimacing, the close-ups on a bug-eyed and ageing, prune-like countenance, and the slowness of delivery, all combined to depress me.

We left the studio in silence and made our way to the car park. Eventually Peter said briskly, 'Yes, well, I don't think we want any of *that* to get out!' and I instinctively knew that was what the verdict of the BBC planners would be too. I suddenly felt revulsion for all my comic endeavours. 'I'd like to be miles away from the whole broiling,' I told Peter, and he said it would be a good idea to take a holiday. 'Do something different,' he suggested. 'Go on a banana-boat or something like that, where you can be scruffy and relaxed. It will be weeks before we get a verdict on this show anyway.'

I took his advice and on the 28th of January 1969 I embarked with Louisa at Liverpool on the *Monte Anaga*, bound for the Canary Islands. I had told my mother that it was not like a cruise liner, it was a merchantman, so she should just bring old clothes and a raincoat because deck conditions would be grubby, all oil and machinery. But when we arrived on board, it didn't look like that at all. After stowing our luggage in the cabins we went on deck to look at the shoreline receding as we sailed out of the port. Louisa looked round at the ship doubtfully, and said, 'It all looks very smart to me – there's a swimming pool and everything. I think you got it wrong about it being a dirty tramp steamer.'

Later on when we went into the dining saloon for our first meal at sea, she gazed at the glittering tableware, the immaculate stewards, the smartly gowned and bejewelled passengers and told me I'd completely misled her; 'They're all dolled up in their gladrags and I'm sitting here in this old frock feeling like Cinderella!' I felt a bit guilty, but I had certainly not expected such luxurious conditions and consoled Louisa with the promise that she could buy some more elegant clothing at the first port of call. This was to be much earlier than I could have foreseen.

On the second day everyone was beginning to find their sea legs and we were sitting in deck chairs enjoying the winter sun off the coast of Spain, chatting to some fellow-passengers and enjoying the fresh air. They suggested a sherry before lunch and we repaired to the bar where we swapped travel stories and I impressed everyone with my account of troopship entertainment aboard the SS *Devonshire*. At 1 pm we all went down to lunch feeling happily at ease with our new acquaintances. We had just reached the pudding, a delicious-looking baked apple, when there was a rending sound and the ship shuddered, sending crockery sliding across the table. I hastily cupped my hands round the dessert plate as the Captain rose from his seat nearby and ran up the companionway to the deck. Several other officers chased after him and the passengers, wide-eyed with alarm, began to follow suit.

'We'd better go, too,' said Louisa anxiously. 'Something's wrong.'

'Well, we can't put it right,' I told her, 'so let's finish our meal.'

'But that terrible noise, it sounded as if we'd hit something. The ship might be sinking.'

'Let's have this baked apple, I haven't had one for ages; it's got all those raisins and brown sugar in the middle.'

Louisa looked round. 'We're the only ones left. The rest have all gone up on deck.'

'So they won't want us adding to the confusion. Crowds always hamper proficiency.'

'What about that safety drill we had yesterday, shouldn't we go to our boat stations?'

'Baked apples are better than boat stations,' I told her, tucking into the sweet. 'This is delicious, try it.'

She tentatively took a mouthful and admitted, 'Yes it is rather good, isn't it,' and we completed our meal in the calm of an empty dining saloon.

Later on we learned that we'd hit a fishing-boat amidships cutting it in half and sinking it. Lifeboats had been lowered and we'd picked up one dead man and six survivors while a companion fishing-boat hove to and its Spanish crew shouted loud recriminations at our ship. We altered course for Corunna, which was where the fishermen hailed from, tying up there at 7 pm. The police came aboard and the corpse was removed to the mortuary. I spoke to the radio officer about my amazement. 'It seems extraordinary, a collision at sea at midday in excellent visibility.' He told me, 'You couldn't see the bow of the ship because we were sailing into the sun. It was blinding. It is a terrible thing but we just have to accept it.'

Spirits were lowered by the incident and passengers talked in low tones about the consequences of such a mishap.

It was a relief when we left Corunna at midday on Friday and by Sunday we arrived in Santa Cruz, berthing at midnight. I'd turned in earlier, though Louisa and several passengers went ashore determined to enjoy a jaunt round the town. They wanted me to join them but I feigned sleep and ignored their knocking at the cabin door. Excursions at the witching hour weren't my idea of a winter holiday.

Next day we arrived in Las Palmas. Disembarkation was tardy because of confusion over the baggage and it wasn't till 6.30 pm that we got ashore. There wasn't a taxi in sight and in desperation I asked a lorry driver if he could take us to the Metropole Hotel. He cheerfully agreed. Louisa was hoisted into the seat beside him and I went over the tailboard with the bags and sat on packing crates. I couldn't help thinking it was hardly the équipage for a cult figure in the Canaries.

The commissionaire at the hotel tried to wave us round to the goods yard at the rear, but I jumped out, and cried, 'Je suis un grand vedette des Anglais' and helped Louisa down from the driver's cab under his bewildered gaze. I'd used quite the wrong French. I should have said, *étoile*, which means star, not *vedette* which signified a twinkler, but my language was as makeshift as the transport and at least it saved us from the tradesmen's entrance.

The rooms at the Metropole were commodious and after unpacking we went downstairs for dinner in an elegant room, where an orchestra discreetly played Gershwin and solicitous waiters served an excellent meal. Most of the people staying there were, like us, English and on holiday, and the friendly atmosphere ensured that we met lots of families. On one excursion to Mas Palomas as many as twenty of us sallied forth. Our refreshment bills became very complicated so a kitty was arranged and I was appointed treasurer. At every restaurant I sat dispensing pesetas from a huge wad of notes asking for receipts and checking every item with such Scrooge-like suspicion that I often got reductions for which I'd never asked. I also rehearsed a chorus of would-be Tiller Girls and they performed a very creditable *bourrée* by the end of the week, though several of them had Spanish tummy for which I recommended Fernet Branca. The revolting taste always convinced them it was doing them good. When children got bored

I taught them word games and they succeeded so well that adults invariably joined in. During our entire stay Louisa and I were never without company and when we boarded the *Monte Umbe* for the return on the 10th of February there was a huge party to see us off. Everyone came on board, toasted us in champagne, and we all sang 'We'll Meet Again' and exchanged sentimental embraces, and by the time they'd gone ashore we felt as bereft as orphans.

Unlike the voyage out the home passage went smoothly enough, but on the third day I noticed an ominous puddle around my feet while I was shaving and had to call the steward's attention to a leaking S bend under the washbasin in my cabin. The following morning the spillage was worse and I got him again saying, 'Muchas inundacion a' cabina.' He laughed, 'You must wear a bikini.' Then a passing passenger peered through the open door and said, 'You've got a leaking S bend there!'

'Tell me something I don't know,' I shouted angrily and they both departed with raised eyebrows.

Eventually I found the purser who assured me he'd get a plumber to deal with the problem and by the evening the leak was at last fixed. I was at the bar, with a campari, congratulating myself on the repair, when the radio officer came up and informed me that the BBC had just announced the death of Kenneth Horne.

That put paid to my good humour. I went up on deck and stared out at the sea. Thankfully there was no one about because they were all preparing for dinner, and I leant over the deck rail, alone with my misery, remembering the gentleness, the fun and the generosity of that dear man whom I would never see again. I was certainly not in the mood for the festive party in the evening. It was all paper hats, balloons, communal singing ending with a speech from the Captain – 'Whenever you see tomatoes from the Canaries, think of the *Monte Umbe*.' I knew I'd think of her whenever I saw an S bend.

Among the pile of letters waiting for me when I returned to the flat was one dated 28/1/69 from Kenneth Horne. It was a weird sensation reading lines from someone no longer with us. He had written asking me to spare a few minutes of my time to see Mollie Millest – for a magazine article she was writing about *Round The Horne*. Molly had done some script writing for *Much Binding in the Marsh* and for *Beyond Our Ken*, and, added Kenneth, she was also a member of the Salvation Army and had a tremendous sense of humour. When Kenneth had talked in the past about this improbable source of his comedy matter, I had always thought it was an elaborate fiction; now I realised that Molly really existed. I subsequently mentioned it when I did a broadcast tribute to Kenneth Horne for the Forces network from Dean Stanley Street on 17th February, an occasion on which I also talked about his impeccable sense of timing and the aplomb with which he suggested an establishment figure. It was largely because of this quality that so many outrageous characters were able to get laughs in the show. Kenneth Horne made everything acceptable precisely because he himself was so respectable. I told the producer afterwards that if it sounded eulogistic, I couldn't help it. The man was unique.

The projected series of *Round The Horne* had to be cancelled of course and the producer, John Simmonds, asked Myles Rudge to write a new show. It was called *Stop Messing About* and since Joan Sims had been so successful in the Bannister saga she was our new girl and, with my old friend Hugh Paddick, we all started at the Paris Studio on the 17th of March 1969, running weekly till June. I was doing TV as well with Denis Norden and Michael Trubshawe in *Call My Bluff* because they had asked me to take Kenneth Horne's place in their team.

Peter Eade informed me that my forebodings about the pilot show had been correct. The BBC said that a fifteen-minute programme did not suit the schedules. Bill Cotton suggested instead a longer show with a revue format and by the time the radio series finished I was back with John Law working on the material for what was to be called *The Kenneth Williams Show*. They wanted six episodes and rehearsals were planned for December, so we had plenty of time to prepare.

On 18th March I started work on *Carry On Again Doctor* at Pinewood and Gerald and Peter not only released me on Monday mornings for the radio show, but Joan Sims as well. This complicated the shooting, because there was a long Easter holiday to contend with as well as a lot of exterior locations. I was playing a surgeon aptly named Carver whose ambitious schemes caused trouble for colleagues and patients alike. The actual shooting of the film was not without its troubles either. In one scene Jim Dale performed an incredibly daring feat

197

careering down a staircase and crashing through a window. Unfortunately he injured himself in the process and had to be taken to hospital.

On the 9th of April we went to Maidenhead for the hospital exterior sequences. Gerald said they were to have been shot three weeks hence but they'd been brought forward because of Jim's accident. I was standing on the pavement in high spirits while the crew set up the camera and I began singing 'Everything's Coming Up Roses'. Bemused passers-by stopped to applaud my antics and, thus encouraged, when I got to 'Light the lights, clear the tracks', I did an impromptu dance with some high kicks. One was a little too high and I landed flat on my back, ricked my neck, cut my elbow and tore my suit. Gerald appeared looking anxious and the wardrobe mistress told him, 'It's all right, we've got a spare suit, there's two of them.' 'But only one of me,' I added piteously. Gerald said one was quite enough, thank you, and asked me what on earth I was doing. I told him it was my impression of Ethel Merman.

'In future, try Ethel Barrymore, she's less exerting. I don't want any more injured actors on the picture.'

To make matters worse, I fluffed several takes after that, and, with the daylight waning, it did little for Gerald's good humour.

'I was too buoyant to begin with,' I told him, after spoiling the third shot. 'That was my undoing.'

'Yes,' he said resignedly, 'so was your impression of Ethel Merman.'

Inevitably in a *Carry On*, Gerald had the last word.

In the end everything went all right, Jim Dale was soon back on the picture, and Peter Rogers gave us all a splendid celebration dinner at the Mirabelle when the film was completed. Most of the cast were planning holidays. Charles Hawtrey said he was going abroad. 'I'm taking a false beard and travelling under an assumed name, to allay suspicion. I'm meeting my companion at Smith's bookstall at the airport. I should be going alone but she was very persistent.'

'You surprise me; you said you didn't want to be lumbered.'

'I know, but she kept on and on. "Please Charles, be my Sir Galahad". I said, all right but it's very bad casting.'

I couldn't go anywhere because I was too busy on the scripts with John Law for *The Kenneth Williams Show*. We had decided on a format in which I would introduce the pro-

198

gramme followed by sketches with no realistic sets, just stylistic outlines and minimum costume changes. The idea was to aim for economic staging so that the entire half-hour show could flow without interruption. In so many television shows the live audiences have to sit through numerous scene changes, their interest flags and the comedy momentum is lost. We were determined to avoid this.

The writing occupied us in fits and starts, however, because John Law had other commitments and his health wasn't too good. Fortunately I too was preoccupied with the *Just A Minute* programmes, the David Frost Shows, more voices for Richard Williams's animation films, more episodes about a Bannister called Freda, and another five *Jackanorys*. Joan Sims and I had worked happily together in the radio shows, and she agreed to partner me in my television series. The preparation of all this material meant that I had to miss the next film with Gerald and Peter, so I was not in *Carry On Up The Jungle*. It was sad not to be working with the team when they began in the autumn but I consoled myself with Bill Cotton's maxim: television is the medium of the future.

During one session with John Law we were working on a sketch about a lecherous gourmet taking a girl to a restaurant. I said, 'I'll play him like George Borwick, he's always ordering sole meunière, so that's what this man will have. He can say "I'll have sole meunière, that's very good." '

John said, 'Then she could ask, "Is this toad-in-the-hole?" and the waiter can say, "No it's punched up the hooter." '

I said, 'No, she must have pheasant'.

'Why?'

'Then when it comes to ordering the wine the man can say, "I'm on the fish and you're on the game, so I think it leans toward a claret".'

John said, 'All right, but make it grander, not just claret, let it be something extravagant like Chateau Beauregard.'

I hastily rewrote the passage and expressed satisfaction with the result. 'We work well together,' I told him, 'because you've got a comic mind whereas I've got a dramatic mind. Would you say my mind was dramatic?'

'No,' he said briefly, 'I'd just say dirty.'

We did a lot of work in September but in October Beryl Law rang to tell me that John had been admitted to hospital. I started wondering. He had not been well lately. Several bouts of 'flu had kept him debilitated and he had complained about asthma symptoms, but I hadn't thought any of this was serious. Two days later Beryl telephoned to say that he was in the intensive care unit of the Brompton Hospital, so visiting was out. I began working on the scripts alone and remembered Stanely Baxter's remark about writing: 'So depressing, all those sheets of white paper, I go snow blind.'

The solitary labour was daunting and I was relieved when Bill Cotton telephoned me and told me to come back to Television Centre and work with another writer he had found, called Austin Steele. He said he also wanted me to write a spot for *Christmas Night With The Stars* to be recorded on the 14th of December and when I demurred about all the line-learning, he said, 'Don't worry, you can have it all on teleprompter.'

'But will it look involuntary?'

'Certainly, you manage it effortlessly on *Jackanory*.'

'As long as it comes over spontaneously.'

'It will, you have a gift for making comedy lines come alive.'

'I think you're very generous.'

'You might change your mind when you hear the fee.'

'Oh, really?'

'Well, it's a tight budget, and there's a big cast.'

'That's all right, my BBC suit has the right pattern.'

'What's that?'

'A very small check.'

Austin Steele and I finished all the scripts for the series by the middle of November and we completed the spot for the Christmas Show as well. He knew about the importance of a story-line and he had a good editor's mind, knowing where to economise and where to ornament. In a saga I was preparing about the Shoeburyness Knitting and Social Circle where I said they had a running buffet, he interjected, 'And I nearly caught up with it twice,' which provided a useful laugh along the way. That's what oils the wheels in a writing partnership. Ideas are bandied about, some suggestions accepted and elaborated, some discarded as impracticable, but each stimulates and encourages the other. Once a sequence was arrived at I would read it back and start acting it and if we found it funny we pronounced it workable. But it always remained a blueprint until we found reassurance outside. That meant buttonholing other writers, asking, 'How does this grab you?' and performing it for them all over again.

Bill Cotton would sometimes visit us and listen to an improbable monologue, occasionally suggesting an improvement or a cut but mostly spurring on the output. When he appointed Roger Ordish director of the show, we sought his judgement too, and he would point out where there was a good gag or suggest a line somewhere else that needed to be stronger. By the time we were approaching rehearsals I felt we were well prepared.

At the beginning of December I was plagued by troublesome noise in the flat and the manager of the property told me that I was living directly below machinery housed on the roof. 'It's for the fans which supply the ventilation for the bathrooms and health regulations demand that they're continually in operation.'

'They're not only supplying oxygen, but timpani as well,' I told him, and said that the endless thumping was driving me mad. My next-door neighbour advised me to move and sell the apartment to a ship's captain – 'He'll be used to the sound of the turbines.' As usual I rushed to Stanley Baxter with my troubles. He had quite a few of his own, having hurt his mouth by walking into a piece of scenery at the PalaceTheatre where he was playing in *Phil The Fluter*. 'I took that flat in Judd Street when I thought we were moving from Highgate but we're staying put so you can move in there if you like,' he said with typical generosity, and we had a delightful lunch together.

He talked about the show which had opened in Novemer and about his affection for Evelyn Laye with whom he was starring in it. 'She's like a million-watt light bulb coming on. Every night the audience has a love affair with her.'

Afterwards we went to a tailor in Brewer Street where he asked my opinion of a suit he tried on. 'Do you like this yellowy-brown tweed?'

'Oh it's more than yellow,' I effused. 'It has a golden effulgence, pastoral and welcoming like the tender bowed locks of the corn.'

'Yes, well, we just want the suit, not Palgrave's *Golden Treasury*.'

I decided to take up Stanley's offer and the prospect of moving filled me with elation. By mid-December I was rehearsing for my television series and we did the first *Kenneth Williams Show* at the Shepherds' Bush Theatre on the 22nd. It was not the most exciting house I've ever played to and when I asked Austin Steele where they got the audience from he thought it was probably the local geriatric wards. The director, however, pronounced himself satisfied. 'Plenty of laughs there, don't worry.' He said we'd build up a better audience reaction in the weeks ahead.

I knew the truth of that from the radio shows at the Paris; once a series became established the reaction got better and better as the run progressed. Yes, I thought, it'll be like wine, and it'll mature in the New Year.

I spent the Yuletide with Louisa. We had turkey and Christmas pudding, and went a little mad opening a bottle of Tokay. In the evening we saw *Christmas Night With The Stars*. My spot had been cut to ribbons. 'Oh, they've edited it with gardening shears' I told Louisa. 'I had much more than that – half of it's gone.'

'Not as good as you were in *Carry On Again Doctor*,' said Louisa. 'I saw it with your Aunt Edith, and we both thought you were marvellous. Better than you've ever been before. You should do more of those straight parts; you're better when you're serious.'

I did a double-take but saw that she was perfectly serious. Suddenly I remembered Perelman's lines, 'When I pointed out to the author that this bore no direct connection with his play . . . he gave me a typically Gallic shrug of the shoulders. "After all", he observed, trimming a goosequill to tickle the leading lady, "you can't give them everything. We don't pretend we're *Chu Chin Chow*." '

We did the second *Kenneth Williams Show* on the 5th of Janaury 1970 and everything went satisfactorily, merriment bubbling along throughout. I was so pleased with the playback which I saw next day that I became uncharacteristically generous and asked Joan Sims, director Roger Ordish and his assistant Tony James to have a drink at the BBC club upstairs. We were in the midst of congratulatory toasts when Austin appeared looking strangely apprehensive. I asked him what was the matter, and he told me that John Law had died.

It was like a bombshell. Ever since he had been admitted to the intensive care unit in the hospital the news had been unchanging – his state was comatose, but there was always the possibility that he would come out of it. Everyone clung to that – hope was like a white sail on a dusky sea:

202

'Though every wave she climbs divides us more
The heart still follows from the loneliest shore.'

Now that hope was dashed. First I had lost the most genial of colleagues in Kenneth Horne, now I had lost the most sympathetic of collaborators in John Law. 'And we were all standing here congratulating ourselves on the show's success,' I said bitterly. Austin corrected me. 'John would want that success. You worked on those scripts together and he'd want you to go on making them funny. Save your tears for later. You owe him the laughs now.' I went back to rehearsal in the afternoon and tried to act on that advice.

On the 12th of January, Number Three went fair but the laughter was all in the obvious places – I felt no reciprocity. Then on the 19th of January, for Number Four, everything was transformed. I don't know if someone gave the ticket unit a hint or whether it was sheer chance but it was as if a magic wand had been waved over the auditorium and their reaction was a joy. From the moment I went on stage the atmosphere was receptive, all the subtler points were taken as well as the tag lines, the sketches with Joan went perfectly and every denouement worked. I thought afterwards in the dressing room that this was the script which John Law and I had thought the trickiest of all to pull off, and I knew he would have said 'Well done'.

The following week, however, it was all back to square one, and when I watched the playback of Number Five I was staggered by the sheer obtuseness of the house. The laughs were there all right but they occurred in the wrong places. It was as if the audience were searching for *double-entendres*, and finding them whether they were in the script or not.

I would have lunched in gloom at the TV Centre but luckily I met Gordon Jackson and he cheered me up. He had watched the show from the theatre circle on the first night and he was unstinting in his praise. 'You're absolutely right to strike out in this new direction. Stick with that concept. Never mind if it's not a hit every week, it's the originality that counts.' When the sixth and last show was performed on the 2nd of February, it was very successful, with a lively and appreciative audience. It was a fitting note on which to end the series. Gordon had been right.

Immediately afterwards I began work on the BBC radio

203

programme produced by Helen Fry called *With Great Pleasure*. It was an anthology of poetry and prose excerpts with explanatory linking passages between each one. For some reason I had assumed I would be sitting in a studio speaking intimately into a microphone. I got quite a shock when Helen told me there had been a big demand for tickets at the Playhouse. Only then did I realize it was to be more than just a radio performance. Anyway it was a perfect opportunity to talk about my favourite poets in serious and comic vein. I used a piece by Stanley Baxter called 'It Was All Done In The Twenties In Berlin', which the audience adored, and Johnson's 'Death Of Dryden' which got laughs as well. Louis MacNeice's 'Bagpipe Music' also aroused a great deal of amusement. I used three illustrations of Hope, quoting Byron, Shelley and Haro Hodson, without fluffing any of them. With Tennyson's 'Lady Of Shallott' I went at a spanking pace after 'the mirror cracked', speeding through the boat sequence and slowing down only for the valedictory ending. And I included Francis Meynell's 'Tissue Of Time' and spoke of its special significance for me. Altogether it was an enjoyable evening and the audience received me warmly. There was literally only one sour note. It was a letter written by a woman complaining that she thought it was extraordinarily tasteless of me to 'expatiate so eloquently on Wordsworth and then clutch your trousers in that vulgar fashion and say you were dying for a pee.' She said she had expected better of me. Since I'd been on stage for two hours she could have expected worse.

After the programme was broadcast I had more letters than I had ever received before. Peter Eade and Helen Fry both helped me and we coped with over seven hundred. Then the BBC put out a repeat and the mail piled up all over again. Haro Hodson wrote very generously about my performance and there was a heartwarming letter from Sir Francis Meynell saying, 'I was proud to be in your company.'

The endless throbbing from the ventilation fans drove me out of Farley Court and by the time I had started on the second *Stop Messing About* series I was temporarily housed in Stanley's flat in Judd Street. It was only a stone's throw from my old junior school and my erstwhile parental home, and there were plenty of people in the area whom I knew from the past. But it was all a bit *déjà vu*. Stanley told me there was another apartment vacant in the block, so I took it, and I asked Brian Dobson to do all the carpentry for me. He said he thought he could complete it by June. I'd met Brian through Richard Williams. I'd visited his studio in Soho Square and commented admiringly on the superb panelling and he'd told me it was all Brian's work and gave me his telephone number. Since then Brian had made a beautiful bedhead for Louisa in aphromosia and the joinery was immaculate. He promised to combine the wardrobes in my new flat with filing cabinet units. In most places I'd never been able to accommodate all my scripts properly. I went back and forth from each flat seeing to everything from electricians to plumbers and was unsettled and totally disorganised.

The radio programmes were barely underway before I was back with Gerald and Peter filming *Carry On Loving*. I was in trouble with my back and visits to Johnny Johnson, the osteopath, started all over again. Eye concretions also plagued me and I was in and out of the Western Ophthalmic Hospital. When I finally moved into the completed apartment I had to cope with an obdurate boil on the leg which required injections of penicillin for ten days and didn't clear up till the end of August.

In September I fled to the Greek Islands again, Corfu, Rhodes and Chiros, ending up in Heraklion where I tried unsuccessfully to relive the happy stay I'd enjoyed there with Beverly. Alas, broadcasts are the only repeats that work.

In October 1970 I was back at Pinewood for the twenty-first film in the series playing Cromwell in *Carry On Henry*. Gerald and Peter greeted me affectionately, my old friend Alan Hume was lighting the picture, and my first scenes were with Kenneth Connor, so it couldn't have been nicer. He made me laugh and I spoiled a take. I had a false arm inside my sleeve. When he asked, 'Are you with me?' I replied, 'You have my hand on it,' and he shook this plastic hand and I walked away, leaving him holding it. His facial expression was so comic that it set me off every time.

During the shooting the electricians in the studio used a jargon for their lighting terms – 'Give us a barn door, Fred,' etc. When they asked for a 'Chinese' Kenny echoed it 'a la Charlie Chan and on the call 'Bring a pup over here,' he began a yelp that was so life-like that everyone began looking around for the dog. I trotted out a few technical terms myself to show off on the set.'I think it wants a Number 5 for this panning shot,' I said to Gerald authoritatively, and when he looked doubtful I added, 'Don't worry, I'm right. I've been around so long I know the wrinkles.'

'I can see that,' he replied, 'Most of them are on your face.'

'Yes, well of course, I should be shot through a gauze. Merle Oberon was always shot through a gauze. It hides all the defects. I should have a gauze.'

'If you're not careful you'll have a blanket.'

I looked heavenward, laughing.

"Keep your chin down for goodness sake, the nostrils are awful in close-up. Worse than the Blackwall Tunnel.'

On a *Carry On* set no one was ever pummelled by ego massage.

The film was completed in November but I couldn't go away for a holiday because the weekly *Just A Minute* shows continued to the end of December; and there were costume fittings and other preparations to be made for a forthcoming stage production because, after much heart-searching, I had decided it was time I returned to the theatre.

Binkie Beaumont, of H. M. Tennent, had told me he was planning a revival of Shaw's *Captain Brassbound's Conversion* starring Ingrid Bergman and he asked me to play Drinkwater. I read the play and thought it was decidedly creaky, but after a meeting with the director Frith Banbury, I thought I might risk it. He seemed well aware of the weaknesses in the piece and pointed out that a well-cast, swift-moving production would camouflage the defects. I was nearly persuaded. Then Binkie arranged a party for some of the cast at his house in Lord North Street during October, where I met Ingrid. I was impressed from the moment she entered the room. The legendary beauty I had first seen in *Casablanca* had lost none of her charm, and her smile was radiant.

After the introductions had been made she apologised about traffic delaying her all the way from the Connaught Hotel. I said it was a star's privilege to be late, but she protested that she hated unpunctuality. We all instanced occasions when we had suffered from it, and Ingrid said, 'Oh yes, it can be very trying. Once in Jennifer Jones' house we were all sitting having drinks and waiting for her to come down for dinner. The time went on and on and the highballs were getting more and more lethal till I lost patience and asked where she was. They said she was still in the bedroom and they didn't dare disturb her. I said that was ridiculous and I went up there. She had these switches by the bed which controlled electrically-operated doors and she was lying there pressing the buttons and the panels were sliding back to reveal hundreds of dresses and hats and shoes. I asked "What's the matter?" "It's no good, Ingrid", she said, "I just can't decide what to wear".'

Everyone laughed over such luxurious vacillation. Binkie wanted to know whether we were going to dither over the play or whether we were keen to do it. When we all chorused yes he said, 'Then why don't I ring the *Daily Mail* and announce it!' But I felt we should wait until contracts had been signed. Even in the presence of this beautiful star, I was still not totally committed.

Eventually it was Peter Eade who decided it for me. He countered my argument about the size of the part. 'You said the same thing about the Shaffer plays and afterwards admitted you were wrong. Never mind about the length of the role, think how effective you can be in it.'

He arranged the contract with Binkie and in January 1970 I began rehearsing *Captain Brassbound's Conversion*. During the first week it was obvious that the work was proceeding in a plodding, pedestrian fashion, and on the 8th of January Ingrid expressed her misgivings to me. 'I thought Binkie would get a young and imaginative director so that the play would have the sort of re-interpretation which Zeffirelli gave to *Romeo and Juliet*.' I said I didn't think we could expect any innovations here. All we got in direction was peripheral instruction, no total concept or integrated design for the play was ever evinced. My depression was largely warded off by Joss Ackland, who played the Captain. He made us all laugh with his uncannily accurate impersonations of Groucho Marx, waltzing up to Ingrid and saying, 'I could dance with you till the cows come home! Come to think of it I'll dance with the cows and wait for you to come home.' When Ingrid said she'd been told about his irrepressible humour, Joss mimed Groucho's cigar and quipped, 'To be forewarned is to be forearmed' – and then added with a frown, 'But who wants to walk around with four arms?' Joss certainly kept my spirits up during the first weeks, but as the opening night on tour approached, even he became tetchy. On the 26th when the director told him not to keep moving about during a scene, he said, 'If I'd been given some moves I wouldn't have to.'

'Yes, well we must get on, don't you see'.

Even Ingrid became a little vexed when asked to rehearse the scene twice. 'Oh don't let's bother to go back over it again. I don't know those lines anyway.'

'I think we should go back over it again.'

'Oh no, let's go on.'

'No, it's important to get this right. Don't you see?'

'But you said earlier there was no time and we must get on.'

'Yes, but we will have to make time, don't you see.'

Sentences frequently ended with this ocular enquiry, but even a cyclops could discern that the production was halting and unexciting. On the 30th the director rehearsed in the morning and then announced his departure for the day.

'But you've called a word-rehearsal for this afternoon,' I said. 'Aren't you going to attend it?'

He said, 'Mr Beaumont ordered the word-rehearsal,' and left.

In the afternoon things took quite a different turn and it was much more than a word-rehearsal. Ingrid suddenly began to assert herself in a way she had not done hitherto. She altered the static speech poses and introduced several moves which gave fluidity and meaning to the scenes. In the trial sequence she plotted it differently so that, very properly, she dominated it as a Prosecuting Counsel really should. The entire process heartened everyone in the cast and Joss expressed his admiration for her patience and her inventiveness. 'She's going to be very good in this,' he remarked. 'She's pulling all the loose strands together now.'

I said, 'There's still a lot of mispronunciation – "clothes" is coming out as "clows" and "Board the ship to look after his wife" as "Wife on board to look after the ship".' Ingrid laughed gaily and told me not to worry: 'I'll get it right.' Later she talked about the actor's need for encouragement during rehearsals. I suggested we should have someone continually in attendance to praise us.

Ingrid said, 'It certainly happened with Lewis Milestone on his first picture with Joan Crawford. He walked down a line of assembled extras and picked out a very handsome one, saying, "Miss Crawford, here is your flatterer. This man will be engaged to tell you how wonderful you are in every scene we shoot."'

208

We opened at the Theatre Royal, Brighton, on the 1st of February 1971 and, in spite of a ragged performance, the applause justified three curtain calls. Peter Eade came backstage saying he thought we'd just about got away with it and Binkie invited most of the cast to a nearby restaurant to celebrate. The actors' relief turned quickly to elation. Ingrid ordered champagne for everyone, Joss proposed the toast to the most beautiful leading lady ever to grace a play by Bernard Shaw and we all said 'Aye' to that. I went round embracing everyone with exaggerated affection. Frith Banbury said, 'What an escape!', echoing the last line of the play, and the occasion began to assume the heroic proportions of Dunkirk.

The play started its London run at the Cambridge Theatre on the 18th of February. I wrote in my diary, 'The performance went reasonably competently and at the end there were nine curtains for the company and Ingrid had to take three solo calls because the house obviously adored her.' The critics were either cruel or cool but certainly not enthusiastic. It counted for nothing because the advance bookings were overwhelming and we played to packed houses for the limited six-month run. There were nights when Ingrid was on form and there were nights when she was tired and didn't adhere to the text. All her film experience never supplied the technique for a sustained performance eight times a week in the theatre, but that didn't really matter. The reception she received night after night proved that the audience hadn't come to see Bernard Shaw's Lady Cicely Wayneflete: they'd come for the magic of Ingrid Bergman and an aura which criticism, good or bad, could do nothing to dispel.

In March, Bill Cotton planned ten episodes of a new show called *Meanwhile on BBC2* under the aegis of Stewart Morris and I was asked to provide the same zany compering material I had used in the cabaret series. After unsuccessful attempts to find a collaborator, I wrote the scripts alone and managed to get several completed before starting on the next film with Gerald and Peter at Pinewood. Sometimes I jotted down ideas in the dressing room at the Cambridge Theatre, but I completed most of the writing at home. I used to walk back and forth from Judd Street to Seven Dials running the dialogue in my head and deciding what voices to use.

On the 15th of March I got to the theatre to find a note from

209

Ingrid asking me if I would go to her flat for supper after the performance, and I went up to her room to say yes. She seemed unusually buoyant and when I watched her from the wings during the second act of the play, I could see she was sailing through it with tremendous élan and confidence. When she came off I said, 'You're on form tonight!' And she replied, 'Yes, I feel the tempo is right somehow . . . and of course Binkie is out front. I always work better when there is a particular person I want to please.'

She lost none of her energy when the curtain descended, taking us off to a splendid party at her flat in Grosvenor Street where she entertained about twenty people. She'd prepared cold Swedish food and chilled white wine and it was all very pleasant. Binkie said the production costs would be paid off by the end of the week and that he'd been greatly impressed by the box-office staff. 'They're as proud as punch to have Ingrid's name out front,' I said. He agreed. 'The enthusiasm pervades the entire theatre.'

I asked Binkie if a story I'd heard about him was true or apocryphal. Years ago he'd gone to the box office at the Globe Theatre and had been aghast to see that the chart had hardly a seat sold on it. The elderly lady clerk in the cubby hole peered over her pince-nez, admitted that the bookings were abysmal, and Binkie said, 'Well dear, you'd better put your fascinator on!' Binkie said the tale was true.

'What is a fascinator?' Ingrid asked, and I told her that it was a Victorian gadget which slipped down the front of a dress making the breasts more prominent. 'Apart from its unsuitability for the lady' I added, 'it was a ludicrous suggestion because you could only see her face through the glass.'

Binkie liked the Globe and I remarked on the tiny lift which bore one to his office from the foyer. 'When two people are in it you're so squashed against each other that reticence is impossible.' 'That's the idea,' he smiled. 'They arrive uninhibited.'

Ingrid washed the dishes as we went along and the guests helped to dry, so there was no collection of dirty plates at the end. I walked home in the early hours thinking what a superb evening Ingrid had given us. After two hours starring on stage, she'd been a hostess for another two, looking as nonchalant as if an army of servants had been at work, when in fact she'd done it all herself.

* * *

210

Carry On At Your Convenience began at the end of March 1971 and my first shot was with Patsy Rowlands in bed, so there was quite a lot of giggling. After that there was a scene in a fortune-teller's booth with a crystal ball between me and the dark-eyed gypsy, played by Sid James in drag. When I saw his face I nearly got the giggles again but I knew that would annoy Sid. He loathed wearing female attire and wanted to finish the sequence as quickly as possible.

At the end of a day's filming I generally got to the theatre early and had a nap before the evening performance. One evening I met Ingrid at the stage door in a very gay mood. 'I have had a marvellous weekend in Paris,' she said, 'just strolling through the trees.'

'It's obviously done you good, your eyes are sparkling!'

She agreed: 'I feel good! A change of scene does wonders for me.' By this time we'd reached her dressing room and she examined herself in the mirror.

'Have you done something different with your hair?' I asked.

Her expression changed. 'No, I'm rather cross about that. They did it wrongly at the hairdressers. I've told them they'll have to do it all over again, that back-combing makes it stand up.'

It didn't affect her performance because she played with such authority and confidence that when she came forward at the curtain people rose in their seats to applaud her. When we came off I said, ' You did some back-combing yourself with that audience tonight!' and that made her laugh.

On the 11th of April 1971 I did the first of the *Meanwhile On BBC2* shows at Shepherd's Bush. Alyn Ainsworth was conducting the orchestra but he found time to take me through my lines before the show, picking me up on mistakes and making me go back till they were put right: he was wondrously patient. Everything went smoothly and the show built right up to the entrance of Howard Keel who got a round of applause as soon as he began to sing those *Oklahoma!* songs he had made so famous years before. By the time I wrapped it up with my last spot the house was in a very good mood. The director, Stewart Morris, complimented me in the dressing room afterwards. 'I noticed a great difference in your delivery tonight, much more relaxed.'

'I had nothing to eat before the show, it makes a difference.'

'Well, your stuff went like a bomb. Better than any of your other shows.'

Then Peter Eade came in and he too said he thought that the linking material all came together very nicely, and that it augured well for the series. I felt especially pleased, since it was the first time I'd concocted a script on my own, and here was endorsement that it had worked.

On the 16th of April I was surprised to see Ken Loach on the *Carry On* set, and we had a chat about the time we worked together in the revue *One Over The Eight*. I knew about the success of his film *Kes*, and congratulated him. He said how much he'd enjoyed working with real people on a picture instead of actors, which didn't please me overmuch, and went on to discuss film-funding, the working-class movement and political revolution.

'You never talked like this when I knew you.'

'Perhaps you weren't listening.'

'I listen very well, I'm a diarist.'

'There are some things we don't always remember.'

'I remember you giving me the Warren book on King John.'

That set the conversation on a different tack and we discussed Magna Carta and were soon back to politics.

When he left the set I said to Bernard Bresslaw, 'He used to be my understudy, and now he's a film director extolling the virtues of the working class.'

'He'll get over it,' said Bernard.

'I don't know about that. He's an idealist, you see.'

'What's he doing on a *Carry On* set?'

'Heaven knows. He doesn't approve of capitalism, so I shouldn't think he's thick with Peter Rogers. Isn't it interesting how the world reacts to success? If an oil prospector strikes a gusher everyone's envious of the newfound wealth. If he drills a dryhole nobody's interested in his lost millions.'

'Nobody's interested in failure.'

'And nobody wants to risk failure. Take our industry. Actors don't want to put their money at risk in a film. Peter Rogers does, and when a *Carry On* is top box office there are headlines about the fortune he's amassing.'

'And no mention of what he's lost on the others.'

'Exactly. If a man sinks his savings into digging a well he's

212

got the right to charge a penny a cup for the water that comes out of it.'

'Socialists say the people should dig the well and then get their water free.'

'Communal effort seldom produces the well, Bernard. It's generally the result of one man's vision and expertise. Art is the same: nothing good is ever produced by committee, it is always the singular talent that creates and excites. People don't go to the theatre to see life – they can see life on any street corner, and a great mess it is. They go to see an artist's vision of life and if it works they share his aspirations.'

'So we're back to ideals,' said Bernard.

'In art, yes, because they're transcendent. Communally they don't work, because ideals are about purity, and men are, by their nature, impure.'

I finished filming on the 10th of May and the following week was full of excitement in the theatre. We raised a subscription among the actors and acquired a silver salver to present to Ingrid on the night of the hundredth performance of the play in London, inscribed to her 'with admiration and affection from the cast'. After the performance on the 17th we gathered in the stalls bar where celebratory drinks were served, and I made a speech praising our star, before presenting her with the memento. Ingrid looked a little taken aback when I unwrapped the parcel and gave her the glittering silver tray. Her eyes glistened as she spoke some words of thanks and she concluded, 'Nothing like this has ever happened to me. I shall treasure it.'

There was another party on Thursday when Ingrid asked some of us to come to her dressing room and meet Noël Coward, when he came to the play with Graham Payn and Cole Leslie. The Master was lavish with his praise and told Ingrid she'd never used a wrong gesture throughout the play. Turning to me, he said, '*You* frequently do, but you're one of the few actors I know who can be outrageous and get away with it, and we love you for it.'

Later on, someone drew Noël's attention to an enormous lithographic print of Eleanora Duse hanging on the wall. 'I saw her', he said. 'She over-acted dreadfully. Even when playing an eighteen-year-old at sixty she never had a shred of make-up, just powder, and her snow-white hair was drawn up into a terrible bun at the back. The entire effect was distinctly

213

discouraging.' Ingrid laughed and said it was a wonder she could remember the lines and then talked about her own difficulty learning Shaw. Noël pointed out that he was impossible to paraphrase, and Ingrid seized on this, saying that when I had once been late on my entrance she'd found it quite impossible to extemporise. The Master agreed.

'She's right, and there's no excuse for lateness. Shaw's dialogue consists of argument and it needs all the voices.'

I said, 'You're right about the argument. Have you noticed, there's no real emotion with Shaw, it's all cerebral, there's no sex.'

'No,' replied Coward. 'Whenever he felt particularly erotic he went round to the Webbs and talked himself out of it.'

As usual with Noël you were amused as well as enlightened and at the end of the evening when I helped Ingrid clear up in the dressing room, I thanked her for making it all possible. 'You don't know how much delight and affection you bring into a room. It doesn't want lights, it just wants Ingrid Bergman.'

I walked home singing all the way, full of elation over one of the most enchanting people in show business.

In June 1971 I was not only doing theatre at night and TV on Sundays, I was beginning a new situation comedy on radio – *The Secret Life of Kenneth Williams* – as well as another series of *Just A Minute*. Nowadays that kind of schedule would exhaust me, but I see from my diary that there were precious few early nights.

On the 4th of June Ingrid invited me to supper after the show with her friend Alfred Hitchcock, and we talked into the early hours. Alfred told her she had given a very assured performance.

'The trouble is', said Ingrid, 'I can never remember *how* I was good, you know! Something happens from inside and the performance comes alive for me, but I can't just switch it on again the next night. I suppose it's all instinct with me.'

'That is better than method acting,' said Alfred. 'I remember Paul Newman in *Torn Curtain* raising endless questions about the death scene with the German. He kept asking where the woman could get the motivation to put his head in the gas oven. I told him she got the idea on her way to the studios to do the filming.'

214

Ingrid said that actors needed to be indulged by the director and she reminded Alfred of a memorable scene with Charles Laughton crying on the set and saying to an uncomprehending Hitchcock, 'Aren't we just a couple of big babies?' and Alfred replying, 'Look, Charles, as Sam Goldwyn says, you can include me out.'

'Of course actors need indulging,' agreed Hitchcock. 'In *The Birds* we had loads of 'em behind some chicken wire and when the scene started, the wire was raised and they all came flying out at Jessica Tandy. Before the scene I could see she was nervous and I said, "Listen, Jessica, if one of them gets up your skirt, grab it. Remember, a bird in the hand . . ."'

Of course he didn't need to finish the line before there was laughter all round the table. Ingrid, however, looked mystified. Alfred turned to me despairingly, 'It's no good telling English jokes to foreigners.'

July 1971 seemed to get hotter and hotter as it progressed. The heat in the auditorium of the Cambridge practically hit you in the face as you went on. The stalls were a sea of waving programmes as people tried to cool themselves. Ingrid always appeared serene but more than once she complained, 'Oh for some air conditioning!'

On the 31st the theatre was packed and the audience tremendously enthusiastic. Ingrid put her arms round me in the wings before I went on, and said, 'So at last, my dear, we come to the final performance. Just think, I stood here and wished you luck half a year ago.'

I had little time to reply because I had to make my entrance but I felt a surge of melancholy as she spoke. I wasn't the only one who was affected by last-night feelings. Several actors became sentimental and invested certain lines with special significance. When I came to my speech, 'Dear me, we comes in with vanity, and we departs in darkness, don't we, guv'nor?' I suddenly realised that when the lights went out tonight on this production it would vanish forever. It had all turned out so differently from what I had imagined. This poor old creaking play and this rickety production, greeted with hostility and indifference by the press, had been kept afloat by a lady who had broken all box-office records for a limited London season, delighted loyal audiences nightly and never missed a performance.

215

During August and September 1971 there were several mishaps in my flat. Water flooded the bathroom from above, the kettle over-boiled, wallpaper peeled off the kitchen walls, and a walking disaster moved in below screeching 'Peg O' My Heart' in a quavering soprano at all hours. I became obsessed with the idea of moving again. I wanted desperately to find somewhere quiet. Brian Dobson and his wife Molly were very helpful and we spent days searching for the right sort of house in the suburbs, but for some reason or other I could never commit myself to move there. Richard Pearson drove me miles into the Kent countryside looking for property. He understood my dilemma. 'You really want rural peace in the middle of the metropolis.'

Stanley took me to several places in Highgate but even when the abode was suitable it wasn't accessible. 'I don't drive and so I'd be at the mercy of public transport and the staring is intolerable – every day I mean.'

'Well you could buy a little car and engage someone to drive you about, couldn't you!'

'A chauffeur! Oh no, that is not my style.'

'Hmm. When it comes to a *modus vivendi* you haven't got any style.'

When October came and I started *Carry On Matron*, I was still in the flat but welcoming every opportunity to go out, so I didn't resent rising at 6 am and leaving at 7 for the studios in Buckinghamshire. My first day's filming didn't exactly go trippingly. It was a long and difficult scene in which I had screeds of medical jargon to deliver; I had to use the telephone, take my pulse and put a thermometer in my mouth. I got it wrong again and again; it was my old failing, inability to synchronise. Gerald complained, 'Oh dear, you're no good with props,' as if he didn't know already. By the time it got to take number seven I heard him say to the cameraman, 'Let's keep that last one and print that, it won't get any better.'

My next scene was with Hattie Jacques so I was home and dry. We had the kind of rapport that made work a pleasure. Unlike me, she was very deft with all the props and the scene went smoothly in one take. I said, 'Very different fom that night at Joan Sims's party when your flamboyant gesture knocked her vase off the mantlepiece.'

'Oh yes,' laughed Hattie ruefully. 'Joan said it was a family heirloom that had been handed down!'

216

'That night it was knocked down!'

It reminded me of Mrs Patrick Campbell examing a hideous vase she'd been sent by a fan. She read the inscription on the base, 'Made in Czechoslovakia'. She dropped it on the floor and said, 'Smashed in Belgravia.'

At lunch time we were joined by Barbara Windsor in the studio restaurant, and she told us how nice it was to be back with all her old chums and how different the *Carry On* atmosphere was from her last film.

'We were on location doing *The Boy Friend* in this theatre at Southsea, it was awful, you could see mice running about in the auditorium. I had a terrible time dancing "So Much Nicer in Nice" with all these beads joggling round my neck. We did take after take wearing ourselves out while the director sat in the stalls having his tea served on a tray with bone china. 'Course we had ours out of paper cups. Never mind the poor old actors.'

'You should have put your foot down.'

'Oh I did,' she laughed. 'I put it down so hard it broke all my beads. They fell all over the stage, it was like dancing on ball-bearings. But I kept going.'

At this point Gerald sent a bottle of champagne to our table and Barbara enthused, 'That's a lovely gesture'.

Hattie remarked, 'On these films you don't get paid much but you're certainly treated well.'

'Yes', I added, 'Peter Rogers sent me a pound of sausages last week, they were delicious.'

Barbara laughed. 'Blimey, Gerald gives you bubbly and Peter gives you bangers!'

Hattie said, 'The vulgar with a bit of oo la la, yes it sort of sums up the *Carry Ons*, doesn't it?'

When the film finished in November, I continued with radio work till the last *Just A Minute* in February 1972 and then went to Nice and motored to Seillans in the Var where Beverly Cross had rented a converted farmhouse. I got the only room in the local pension with a private bath, and though the first few days saw an influx of racing cyclists, the odious smell of whose linament permeated the corridors, once they had gone the place was a veritable haven of peace. Every day I used to make my way across fields and up a steep gravel path to Beverly's house and we would sit in the sun on his terrace talking over old times.

217

We went to St Tropez where Beverly ordered some very expensive wine and a delectable meal and insisted on paying for everything. 'But it's a huge bill!' I exclaimed. 'Rubbish, it's your birthday,' he reminded me. I didn't protest.

Next day we visited Bargemon in the Alpes Maritimes, and the day after that Fayence. Bev told me, 'I was in the supermarket here that I saw an Englishman we both know; he was protesting about the prices – like you. He said, "Lobster at fifty francs a kilo! Good heavens, I'll have to make another film!"'

Bev's indignant delivery of the line made me laugh. 'Who was it?' I asked, and he said, 'Dirk Bogarde'.

It was a pleasant reunion and the sunny south of France was a delightful change of scene. I was sorry to leave and didn't fancy chilly England at all, especially as London was beset with power cuts and industrial problems over the miners' strike. But I returned in March, and when I rang Gordon to ask how rehearsals were going for his play *Veterans* I found that he had problems, too. 'At the dress rehearsal', he said, 'there were about 25 notes and I think 24 of them were for me.' It was clear that he was deeply unhappy in the part and when Rona came on the line she told me how much his depression had upset her.

I telephoned Stanley and said we should all rally round and take Gordon to supper in a restaurant near the Royal Court. 'We could collect him after the show and whisk him away. I think it would cheer him up if we called on him, act as a sort of therapy you know.'

'You make us sound like prison visitors.'

'I think that's what we'll be.'

On the appointed day Stanley rang and said the power cuts had wreaked havoc in Highgate. 'I was trying to check whether the heat was working. I put this candle in the oven and there was an explosion which practically blew my head off. I had to rush to hospital.'

'How dreadful.'

'Yes, it's burned half my hair off and I've got no eyebrows.'

'Oh dear, do you want to cancel tonight?'

'No, I think it's important that we see Gordon if he's cast down like that. When you're unhappy in a performance you need your friends.'

'But what about your bald head?'

'I'm not entirely bald, just the front. I'll keep my hat on.'

'I've got an eyebrow pencil somewhere in the make-up case.'

'So have I. See you outside your flat in an hour.'

It was a cold evening and when we arrived in Gordon's dressing room clad in heavy overcoats with wide lapels and epaulettes he said, 'You both look terribly Deutscher – like a couple of heavies come to give me a grilling.'

'That's right,' I told him, 'we're taking you for a pep talk,' and we bore him away to the restaurant.

Stanley asked him about all that had happened at rehearsals and Gordon recited a list of woes. It seemed the play was full of comic lines but the director was telling him to play it seriously. He was using a Scots accent whereas the author had envisaged Cockney. Rona had been telling him it was too burlesque, others said it should be Chekovian and altogether they'd created confusion and havoc for him. Stanley told him that psychological madness lay in listening to dissenting voices. 'You must play it your way and ignore all the outsiders.'

I said, 'Yes, look what happened with *Twang*! Lionel Bart told me there were so many rewrites and different interpretations they'd ruined it.' I quoted Coward: 'Never let anything come between an artist and his personal vision,' and I added, 'If you listen to committees it will drive you insane; they're not up there on the stage doing it, you are. Critics are like the eunuchs in the harem. They're there every night, they see it done every night and they know how it should be done every night. But they can't do it themselves.'

The pair of us bombarded Gordon with our advice, advocating self-preservation, and then saw him to his car. He departed looking dazed but promised to bear in mind all that we had said. Afterwards Stanley said, 'Do you think we overdid it?'

'Yes, he looked a bit drunk.'

'But he's teetotal, he only drank milk.'

'I meant punch-drunk after our verbal attack.'

'Yes, perhaps we did go too far, but he must be made aware of the danger. He mustn't let them undermine his confidence.'

I said I would go and see a performance with Rona, and have another go at him after that.

'But he's told us he doesn't want us to see him in it.'

'Yes, well, I will arrange that he doesn't see me.'

I persuaded Michael Codron to let me have seats and told him of my desire not to be observed. 'Gordon musn't know

I'm out front, it will put him off. It will be all right when I go round afterwards 'cos then it will all be over.'

'Then you'd better not sit in the stalls.'

'No,' I agreed. 'Upstairs would be better. The dress circle.'

'So you want two in the Dress.'

'Yes please.'

And that was agreed. I told Rona that Michael Codron had said I should go in the Dress and not in the stalls. At the conclusion of the play she went backstage alone because I first had to go to the lavatory. When I arrived in his dressing room Gordon was convulsed with laughter.

'What's so funny?' I asked.

'Rona told me about the conspiracy.'

'Well?'

'Michael Codron telling you to go in the Dress.'

'Yes, well, the Dress Circle is where you can't be seen by the actors.'

'No, it sounds like you were to go in a frock – dress, you see.'

'Oh,' I said, as the penny dropped. 'I see what you mean.'

'Oh it's terribly funny, the idea of you in drag at the Royal Court to avoid attention. Rona said it would probably have quite the opposite effect.' I was inclined to agree, but the incident, and my visit, had the intended effect of putting Gordon into good humour and we ended having a very enjoyable supper together.

Carry On Abroad began in April and I wasn't best pleased on the second day when a workman passing me in the corridor at Pinewood said, 'Morning Mr More.' I saw Barbara Windsor and Joan Sims in the make-up room and told them. 'I've been coming here since the '50s and today I was called Kenneth More.'

Joan said, 'It happens to all of us. I was having lunch in a restaurant, and a woman asked me for my autograph, saying, "It is Shirley Malane isn't it?" She even got the wrong name wrong.'

Barbara laughed. 'Well, I can beat that. In a cinema last week the usherette said, "Would you like me to order you a cab at the end of the show, Miss Sims?" I said, "No, but you can get me a plastic surgeon if you think that's my name."'

Joan pulled a face and moaned, 'Charming; just kick me as you pass.'

I told them that one of the funniest mistakes over names was when the government decided to honour Isaiah Berlin, who was in America, and they cabled Washington 'Offer knighthood to Berlin', whereupon our embassy promptly approached Irving Berlin who was delighted and thought he was getting the same treatment as Fairbanks as a reward for boosting army morale with his troop entertainments. When the mistake was realised they had to withdraw the offer.

'Quite right', said Barbara. 'After all he wrote "Call Me Madam", not "Call Me Sir".'

We had to do a coach sequence that morning with everyone boarding to depart for the holiday. When most of the actors were in their seats, Kenneth Connor, who played June Whitfield's husband, struggled on the bus with her and several suitcases. As he passed Sid James he asked, 'You wouldn't happen to have a spare bottle of bromide, would you? You see the jogging of the coach excites my wife.' He spoke with such devastating seriousness that there was quite a beat before anyone got the joke.

Gerald was anxious to take advantage of what little sunshine there was and shot through all the scenes very quickly. At lunchtime Joan Sims complained, 'It would help if the director told you where to put your face for the camera', and when we got back on the set afterwards I rushed to Gerald with the story. 'Joan Sims says you failed to give her an eyeline —'

'Yes, she's just been and told me that and she smells very strongly of onions.'

I primped and smirked and went back to Joan. 'Gerald says you smell of onions! I warned you at lunchtime when you were mixing the salad!'

'I should have given you the spoons — you're one of the biggest stirrers round here, carrying all the tittle-tattle back and forth.'

'I believe in airing these things.'

'Don't we know it! You're one long clothes line. You want to be careful your own smalls aren't dangling on it one day.'

'They'd be spotless. No one can besmirch my good name.'

'You told us this morning that people don't know your name,' Barbara said.

'Yes, well, that was an insult I have decided to swallow,' but their laughter drowned my reply.

By the end of May we were shooting scenes of holiday-makers sunbathing on the terrace. It was all supposed to look like a Spanish hotel on the Costa del Sol, and I was playing the courier for the package tour. For once, the weather was not on Gerald's side, and he was shooting with the aid of huge arc lamps to suggest the sun, while the actors were trying to cope with gale-force winds. Stella Rivers, the hairdresser, had to keep rushing on to the set to effect lightning repairs in between takes.

There was a scene in which I had to tell all the guests, 'Enjoy the sunshine!' and then there was supposed to be a cloudburst. The first time I tried to speak the wind was howling me down an my hair was all over my eyes. I told Gerald, 'It's ridiculous trying to pretend it's halcyon weather under these conditions. Stella is furious, she says Charlie's wig's nearly been blown off and you know how bereft he feels without it. He's like Samson.'

'Tell Stella the wind took his hair, not me,' said Gerald tartly. 'I'm not Delilah.'

'Oh, I don't know,' I said. 'With the right drag and a few tips from Danny La Rue you'd be home and dry!'

'That's more than you'll be in the next scene,' he said. 'It's the cloudburst, the rain will be running down your nose.'

Sure enough, they played firehoses onto the set to create the cloudburst and within seconds we were all soaked to the skin. Gerald called through the loud-hailer, 'Act like the captain of the ship braving the elements, Kenny! Tell the guests it's just a shower, it'll be all over in a minute.'

I ran under a table parasol and sheltered there bawling ad lib dialogue over the roaring wind and torrential downpour. It wasn't quite what he wanted, but he didn't reshoot it. To do that we'd have all needed to dry out and be re-costumed and made-up and there wasn't time for any of that. When the first assistant shouted 'It's a wrap', everyone rushed off the set swathed in dressing gowns and towels grateful that the ordeal was over. When I said, 'Wasn't it wet?' to Gerald, he muttered, 'So were you.' But I affected deafness and replied, 'Yes, wet through', before fleeing back to the dressing room.

In June 1972 there were long discussions with David Hatch and various scriptwriters about a revue-type radio programme, which resulted in *The Betty Witherspoon Show*. I was particularly enthusiastic because Ted Ray was starring in it, and I had a profound admiration for his work. We had a marvellous comedy character lady in Miriam Margolyes, and we eventually performed a pilot show at the Playhouse on the 25th of June. It went well enough for David Hatch to tell us he thought it stood a good chance of success and I said that radio needed the sort of comedy which Kenneth Horne had made so popular. Ted had a comparable geniality and was never short of an amusing aside. I had high hopes of this projected series becoming a reality.

The screeching tenant below succeeded in driving me out of the Judd Street abode, and I decided to move into the same block as Louisa where a flat had become vacant. This immediately involved me with removal men, carpet layers, electrical and telephone engineers, furniture shops, curtain makers, endless visits to the solicitors researching the lease, and all the imbroglio of moving house. There were snags galore, but everything was sorted out eventually and I had moved to Osnaburgh Street within a few weeks.

It seemed a propitious moment because Peter Eade told me the BBC had accepted the pilot programme and wanted ten episodes of *The Betty Witherspoon Show* starting in October. They also wanted me for the *Just A Minute* series, starting a month before, and Michael Codron sent me a new play entitled *The Fat Dress*, by Charles Laurence. As soon as I read it I knew it was my kind of script and sent him a note expressing my delighted thanks. It was an amusing and literate piece in which I was offered the part of Henry – an endlessly wise-cracking man hiding inferiority under acid-tongued humour, crushing all opposition but acknowledging in the end that it led him to a twilight of loneliness.

In September I was back with Derek Nimmo, Clement Freud and Sheila Hancock on *Just A Minute*, and in between I was doing another five episodes of *Jackanory* for BBC Television. During the month there were several sessions with Michael Codron about *The Fat Dress* and on the 26th of September I attended a meeting at the home of Eric Thompson who had been engaged to direct the play. I was alarmed when he began to talk of making cuts on the first page, and later Michael Codron frightened me further by saying he wanted several cuts as well. I looked warningly across at the playwright when Eric said, 'There are too many words. The audience will be sick of hearing all this dialogue, we must cut out these verbal conceits and make it real, keeping only what is essential to the plot.'

Next day I went to Peter Eade and voiced my misgivings. 'Look, if you do this play', he said, 'you must take direction. When you think comedy needs gingering up a bit you start acting outside the framework of a play and that damages it. You have got to get back to the discipline you had in *Saint Joan* and the Shaffer plays. That's what people remember. You must give Eric Thompson a chance.'

I nodded agreement but two days later the disquiet surfaced again and I telephoned Michael Codron and said I was apprehensive. 'Do you want to do this play?' he said.

'Yes, of course I do.'

'Then please understand it has to be done my way. You are self-destructive. I have always thought that about you. Charles Laurence is very happy about it and he is going ahead with the rewrites.'

In October I had to have a molar extracted and I told Louisa, 'It makes me feel so old – bits of me are decaying all the time' – but she said, 'Don't worry, you'll feel quite differently once the false one is put in.' At the radio show I moaned to Sheila Hancock about the agonies of starting a stage production all over again. 'It's best to just get on and do your job', she said, 'and not take any of it too seriously, it hardly ever warrants it.'

On Monday the 16th of October I did the *Betty Witherspoon Show* at the Paris Studio but it was a small house and though the cast worked vigorously it wasn't exactly scintillating. Peter Eade came backstage afterwards and said that Monday mornings were not the most opportune times for comedy shows. I went to his flat for coffee before rushing to St James's Church Hall in Piccadilly for the first rehearsal of *The Fat Dress*, which was now being called *My Fat Friend*. We started setting Act One and it wasn't long before my playing was questioned. On my speech beginning 'Victoria Hope, Spinster of this Parish . . .' the director said 'Now go through that all again only this time speak it *naturally*. Don't act it. Just be it. Say it as if you were almost thinking it for the first time, say it to yourself!' So I did, and of course the comedy went out of the window, but he seemed very pleased with the result. 'That's it,' he said. 'Now

224

this is what we must continue to do – pare the whole thing down, pare and pare until we get to the bones of these people. Forget all about the *acting* bit. Just let it happen.'

I walked home very depressed afterwards and Michael Codron telephoned me to find out now rehearsals had progressed. I told him the instruction I'd been given and added, 'I think the director feels that nothing must be glib and he's concerned to get at the truth of the characters.'

'Does this method inhibit you as an actor?'

'Yes, but I'm just going to do what I'm told.'

On Tuesday we came to some funny lines about a Scotsman's kilt. The director said, 'Let's cut it altogether. It is such an old joke everybody knows it,' and I protested, 'The scene will be left without a tag.'

'Oh, all right. Leave it in for now,' he said reluctantly, and I began to wonder just how much fun was going to be left in the script. At the Wednesday rehearsal, in a scene ending with the lines, 'I have a large chicken, what shall I do with it?' followed by 'Stuff it, let's go and do some work,' he suggested we cut that last line, and substitute 'I don't know' for 'Stuff it'.

I could hardly believe it. That was the curtain line in a comedy. Then he told the cast, 'During the last few days you've all been acting and doing all sorts of things and it's all been interesting and lovely. But I don't want to see it ever again. Think of ease, cut out all this acting bit.'

In my diary I wrote, 'I don't think anyone who knows about the vulnerability of actors could ever make such a silly speech.'

On Thursday there were more cuts. On Vicky's curtain line, 'Well, it's bloody well worked,' Eric said, 'We'll just have the crying – cut the line, it doesn't need it.' No one asked why, in that case, the author had written it. When yet another funny line about the galloping Scotsman was cut, I began to wonder if we weren't going to eschew dialogue altogether and end up with a mime. Every time a scene got under way and the actors started instinctively developing an idea, the director stopped it – 'Careful! We mustn't lose the truth of this situation' – and the players went stumbling back to the script and the spark of comedy guttered. I became self-conscious and inhibited, just speaking the lines and trying to look thoughtful. Not that there was much opportunity to rehearse because we had endless theorising from the director about the characters. He would give them imaginary backgrounds and make up stories about them.

225

That evening I told my worries to Stanley who advised me not to work under those conditions. Gordon said on the telephone that it sounded like *Veterans* all over again. And then I realized why our advice to him at the Royal Court had been useless. In rehearsal the actor becomes invalid; in the birth-pangs of creating a character he needs reassurance of his own worth within the company. Ideally this should come from the director; without it the seeds of doubt are sown, hesitancy takes the place of decisiveness and confidence is undermined.

On Friday the same dreary atmosphere prevailed and we had to listen to more speeches. 'Now I am going to keep on and on at you about the serious moments in this play that have got to come through, otherwise it will all be very glib and gagsville.' Specifically to me Eric said, 'Don't lay anything on in these descriptive passages, just let them come out as natural conversation.'

After I'd attempted to do this in performance he said, 'Yes, that's it, but the trouble is that you don't seem to be enjoying yourself enough when you tell us these things. Henry in the play would always be enjoying himself you know.' I felt like shouting, 'Of course I know, I was enjoying it before you killed all the fun in the part stone dead.' But in fact I simply said, 'Yes, I see,' and went home just as depressed as before.

That evening the author telephoned me to ask about rehearsals and I told him what had occurred. 'Well, I hope you're not going to play it on that level,' he said. 'I've written a comedy not a kitchen-sink drama.'

'I am not arguing with the director,' I told him. 'You can only have one captain of the ship.'

Disconcertingly, Charles said, 'But he won't be with you when you put out to sea.'

There was a run-through of the play at the end of the second week of rehearsals and the cast dutifully acted with serious naturalism. Charles was out front watching but left the theatre without comment. In the evening he telephoned me. 'That run-through was total disaster. The opening looks like *The Fall of the House of Usher*. There is a sense of impending doom. Everyone is down, lacking energy or drive. You would never dream you're supposed to be watching a comedy.'

On the 30th of October I did the *Betty Witherspoon Show* at the Paris and it went very well. I was glad because I was beginning to wonder if I'd ever know how to get laughs. But I

226

went to rehearse *My Fat Friend* afterwards with my heart in my boots. This time there was a run-through attended by the author and management. At the conclusion Michael Codron said it was moving and beautiful. Charles Laurence indicated he wanted to have a discussion about the play and I walked with him and Eric Thompson to Michael's office. Charles said *My Fat Friend* didn't look like a comedy at all and I added that I was bitterly unhappy playing it in a style that was alien to me. Michael Codron felt that was foolish and silly of me. Whereupon Charles said that if I was unhappy I must have my reasons.

'How can he be unhappy? It's such a beautiful production!'

Eric Thompson turned to me. 'You're unhappy because I've taken away all your tricks and your funny voices. I don't want them. I thought your first reading of the role was *awful*. I never said so because I thought you'd say you didn't want to work with me, but if this play is done it's going to be done my way, otherwise I'll go right now!'

Michael Codron told me, 'I am not going to allow you to cheapen my production, to turn it into a vulgar little piece.'

There wasn't much discussion after that. I felt demolished. The rest of the week I went through the motions thinking of Sheila Hancock's advice to just get on and do one's job but I found it brought no comfort. All my convictions had been steadily eroded. Was I wrong and the director right? Was the author wrong and the manager right?

On Saturday the 4th of November, I sat in the flat going over the lines feeling naked and unprepared. I kept thinking, 'You open in two days, you can't go on dithering, you'll have to make up your mind.' And the lines of a poem kept intruding upon me:

What banners are hung out to greet you here?
None, save the pallid tattered rag of fear.

On the 6th of November I did the *Betty Witherspoon Show* at the Paris with Ted Ray and then journeyed down to the Theatre Royal at Brighton. I got through the dress rehearsal feeling like a zombie.

By the time the curtain went up on the first performance, nervousness had wreaked such mental havoc that I walked on stage without the props. I forgot my briefcase entirely. The opening of the play depended on certain feed lines and since they were spoken off-stage they weren't heard so I repeated them and replied to myself. Straightaway I got the laughs. Suddenly it was as if everyone out front liked me and I began to play the part as I had always intended, ignoring the shackles of direction and using the lines for all they were worth. The rest of the cast were not so unbridled but I set a different pace remembering Charles Laurence's description of Henry —'He freewheels through the action' — and the resulting bifurcation somehow worked.

The reception was enthusiastic and George Borwick appeared backstage saying, 'It's marvellous! I'm trying to acquire the overseas touring rights.' Peter Eade followed him and said, 'By coming up in performance tonight you really helped the show.' Michael Codron also said, 'You were marvellous!' Eric Thompson said nothing.

On the following night I felt a little easier in the role, though the day had been taken up with more abortive rehearsals, Eric Thompson demanding more cuts. When Wednesday came, he appeared in my dressing-room after the show looking preoccupied. I chatted about the audience reactions in certain scenes and he suddenly burst out, 'Michael Codron has been terribly rude to me and said he's not going to have me mess up this play with sentimentality!' I was staggered. This seemed a great *volte face* after all the talk about a beautiful and moving production, but by Friday Michael had agreed that the play was better for the lightness and speed which had been injected into it, and that I had been right about some aspects of the comedy.

By the 13th of November we were playing at Wilmslow in a theatre originally built as a cinema. The auditorium stretched before us like a tunnel and the acoustics weren't helped by amplifiers fed from microphones in the footlights. Nevertheless the show was very well received. Eric Thompson came backstage and told me there was too much pace and too many laughs and then he took the cast for a meal to a nearby restaurant where he told us we were to rehearse tomorrow at 2 pm, adding, 'I was stampeded into altering this production by Michael Codron when he exploded on Wednesday at Brighton. I was trembling when I got into Kenneth's dressing room. Well, we are not going to put it all back. I am going to restore the original curtain and we must get back all the

228

seriousness into the characters. When James Anderson goes shopping in the play, we've got to believe he really went shopping – not that he got bags of food from an elf.'

On the 14th we were back to square one. More cuts were suggested but this time, as the actors saw their lines disappearing, they started to object, and there was some tetchy argument. When Eric told me he was cutting a speech of mine, I didn't argue at all, I just said 'no'. Eric went on: 'Unless I am obeyed, it will simply result in chaos.' I thought chaos had resulted anyway but I didn't say so. I replied that I liked the speech and wanted to keep it.

'You're not discussing this objectively, you're being emotional.'

I remember clearly how far I was from emotionalism. Tiredness had drained me, my voice was an octave lower than normal and I spoke in a weary monotone.

'I like the speech and I think I do it well. Obviously you don't, but then of course you've never approved of me in this role. You've never even said I was good in it.'

He turned to the cast. 'Hands up anyone here who I've told that to.'

No hand was raised. He smiled triumphantly. 'There! You see! I never go around telling people they're good!'

That night I went on and did it his way. I lost ground everywhere. I lost laughs, lost command, lost presence, and lost lines. Eric came round afterwards with the author and said, 'That was marvellous! That's the best you've ever done!'

'But all the laughs were lost.'

'No, that doesn't matter.'

Charles Laurence said it did and that he was going to speak to the management about it.

At the Wednesday rehearsal more cuts were attempted and Eric Thompson indulged in more theorising about the reality behind the comedy and reiterated the need to pare down to the bone. He quoted one passage as being extraneous saying it was 'weak and contrived'.

'All comedy writing is contrived', I said.

'Not as contrived as this.'

'Endless denigration of the script is dangerous. We've got to go on at night and perform it.'

'All right. That's it. Get on with it. Do it yourselves,' he said and left the theatre. I vaguely hoped the departure was permanent but he reappeared for the evening performance and ironically the section he'd wanted to cut got more laughs than ever before.

At the end of the week Peter came to Wilmslow to see the show and drove me back to London afterwards. In the car he said he thought the play had subtly altered since he saw it at Brighton. 'You are setting a pace that is too fast in the beginning and it could run away from the others. This is why I warned you in the beginning about obeying direction.'

'But most of the direction is at loggerheads with what the author intended.'

'Nevertheless it is the objective outsider who can best judge the overall effect and that's why Michael Codron wanted Eric to do this play.'

'It's been no good for me. It's made me teeter 'twixt one idea and another. Half the time I don't know where I am. All I know is that my instincts and my reason tell me the situation is wrong!'

'Perhaps it's you that's wrong. Michael Codron said at the beginning that you'd been away from the theatre such a long time that you wouldn't know how much it had changed and therefore you should obey Eric.'

'Michael said *that*?'

'Yes.'

'I don't think it's changed at all. *La Dame Aux Camélias* just gets renamed *Love Story*.'

At that point we rounded a bend in the road, the door opened and I nearly fell out of the car. Peter quickly reached across and slammed it shut. 'I should have locked the door when we got in. My mind was full of the play.'

'So was mine.'

Later on we stopped at a motorway cafeteria for a coffee and he was solicitous about the mishap. 'Did it frighten you?'

'No, but the thought of a London opening does.'

After the week in Wilmslow, the company had two weeks free before the London opening. I continued with the *Betty Witherspoon Show* and Ted and Miriam became as doleful as me over the sparse audiences which provided little or no reaction to the comedy material. It became a tedious chore and the scripts started taking a lot of the blame. By the 27th of November the producer told us that the BBC was trying to find new writers. After all the inquests about the writing of the play

230

I felt punch-drunk as far as literary analysis was concerned, but I noted in my diary: 'The people who are the quickest to fault comic endeavours are invariably unfunny themselves.'

I was back and forth to the dentist undergoing all the drilling and preparation for a cantilever bridge to support the false molar and soon I'd been fitted with temporary plastic caps to hide all the surgery. The bite didn't fit and every time I tried to eat I kept cutting the inside of my mouth and ulcerating the skin.

I was full of fear about the play, miserable about the radio show and my spirits were at zero. Peter Eade telephoned and said that the Parkinson show wanted me on the 2nd of December. I told him, 'Oh no! I've got a mouth full of plastic, and the old rectal problems have returned with a vengeance. I'm full of pain-killing tablets, I can't be funny.'

'I think it's important that you do it. *My Fat Friend* opens on the 6th and an appearance just before would help the play.'

So I did the television programme and it went surprisingly well. Michael Parkinson talked with me at length before we went on and we roughed out the themes. 'Don't bother yourself with the details,' he told me, 'leave it till we're in front of the cameras, I've got no worries about you being funny.'

He not only relaxed me, he gave me confidence. Luckily the programme was directed by Roger Ordish who'd worked on the *Kenneth Williams Show* so I had an ally, and the producer was Richard Drewett who was very reassuring. 'You are perfect for the chat show, you won't put a foot wrong,' he said.

Everything conspired to help me, and the audience was sympathetic throughout. Later on I was sent a newspaper cutting about the evening in which the MP, Ivor Jay, wrote, 'Mr Williams made you cry with laughter and weep with pity ... it was comic talent walking blithely and brazenly on a tightrope.' Peter Eade said he liked what he had seen and Gordon and Rona telephoned me and were fulsome in their praise. Nobody noticed the plastic teeth.

On Wednesday the 6th of December 1972, the day of the opening, the dentist took off the plastic caps and fitted the ceramic teeth. They looked as good as the real thing and that gave me a boost, I went on to the Globe Theatre where we had more rehearsals and then we were at the point of no return, when the doubting had to stop. A London opening night. I had asked myself so many times if I was right or wrong that my

231

brain had become a treadmill. Now it was left to desperation, and desperation said go on and do it your way. The performance was hard work. It was a difficult house, not lavish in reciprocity, but the script triumphed. Charles Laurence's lines sent the barometer up again and again and stopped us plummeting. There was the usual first-night bedlam after the show but eventually I got away and had supper with a party of friends. I finished up in Louisa's flat drinking coffee at 3 am, listening to her telling me how good I'd been and marvelling to myself that I had got through it at all.

When I arrived at the theatre the next day there were stacks of letters and telegrams congratulating me and I had already seen most of the reviews which were all favourable, but the most prized missive of all was from my beloved Maggie who was starring next door at the Queen's, in *Private Lives*. She wrote, 'I've never seen such a wonderful crop of good notices. You may have been away from the theatre for a long time but you've certainly come back with a bang!'

We had supper together on the following night and I told her, 'It's marvellous having you next door at the Queen's Theatre just like it was ten years ago when you did *Mary Mary* there and I was still in the Shaffer plays at The Globe. Of course, it isn't a coincidence. God intends these things. It's the divine nature of special affections. Some of my fondest memories are of our early days together in revue.'

'It was all so carefree then, wasn't it!' she said. 'But the awful thing about success is that it gets harder every time, not easier. When we were young arrogance blinded us to the pitfalls.'

'Yes, and age brings all the misery of decay. I've just been through agonies with these new molars on a cantilever bridge.'

'Don't talk to me about teeth. I'm so full of lead fillings my head keeps falling forward. People think I'm nodding profoundly but I'm just top heavy.'

I had another happy reunion on Christmas Day when I went to Hattie Jacques's house. She had a lot of friends round a groaning table and presided over the meal with that special warmth and affection which so endeared her to everyone. We all got a present – some even got two – but Hattie was given so many you couldn't count them. Joam Sims did the distributing, playing the Fairy of the Christmas Tree and calling out the names and good wishes, coupled with rude asides; as Hattie's pile of gifts mounted in front of her on the table, her face was gradually hidden by the parcels, and everyone was giggling as she protested, 'It's getting dark behind here.' But Joan went on producing the packages and eventually cried, 'And yet another tribute to the over-endowed Miss Jacques,' as she put a caged bird of paradise on top of the lot, adding, 'and it couldn't happen to a nicer person!'

Hattie's present to me showed special thoughtfulness. Months before I had told her how I had lost a greatly loved 78 rpm recording of Coward reading 'Welcoming Land' by Clemence Dane. She'd scoured half the gramophone exchange and mart shops in London to find it for me. There it was on my plate on Christmas Day with a special message written on the sleeve. It was a joy to have it back again and when I played it and heard those precisely modulated tones talking about the hunted people who fled from persecution to this wise island – 'Climbed the soft hills to the downs, and smelled the may sweet as a kiss on a winter's day' – I knew that the last line would forever symbolise Hattie for me.

Louisa had gone away with friends to the coast for Christmas and New Year and I spent Hogmanay appropriately with the Jacksons at Hampstead where I tasted haggis for the first time. 'It is delicious,' I told Rona. 'Your Scots culinary skills are still intact. How clever of you to remember the complicated recipe!' When she laughed at that Gordon explained 'We got it from Harrods!'

'Well, of course,' I said, extricating myself smoothly. 'I expect they've got a Scots chef, someone called Fraser.'

After dinner Gordon played 'Ich Grolle Nicht' from the Dichterliebe, then we went through the Coward songbook and tradition demanded that we finish with 'Waltz Ultime'. We sat talking after the New Year toast. Gordon made me laugh about a fund-raising appearance he had made. At the end, the organiser had seen him to the car, and surreptitiously pressed something into his hand before closing the door. Gordon said, 'I was horrified at first because it felt soft and rubbery, and I just kept my fist closed. It was about a minute later when I actually opened it and looked. I'd been given a handful of little balloons which advertised the charity'. He told us that it had been arranged by the publicity people with the show he was doing.

I said, 'I've had loads of that with the play opening:

interviews on the radio, interviews with newspapers and magazine writers. One question always comes up "Why don't you do some serious acting?" As though *Carry On* films and comedies in the commercial theatre are somehow meretricious.'

'That's because real respect is reserved for acting in the classics, not bums and tits films and plays about fat ladies.'

He was summing up the sort of critical disdain which I have always abhorred. It smacks of the same snobbery which rejects drawingroom ballads and operetta as unworthy alongside Mozart or Beethoven. I have enjoyed both. It is the same with poetry. As well as Shakespeare, it's important for me that I hear Housman triumph with a tiny poem. As a jobbing actor I've taken what has been offered to me. Sometimes the writing has been inspired, sometimes it's been hackneyed, but if either has given me a chance to create laughter I've used whatever tools I've got to make it work. The original dream of working with a group of people whose shared affections counted for more than personal ambition has never quite died. Embers still flicker into flames. But a part of me has always admired the cloistered virtue rather than the dust and heat of the race where Milton tells us that immortal garland is to be won. In any case, I think I've always preferred ambling to running. I've never enjoyed heat and dust and I've certainly never cared much about winning. I cling to Rilke's thought: 'The big words from those ages when as yet/Happening was visible, are not for us./Who talks of victory? To endure is *all*.'

Chapter Twelve

The last of the *Betty Witherspoon Shows* was done on the 22nd of January 1973 and went so well it was like the old *Round The Horne* days. The reason it was so successful was that this was one of the few occasions during the series when the studio had a capacity audience. Averagely we played to near-empty houses, and a handful of spectators in an auditorium inspires unease, not merriment. In February I went on the *Parkinson Show* again, this time with Maggie Smith, and together we read the Leamington Spa poem by John Betjeman because he was on the show too and we wanted to pay a tribute to him. After the show we talked about favourite lines and he asked me, 'Do you know who wrote: "And in my heart some late lark singing?"'

I said, 'Yes, it's W. E. Henley.' That seemed to surprise him. Then I said, 'Now I've got one for you. Who wrote, "Beneath the rule of men entirely great, the pen is mightier than the sword?"'

'Ah, don't tell me. I know, it's Tennyson.'

'No,' I said, 'it's Edward Bulwer Lytton.'

He repeated the name wonderingly, and then said, 'Our choices *are* revealing, aren't they!'

During the show I spoke about the fallacy of egalitarianism, and as a consequence I was asked back in March when I was confronted with a rabid communist who delivered some heated rhetoric about the wickedness of capitalism ensuring the deprivation of the working classes. After he'd condemned the rich, I said that I rather admired them. 'I think Rolls-Royce motor cars are very impressive, and if people enjoy going round in mink-lined jock-straps, good luck to them!'

Michael reproved me, saying that was a superficial and frivolous remark, but I knew that this wasn't going to be a serious discussion, it was going to be a propaganda exercise, where you played it all out front. The Marxist picture of power to the people always leaves out the stream of refugees, whether it's East Germans scaling the Berlin wall or Vietnamese braving the seas. Acton's maxim about power tending to corrupt is most clearly illustrated when the power is newly acquired. The traditions of inherited wealth breed indifference to bribery. As we've seen in America, presidents will profit from their temporary tenure in a way that monarchs would disdain. Bernard Shaw had no illusions about rule by the commonalty: 'Government by the people is not and never can be a reality: it is a cry by which demagogues humbug us into voting for them.'

In 1973, as well as playing in *My Fat Friend*, I did a new series of both the *Secret Life of Kenneth Williams* and of *Just A Minute*. But it was the play which broke the camel's back. It was a lengthy role, and though I captured some of the humour and pathos in the part I could never win against the framework of the production. The foundations had been too firmly laid for that. For me the bricks were all in the wrong place, but they were bricks, and while I might occasionally raise the roof, that would never dislodge the floor. I certainly never tried: it might have pulled the house down. As the run progressed the dichotomy became increasingly irksome. I had made the initial mistake of listening to conflicting counsel. What should have been joyous performing became miserable drudgery. To hide the wounds inflicted by destructive criticism I acted off stage as well as on stage, and in the end the strain produced a crisis.

Usually, it was only on opening nights that I experienced the kind of nervousness which affects digestion, but this condition now became ever-present. Meals were followed by pain and discomfort so often that I frequently went without food in order to get through the day. In the end the doctor expressed concern about the symptoms and I went back to Mr Mulvaney. There was another barium X-ray and this time it showed inflammation of the colon. I went back into hospital and the surgeon advised that I should not return to the production.

After a month's treatment and rest I finished the *Just A Minute* programmes and by August I was with Isobel Barnett in a revamped BBC television version of *What's My Line?* I think the only reason I wanted to do this was because of Isabel. Her deductive ability and her elegance were an asset to the show, but I liked her for something else: a courageousness she was never anxious to publicise. She was once flagged down on the road and asked to help a man who was in considerable pain. Eventually she got him to a local hospital where she diagnosed appendicitis. The matron asked, in the absence of a surgeon, if

236

Isabel would operate. 'It was years since I had trained as a doctor,' Isobel said, 'but it was an emergency so I had a go. The patient was anaesthetized but it took quite a time for us to find the right bits and tie them all up and do the stitching. In the end all was well and I left him comfortable. But it had been an unconscionable time! I don't think I'd have found the bits at all but for the matron's help. The next day I had a telephone call from their resident surgeon who thanked me profusely for doing such a good job, but asking why a straightforward appendectomy had taken over half an hour to perform. I said it was ages since I was in medical practice and I was a bit rusty. He said, it was a good job the instruments weren't!' And in this way she lightly deprecated the saving of a life.

The programme was televised from Manchester, where we stayed at the Midland Hotel. I used to walk out in the morning with Isabel, but after one turn round the block she would say, 'Yes, well, that's quite enough exercise for one day,' and we'd return to the hotel. Like me, she disliked unnecessary exertion. She was delighted when I quoted Peter Cook's line – 'Every morning there's the toothpaste to be squeezed, the laces to be tied: it's a full life.'

'Too full, my dear,' she laughed, 'and must forever be emptied.'

One of the mystery guests on the programme was Marty Feldman whom I hadn't seen since *Round The Horne* finished. We travelled back together on the train to London and had a long talk. 'You've changed a lot,' he told me. 'You're much more relaxed, much less frenetic than the old days.'

'I was afraid of the silences so I filled them with stories.'

'Very funny they were.'

'Dressed-up confessionals really. The comedy which Stanley Baxter calls the channelling of a private misery.'

'Nothing wrong with that if it results in laughter, but don't overdo the analysis-bit, society is getting fragmented enough as it is.'

Shortly after this I met Helen Fry again. She'd produced the poetry programme I'd done in 1970 and when I touched on the sentiment voiced by Marty Feldman she eagerly took up the theme of fragmentation. 'It's one of the most dispiriting aspects of our age,' she said, and when I pointed out that poetry provided an ontological defence from Xenophon to Eliot, she said she'd like me to do a programme about it.

I went home and made some notes. I wrote about man's belief in truth, a truth he recognizes as being outside of himself, incorruptible and only occasionally revealed. Therefore it remains a mystery, not the conjured mystery of the ghostly or the occult but the mystery of human affections. I chose excerpts from philosophers and poets to support the concept and by the time I had added all my linking arguments, the script began to look overlong. But Helen Fry had lost none of her enthusiasm, and in November 1974 we recorded the programme at the Playhouse Theatre. Helen decided to call it 'The Crystal Spirit' from an Orwell poem I'd used and it was under that title that it was broadcast.

Later on there was a review in *The Times* by David Wade with an interesting reaction:

> It was a slightly bizarre experience listening to Kenneth Williams' 45-minute solo 'The Crystal Spirit'; here was the voice, which, try as it may, cannot entirely shake off all those inflections which in other circumstances breathe inneundo, the distorted vowels and the nasal twang which calls to mind at once the characterful Williams' nose. Here it was for all that time, speaking a mixture of verse, personal comment and reflection to an invited audience which must have laughed all of two and a half times . . .You had to set aside the filters of expectation built up by years of exposure to *Round the Horne* et seq, and grasp that if you found yourself unable quite to credit Kenneth Williams in philosophical vein, then perhaps you were in need of registering his remarks on the departmentalisaton of thought – with which incidentally he had already anticipated you. To those, he added others just as cogent: on how we blame material things for faults which lie elsewhere – in, for example, our sense of fragmentation; how we attempt to cover that over with activity, by travelling, let us say, but more for something to do than for any other reason; we examine our own particular wood so minutely in order to discover what is wrong that we end up obsessed not just with trees but with twigs and are then inclined to say that no wood exists.

238

I do not want to exaggerate Mr Williams' role as commentator on our lives and times, for in a comparative desert a cup of water can get to look like a lake . . . at the same time I cannot help calling to mind how often in stories and plays it is the fool, the professional clown, who suddenly says to us 'Look . . . !' and we do because we thought we were in for another easy laugh. But the expectation of laughter is not fulfilled and because of that we hear and remember what it was that took its place.

Peter Eade's secretary, Laurena, cut this article out of *The Times* for me and I pasted it in my journal because it provided the first press comment on something I'd written in a serious vein.

1974 began with more episodes of *What's My Line* for BBC television, and in March and April I was back with the team at Pinewood for *Carry On Dick*. Then the *Just A Minute* programmes began again in May and by June I had an invitation from Stewart Morris to prepare the linking material for another series of *International Cabaret* which he asked me to compere.

During the same month I met Geoffrey Cannon, the editor of *Radio Times* who asked me to write a column called 'Preview' for the paper and I began to have an inkling of the problems involved with the written word. My brief was to air the views of anyone involved in a BBC production, from producers and cameramen, to presenters and studio managers. My research turned up some weird comments. Pamela Howe who produced *Talking About Antiques* told me she'd had a letter from a listener who wrote: 'My aunt has a painting. It is by Rembrandt, of Lady Hamilton and her dog. She bought it at Boots fifty years ago. Is it valuable?' For a television adaptation of *Madame Bovary* Tom Conti had to ride a horse and he said, 'They make these chalk lines in the road which you have to follow for the camera to get you in focus. My horse was obviously a trained film actor whose whole *raison d'être* seemed to be to stop at every chalk mark on the road. The only trouble was he stopped on everybody else's chalk marks, not mine.' Ronnie Barker, speaking on TV studio conditions, said, 'It's not easy for thin people to laugh on hard seats, they get very numb. Fat people laugh more readily, they don't feel it

239

you see. It's the bony ones who suffer. Instead of offering silly prizes at quiz shows they should award a cushion to the best bony laugher.' And I quoted the producer of a programme about the alarming rate of inflation in Tudor England who said to me, 'It was 100 per cent when Shakespeare was writing about usury in *The Merchant of Venice*.' When I replied, 'That's where he wrote: "How sweet the moonlight sleeps upon this bank",' the producer said, 'Yes, he was probably after an overdraft.'

I completed all the scripts for the television series in July and August and in September started performing *International Cabaret* at the London Hippodrome. Not one of them was a dud. They were all good variety bills and my linking material got its proper quota of laughs. At the last one of the series in November my dressing room was packed and George Borwick bought us champagne to celebrate. At least twenty people were crammed into the tiny space complimenting me and laughing about the script when a security guard appeared and said, 'Everyone must leave the building because we've received a bomb threat.' I have never seen a room empty so quickly. Within seconds everyone was gone except for George and me still forlornly clutching our drinks.

'That evacuation panic is worse than the bomb threat,' I said. 'You could get crushed in the rush.'

'Yes,' he assented. 'And anyway we can't leave, I was just opening this bottle of Krug.'

When he did there was such a loud report from the explosive cork that the building emptied even more quickly.

Because it was something she had always wanted to do I went with Louisa on a Christmas cruise that year. She wanted to get away from the wintry weather and she didn't want to do any cooking. I booked two single cabins on the *Canberra* and we sailed to Madeira and thence to Senegal and the Equator for Christmas Day. Louisa loved it, but I found it increasingly irksome. Constant recognition meant I couldn't sit in a deck chair and enjoy the sea without being asked to sign autographs or pose for photographs with fellow-passengers, pretending I was enjoying every minute. I thought of Eliot's line, 'Find a face to meet the face that you must meet.'

One of the ship's officers asked, 'Don't you find it annoying, all the pestering that goes on?'

'It's like having a wart or a birthmark on your face – after a while you get used to it.'

'Not much of a holiday, though, is it?'

'Well, I thought it would die down after a while, I didn't realize there'd be nearly two thousand passengers on board.'

'You must come up to the bridge, you can get away from them there.'

He meant well and it would have been graceless to say, 'Why change one lot of bores for another?' But it was an experience I never want to repeat.

The cruise liner was like a vast floating hotel with a monotonous simulated party atmosphere. There was an endless round of eating and drinking with organised entertainment of the holiday-camp variety: paper hats, bingo, deck games, physical jerks, sing-songs and concerts. To avoid any one of these was like trying to traverse a minefield. Every night I watched amazed as women appeared in the dining room wearing yet more different dresses, sat down with their dinner-jacketed companions and worked their way through course after course of gastronomic delights. During the day the sight of ponderous bellies squeezed into swimsuits was evidence of their gluttony. Again and again I found myself admiring their courage. On the evening when the ship arrived at Dakar it anchored off the coast and the passengers were taken ashore to a Senegalese night club. Lifeboats were lowered from the *Canberra*'s davits and the sight of elderly ladies in furs and long dresses traipsing down the companionway to the small craft bobbing on the choppy sea under the steep sides of the liner, and jumping into the arms of sailors helping them bridge the gap, was curiously touching. When the boats turned for the shore their bows crashed up and down in the water and the spray soaked them all liberally. Women patted their bedraggled hair-dos and cried 'Oh dear!' but they struggled ashore and repaired the ravages on the coach which conveyed them to the night spot.

This was an open-air venue with seating arranged around an illuminated stage on which some local dancers cavorted. At every table there was a spit on which a whole lamb was roasted. Senegalese maidens did the serving dressed only in skirts with a toplessness that was disconcerting as they leant over the guests proffering canapés and nuts. One man laughed nervously, 'Oh, we're starting with the nuts,' and his

241

companion cried, 'Couple of coconuts by the looks of things,' eyes goggling at the nubile, ebony nymphs.

When one turned from the brilliantly lit scene and looked behind it was very different. The night club was surrounded by a barbed-wire fence through which you could see hungry and curious black faces peering at the plentiful repast. A white-haired English grandmother rose indignantly. 'I am going to give them some of this food,' she said, and took a knife from the table with which to cut some of the lamb from the spit. The knife bent as it sank into the meat and she struggled fruitlessly.

'You want a carving knife,' cried one of the men and asked a waitress to get one, telling her, 'Carve some meat for those people over there,' but she told him that wasn't her job, that the lamb needed more revolutions on the spit and that other courses had to be served first. The man furiously shook a pepper pot protesting at this lack of charity. Most of the pepper blew into my gin and tonic. I left the scene and went to the bar to change my drink. A disgruntled passenger complained, 'I don't think much of this for a night out – like eating in a zoo with all these beggars staring at you over the fence – some of them half-naked.'

'So are the waitresses.'

'Yes, but they're pretty.'

On the way back to the ship there was much talk about deprivation in underdeveloped countries and I began to wonder if P & O had arranged a pleasure trip to arouse guilt, but my friend from the bar was unmoved. 'Europe has put a lot of money into the Third World and most of it ends up in the pockets of corrupt administrators and Swiss bank accounts.'

By the New Year the *Canberra* was headed for home and when we got to Gibraltar, a lady reporter came on board and asked me for an interview. 'What are your plans for 1975?'

'Another series of *Just A Minute* and another film at Pinewood.'

'What is it to be called?'

'*Carry On Behind.*'

'Why *Behind*?'

'It's about some archaeologists who tow their equipment on the back of their Land Rover.'

'I expect people will read something rude into that title. It's a *double entendre.*'

242

'A lot of humour is derived from a play on words,' I pointed out. 'Bernard Shaw declared that the Christian Church was founded gaily with a pun. Christ said to Peter, "On this rock I found my Church." Petra and Peter, you see.'

'Do you enjoy acting?'

'I used to when I was young, that's when the enjoyment is most lively. The older you get the less interested you are in pretence.'

'But you've always enjoyed comedy, haven't you?'

'When I started it was all very different. Comedians topped the bill, with the impersonators, singers and magicians as supporting acts. But now the comic is like a vicar with a dwindling congregation. Television has usurped the place of the variety theatre, so you now have programmes built around the erstwhile supporting acts and the shows star the impersonator, the singer, the magician.'

'Would you like to do something else?'

'Well, I have started doing a bit of writing – the odd magazine article and a column for *Radio Times* and it's given me one or two ideas. Perhaps I will tackle something more substantial.'

'Become an author?'

'Oh, I don't know about that. We're in 1975 now. Next year I'll be 50 – too late to start another career. People think of me as a performer, not a writer. They tend to put you in a pigeon hole.'

'You can always fly out of it,' she laughed. 'It's never too late.'

When she'd gone her words stayed with me. I think she was right. It's never too late. Just because you've made your bed, you don't have to lie in it, you can get out and remake it. A lot of maxims are lies, or at any rate misleading: watched kettles do boil, and rolling stones can gather moss. The man who cannot change his mind is in danger of losing it altogether.

There is not only one second chance, there are thousands of second chances, just as long as we wonder at the sunset, the numberless stars in the heavens and the glory of a new day.

Index

248

249